History of Financial Institutions

Globalization is not an external force but a result of concrete business decisions made by millions of entrepreneurs and managers across the world. As such, the modern corporation has completely altered the economic landscape; business and finance have shaped the international order of the modern world.

History of Financial Institutions contributes to the analysis of how the modern corporation, business and finance have shaped and keep on shaping our world. In a collection of nine succinct essays, this volume looks at the role of finance in European history from the beginning of the 19th century to the period after the Second World War. Archivists and financial historians, who are also leading scholars of banking and financial history, investigate the ways in which the international post-war order developed. They draw on often hitherto unused archival sources from central banks and other institutions to reveal the unique histories of a variety of European countries and the paths that have led to the contemporary economic and financial system. The collection includes reflections on (monetary) stabilization, inflation, hyperinflation, globalization and public relations in banking and commerce.

This book is essential reading for banking and finance executives, as well as policy makers with a historical interest. It will also be of importance to academics with a particular interest in economic history, financial or banking history, and European history.

Carmen Hofmann is Secretary General of *eabh* (The European Association for Banking and Financial History e.V.), Germany.

Martin L. Müller is Director of the Historical Institute of Deutsche Bank and chairman of the German Association of Business Archivists (VdW), Germany.

eabh maintains a global network of financial professionals and academics. Banks, insurance companies and other financial institutions are members of *eabh*. *eabh* places current challenges of the financial sector into a historical context. Our historians work on long-term topics that matter to the management of financial institutions and policy makers. To this end *eabh* promotes archives, organizes workshops, conferences and trainings and publishes in-house and in cooperation with renowned publishers.

Banking, Money and International Finance

For a full list of titles in this series, please visit www.routledge.com/series/BMIF

1. Alternative Banking and Financial Crisis
Edited by Olivier Butzbach and Kurt von Mettenheim

2. Financial Innovation, Regulation and Crises in History
Edited by Piet Clement, Harold James and Herman van der Wee

3. Asian Imperial Banking History
Edited by Hubert Bonin, Nuno Valério and Kazuhiko Yago

4. Colonial and Imperial Banking History
Edited by Hubert Bonin and Nuno Valério

5. Financing California Real Estate
Spanish Missions to subprime mortgages
Lynne P. Doti

6. History of Financial Institutions
Essays on the history of European finance, 1800–1950
Edited by Carmen Hofmann and Martin L. Müller

History of Financial Institutions

Essays on the history of European finance, 1800–1950

Edited by
Carmen Hofmann and Martin L. Müller

Routledge
Taylor & Francis Group
LONDON AND NEW YORK

First published 2017 by Routledge

2 Park Square, Milton Park, Abingdon, Oxfordshire OX14 4RN
711 Third Avenue, New York, NY 10017

Routledge is an imprint of the Taylor & Francis Group, an informa business

First issued in paperback 2018

British Library Cataloguing in Publication Data
A catalogue record for this book is available from the British Library

Library of Congress Cataloging in Publication Data
Names: Hofmann, Carmen, editor. | Müller, Martin L., editor.
Title: History of financial institutions : essays on the history of European finance, 1800-1950 / edited by Carmen Hofmann and Martin L. Müller.
Description: New York : Routledge, 2016. | Includes bibliographical references.
Identifiers: LCCN 2016015420 | ISBN 9781138666511 (hardback) | ISBN 9781315619347 (ebook)
Subjects: LCSH: Financial institutions--Europe--History--19th century. | Financial institutions--Europe--History--20th century. | Banks and banking--Europe--History--19th century. | Banks and banking--Europe--History--20th century.
Classification: LCC HG186.A2 .H574 2016 | DDC 332.1094/09034--dc23
LC record available at https://lccn.loc.gov/2016015420

ISBN: 978-1-138-66651-1 (hbk)
ISBN: 978-1-138-32500-5 (pbk)

Typeset in Times New Roman
by Taylor & Francis Books

Contents

Tables

Contributors

Hubert Bonin is a researcher in modern economic history at Sciences Po Bordeaux and at the GRETHA research centre at Bordeaux University. He is a specialist in the history of services companies (Suez Canal company, colonial and overseas trading houses and their maritime affiliates), and, moreover, in French banking history. Hubert publishes widely and extensively – his most recent work being: *Colonial and Imperial Banking History* (2015).

Philip Cottrell was Emeritus Professor of Financial History and Honorary Visiting Fellow at the University of Leicester. His research interests included finance from a British perspective, British overseas investment in the 19th century, international finance (Europe in the interwar period) and European business history. He served as chairman of the academic council of *eabh* and was one of the founders of the *Financial History Review*. His publications include *The Ionian Bank: An Imperial Institution, 1839–1864* (2007), *Investment Banking in England*, 1856–1881 (1985), *Industrial Finance, 1830–1914* (1980), *British Overseas Investment in the Nineteenth Century* (1975) and *Money and Banking in England* (1974).

Jeffrey Fear is Professor of International Business History (Economic and Social History) at Glasgow University. His research interests include: 20th-century German business and economic history; competitiveness and internationalization of family/small and midsize businesses; history of multinational business and international cartels; comparative corporate governance and organization; and, finally, immigrant entrepreneurship. He is on the editorial board of *Business History Review* and *Essays in Economic and Business History*.

Peter Hertner is Professor of Economic and Social History at Martin Luther University Halle-Wittenberg. Previously he was Director of the Library of the European University Institute in Florence and taught at the universities of Naples, Ancona, Genua and Milan. His research focuses on Italian economic history of the 19th and 20th centuries with a particular focus on Italian business history and the history of multinational companies until

1945. He acts as an editor of *Società e Storia, Rivista di Storia economica* and *Jahrbuch für Wirtschaftsgeschichte.*

Carmen Hofmann is Secretary General of *eabh* (The European Association for Banking and Financial History e.V.). Previously she worked for Eurogroup Consulting and the Frankfurt Fair. She studied economics, Roman and Arab studies and is a regular editor of *eabh* publications.

Ranald Michie is Professor Emeritus of Financial History in the Department of History of Durham University. He primarily focuses on the history of the British financial system, however, he also takes a global perspective in much of his work. He has also investigated the history of global securities markets and the City of London as a financial centre. His publications include: *Guilty Money. The City of London in Victorian and Edwardian Culture* (2009), *The Global Securities Market: A History* (2006) and *The London Stock Exchange: A History* (1999).

Martin L. Müller has been director of the Historical Institute of Deutsche Bank since 2006, where he also started his career as a historian and archivist in 1992. He has published and edited several volumes in his area of interest: banking, financial history and corporate history, including a history of Germany's biggest mutual fund company DWS. In 2014 he was elected as chairman of the German Association of Business Archivists (VdW).

Dieter Stiefel is professor at the Department of Economic and Social History at Vienna University. His academic work focuses on the economic history of Austria, as well as privatization and bankruptcy in history. He is a member of the Board of *Ludwig Boltzmann Institute for Economic and History Analysis,* a member of the Academic Advisory Board of the *German Association for Business History* and the Austrian *Marshall Plan Foundation.*

Nuno Valério is Professor at the Lisbon School of Economics and Management. His special research interests include: the financial and economic history of Portugal; banking in the Portuguese colonial empire; and the Portuguese capital market during the Second World War. He recently published *Colonial and Imperial Banking History* (2015).

Ulrike Zimmerl is Head of the Historical Section at UniCredit Bank Austria. She was also the main force behind the creation of the archive. Previously she was a lecturer at Vienna University, Department for Economic and Social History. She is a member of the Board of the *Austrian Society for Business History* and of the Association *Freunde der Stiftung Bruno Kreisky Archive.* Her publications include: *Die Bank am Schottenring* (2012), *Österreichische Banken und Sparkassen im Nationalsozialismus* (2006), *Bank Austria Creditanstalt. 150 Jahre österreichische Bankengeschichte im Zentrum Europas* (2005).

Preface

This book is dedicated to Gerald Donald Feldman. Gerald Feldman was a historian at Berkeley University (California) who specialised in 20th-century German history. He died on 31 October 2007 at his home in Berkeley at the age of 70. During his lifetime he authored, co-authored or edited more than 27 books – and more than 100 scholarly articles.[1]

Until his death in 2007 he was Chairman of the Academic Council of *eabh* (The European Association for Banking and Financial History e.V.).

Feldman was probably the most prominent figure in America to make business history relevant to the larger 'German question'. In his view, there was simply no way to understand German history, particularly the horribly evil course that Germany took in the mid-20th century, without understanding the central role of business. But this topic was only one of Feldman's big topics. Like the authors of the essays collected here, he was concerned with understanding how different 'varieties of capitalism' around the world emerged. They understand globalisation not as an outside force but as a result of concrete business decisions made by millions of entrepreneurs and managers across the globe. Analysing how the modern corporation altered the economic landscape of our world requires, in the view of these authors, a focus on how business and finance have shaped and keep on shaping our societies. The role of business is more important than ever before. However, creating recognition and understanding of the centrality of the modern corporation and the business community to our understanding of the modern world remains an important task for practitioners of business history.[2]

Business archives are crucial when it comes to explaining 20th- and 21st-century history. That is why this edition and the collaboration of business archivists and historians is crucial. It is a deep respect for the archives and their power to reveal the truth that provides a space for hearing how contemporaries viewed their own situation; it helps to put together the puzzle of the past; makes history into a space for debate on commonly held pieces of evidence; reveals the intersection of economic and political power; and sometimes even the complicity of business and crime.

This work is a collaboration of some of the most renowned European financial historians and archivists. It is a collaborative effort that bridges academic and national cultures in order to remember Gerald D. Feldman and his vision of history as a continuity – the value of the descriptive which allows openness for new approaches and re-interpretation over time.

The collected contributions shed new light on Feldman's predominant research fields: the role of finance in European history from the beginning of the 19th century to the period after the Second World War. Feldman's empirical approach to history mostly betrayed a careful wariness toward large theoretical constructs. Different case studies of a variety of European countries reveal unique histories that can be read separately. The chapters are based on original research, often drawing on hitherto unused archival sources (Historical Archives of Bank Austria, Deutsche Bank, Bank of England, Bank of Italy, Intesa Sanpaolo, etc.). These chapters have all been researched and written by recognised authorities in their field. At the same time, these chapters are loosely linked, highlighting Feldman's pursuit of 'big topics': inflation, stabilisation, globalisation and modernity – all of which are examined from a business perspective.

Contributions deal with questions of contemporary relevance such as the extent to which finance is really about politics; and to what extent local business is affected by decisions of international financial actors and vice versa? They reveal a clash of cultures between creditors and debtors at the beginning of industrialisation in regions with different levels of development and deal with the importance of business culture for the overall economic development of a nation. Other contributions look at the cultural impact of banking and combine cultural history and business history in order to resituate financial history within a larger framework of sociological and institutional history as well as the history of the arts and literature.

In the end, none of the authors has provided definite answers or conclusions of what exactly happened and why. It is precisely that space between black and white, which they examine, that is so utterly important when talking about the history of the 20th century. The truly bad and ugly happened, but the why and how is in the space between – the grey zone – the daily business of the businesses that dominate the modern world. Almost certainly, Mr Feldman would have appreciated the room for interpretation.

Notes

1 Anderson, M.L., Brady, T.A., Connelly, J., 2007. *In Memoriam, Gerald D. Feldman.* [online] Available at http://senate.universityofcalifornia.edu/inmemoriam/geraldfeldman.html [Accessed 28 March 2016].

2 Feldman, G.D., 2001. *Allianz and the German Insurance Business, 1933–1945.* New York and Cambridge: Cambridge University Press.

Acknowledgements

This work is a collaborative effort. Therefore, first and foremost we should like to thank all authors for contributing – and doing so at such a high standard.

A few individuals played a major role in making the edition happen. This work has only been made possible by the great support and initial effort of Peter Hertner and Dieter Stiefel. They carefully approached other colleagues and encouraged them to contribute.

Moreover, throughout the work on the volume we benefited substantially from the co-operation of Norma Ragenfeldt Feldman – we are most grateful!

In a broader sense the international network of historically knowledgeable and supportive individuals and corporations *eabh* has created over the years has provided a magnificent basis of support for this work. In particular, we would like to thank Hugo Bänziger, Harold James and Manfred Pohl for their support, patience and advice.

We would also like to thank Gabriella Massaglia of *eabh* for her indispensable support in general and her valuable assistance with all the details required. Last but not least, we are most grateful for Jonathan Ercanbrack's generosity with his editorial advice and the essential support needed while approaching the finishing line.

1 Gerald D. Feldman

An appreciation

Jeffrey Fear

We lost one of our great ones.

Gerry had reached seventy years of age, but remained vigorous and mentally sharp as ever. (As appropriate in this circle amongst friends and close colleagues in the European Association for Banking and Financial History, I will use 'Gerry' when speaking in a personal sense – 'Feldman' refers to discussions of his scholarly career – even as a graduate student he was simply Gerry to me – which speaks volumes about his accessibility and personability.)

As many in the *eabh* can attest, Gerry's travel stamina was legendary: he regularly participated in conferences on both sides of the Atlantic. One historian based in Germany saw him on two consecutive weekends in two different parts of Germany even though Gerry was living in Berkeley and not on one of his many extended visits. How he managed to travel as much as he did, arrive ready to work, run the Center for European Studies at Berkeley, entertain outside visitors, mentor innumerable graduate students, work on the editorial boards of at least eight major journals, participate in conferences and still write as prolifically as he did is one of the great mysteries of his life.

At a point when most historians slow down, Gerry went on a remarkable run of high quality scholarship with the publication of an award-winning book on the insurance company, *Allianz and the German Insurance Business 1933–1945* (2001).[1] He also edited and co-wrote *Networks of Nazi Persecution* (2005),[2] *Österreichische Banken und Sparkassen im Nationalsozialismus* (2006),[3] and *Finance and Modernization* (2008),[4] the latter appearing posthumously. This pace would tire even a younger scholar. The productivity of this last decade was simply stunning even by standards of Feldman's distinguished career characterized by quality scholarship and major works that helped to shape the field of German history for nearly five decades. Before illness incapacitated him, he was researching Austrian banks during National Socialism, planning to work at the United States Holocaust Memorial Museum in Washington, DC, and beginning to write about the history of Jewish businessmen before and during the Third Reich. According to his wife (a historian herself), editor, translator and true partner Norma von Ragenfeld-Feldman, the work on the Austrian Creditanstalt in particular brought the thousands of Jews who lost their property and later their lives to his attention.

'He wanted to give these people back their voice and place in memory; their stories "broke his heart."'[5]

We lost one of our great ones.

Gerry's fame in Germany was so great that almost every major newspaper covered his death. The *Frankfurter Allgemeine Zeitung* called him '*Der Unbestechliche*', a great German word: *unbestechlich*, which translates as 'incorruptible' or 'untouchable'. Gerry was one of the 'untouchables' among German historians, belonging to the very, very top intellectuals of his generation. In fact, *prior* to his book on *Allianz*, in 2000 he received the Commanders Cross of the Order of Merit from the German government for his life work – and he wasn't finished yet!

Bridging academic and national cultures, Feldman was able to intellectually cross the Atlantic, serving as one of the primary Anglo-Saxon contributors who have done so much to enrich our understanding of the turbulent course of German history. Born in New York City on 24 April 1937, Feldman studied at Columbia University for his undergraduate degree and received his doctorate at Harvard University before moving on to the University of California, Berkeley in 1963. There his career overlapped with that of the great Hans Rosenberg who had a profound influence on him. Rosenberg's linking of politics, interest groups, economic policy, and important business decision-makers also characterized Feldman's general approach to German history. Feldman remained flexible, open, and innovative in his interpretations of German history. For instance, *Army, Industry, and Labor in Germany 1914–1918* (1966)[6] precedes and fits well with the then nascent *Sonderweg* (special path) interpretation of German history that Hans-Ulrich Wehler synthesized in his classic, *Das Deutsche Kaiserreich 1871–1918* (*Imperial Germany 1871–1918*, 1994).[7] The *Sonderweg* interpretation of German history in particular explored the social and economic foundations of German dysfunctional politics.

However, despite his stress on industrial interest group politics and authoritarian political culture, Feldman remained somewhat distant from the new consensus forming around the notion of 'organized capitalism' as then argued especially by Hans-Ulrich Wehler, Heinrich August Winkler, and his close friend, Jürgen Kocka.[8] Feldman found the structural patterns that had been established by the group that supported the idea of organized capitalism overly rigid as categories and thought the often sublime and not easily comparable interactions and conflicts between individuals and businesses too important to be overly simplified and grouped together. He did not think finance capital dominated industry, and thought that tensions between the government and wilfully autonomous firms were too great to speak of a cohesively 'organized capitalism'. This distance also grew out of Feldman's empirical approach to history that betrayed a careful wariness toward large theoretical constructs (more on this below). When a new 1992 edition of *Army, Industry, and Labor* was published, Gerry wrote a new foreword to the 1966 original, the body of which he left fully intact as it (rightly) holds up well:

> If I were to write this study today, I certainly would moderate the emphasis on the continuity in German history that is especially present in the [first 1966] introduction. This is not to say that I would join those who argue against the notion that there is a German *Sonderweg* or special path that led to National Socialism. I would continue to emphasize the fatal role played by institutional backwardness, above all in the realm of parliamentary institutions and forms, and by the absence of a liberal political culture in determining the course of German history. At the same time, I am less inclined to take as bleak a view of the pre-war German Empire as I did earlier. The so-called blocks and alliances, above all the alleged alliance of the Junkers and heavy industry, have been shown by recent scholarship to be anything but monolithic and stable, and they were by no means as effective and powerful as was previously thought… Moreover, Germany was more of a bourgeois society and much less feudal than my introduction suggests… My view of industry is overly simple, concentrates almost exclusively on heavy industry, and underplays the variegation and conflict in the business community and the significance of regional groups and differences. I would also be less inclined today to emphasize the notion that German corporatist tendencies were pre-industrial, especially in view of the significance of corporatist arrangements for the stabilization of advanced capitalist industrial democracies since 1945. In short, pre-1914 Germany, as Thomas Nipperdey has argued, opened the way to more than one future.[9]

Throughout his life, Feldman continued to evolve in his own thinking about German history. Gerry once told me half in jest that it was sometimes remarkable to pull out one's old lectures and with those in front of him, lecture with almost the opposite interpretation.

Feldman was probably the most prominent figure in America to make business history matter to the larger 'German question' about its troubled past. Surveying his major works since the appearance of his first classic book, *Army Industry, and Labor in Germany*, all of his writings made extensive use of business archives or placed business front and centre in explaining the course of German history. In his view, there was simply no way to understand German history, particularly the horribly evil course that Germany took in the mid-twentieth century, without understanding the central role of business. Germany's rise to industrial power, the shift from a commitment to international liberalism to a frightening vision of a 'victorious peace' during World War I, the wrenching economic, social, and political consequences of the hyperinflation, how the Weimar Republic was stabilized through corporatist compromise, the effective undermining of the Weimar Republic from within by conservative elites, and especially how Jews died first a social death through ostracism, the Aryanization of Jewish property, and how they were eventually murdered in the Holocaust during the Third Reich, could only be understood through a thorough examination of the active involvement of business. Gerry stands at the forefront of pioneering historians documenting the missed opportunities, the disappointing lack of an ethical backbone, and awful complicity of business in the worst crimes of the Third Reich.

There was no one who promoted the field of (German) business history as effectively as Gerry over the last forty years – particularly on this side of the Atlantic. Gerry probably felt himself more of a German historian than a business or banking historian *per se*. Indeed, he probably mentored more new doctoral students of German and European history than anyone else in America, regardless of their focus on cultural, military, political, or even economic and business history (his home territory). Always supportive of his students' choice of direction, he did not force his own particular brand of political economy approach on his students. Nor did he act as an imposing *Doktorvater* (doctoral supervisor), but treated new doctoral students as up-and-coming equals who could contribute immediately to our knowledge of Germany – myself included. Since the mid-1980s, he advised major workgroups of young historians on topics like hyperinflation, Nazi Gold in Switzerland, and businesses during the Third Reich. If not for his illness, he also would have advised more thoroughly a recent project on Friedrich Flick.[10] I first met Gerry as a graduate student in a series of roundtable discussions organized by the Berkeley–Stanford–UC Davis reading group led by James Sheehan, Margaret Lavinia Anderson, Gerald Feldman, and William Hagen. There we read draft chapters of our dissertations, which proved an intense and stimulating experience. What I found most remarkable was the wide range of knowledge about all sorts of history that Gerry brought to the table in these discussions. A wonderful sense of collegiality and helpfulness permeated this group. Gerry always warmly welcomed new ideas and younger colleagues to the field.

Feldman was a master at making the study of industry and business matter to the general questions asked by other historians, who often held an antipathy toward business and economic history. Recent trends marginalized business and economic history in American history and economics departments, which Feldman found inexplicable. Taken from the preface of his book on *Allianz*:[11]

> Until recently, historians like myself with an interest in economic and business history have formed a small and somewhat isolated group in the profession. Historians, like most intellectuals, have often taken a somewhat dim view of the object of our interests – namely, business – which they have treated either with intellectual disdain or with profound suspicion and even hostility. Prior to the end of the Cold War, the subject of business history, especially in Germany, was caught up in ideological debates about the purported responsibility of business for bringing Hitler to power and the question of whether the Nazi regime could be viewed as an instrument of big business. Neither of these positions can be seriously maintained today, but the question of what the actual relationship was between big business and National Socialism has only been made more pressing and important by now being considered and answered in different terms.

> Indeed, the role of business is more important than ever before, and it still remains for practitioners of business history to assert – and for general historians to recognize – the centrality of the modern corporation and the business community to our understanding of the modern world....
>
> Nevertheless, it is my hope that the lessons learned from recent experience [the opening of archives and permitting historians unfettered access] include these: ignorance is not bliss; and the promotion of critical business history is a public responsibility and a wise policy as well. The business community can only benefit from a sober appreciation of its own history. At the same time, it is essential that historians pay more attention to business history as a crucial area of general history in the modern age, since they do, after all, have some responsibility to their students and the general public to explain the real world in which we live.[12]

For nearly fifty years, Gerry stood on the cutting edge of historical scholarship on these issues – and at an active seventy he remained so. That is the tragedy of his death. The above statement should also be read as a challenge for us practitioners of business history to assert the field more strongly, and not only for documenting the role of business during the Third Reich that has provided business history with considerable momentum in Germany in recent years. Understanding how different varieties of capitalism emerged around the world, understanding globalization not as an outside force but a result of concrete business decisions made by millions of entrepreneurs and managers across the world, analysing how the modern corporation altered the economic landscape of our world (not always for the better!), and understanding how three billion people are moving out of poverty, requires focusing on how business and finance have shaped our world. Across the world, students are flocking to the business major, but the training is often without any historical perspective. After the recent (2007–2009) and ongoing financial crisis, *The Economist* stressed the need for more economic and financial history to counteract the short-term reactions and lack of experience by many market participants. If Gerry had lived to experience this crisis, one can easily imagine his reaction after studying some of the major economic and financial crises of German capitalism.

Feldman leaves behind a mere twelve authored books, fifteen co-authored or edited books and around 130 scholarly articles. Three of those books he solely authored are certifiable classics, when other great historians might hold just one or two: *Army, Industry and Labor in Germany 1914–1918* (1966), his masterpiece *The Great Disorder: Politics, Economics and Society in the German Inflation 1914–1924* (1993)[13] and *Allianz and the German Insurance Business 1933–1945* (2001). All were award-winning landmarks that defined the state-of-the art in the field of business and financial history for decades to come.

Army, Industry, and Labor, which examines the manner in which unions and industry introduced collective bargaining and created a new social-political contract by the end of the war, still holds up well in its basic narrative after forty years due to Feldman's close attention to grounding everything in historical documentation. It remains a standard work after all these years. No one can study the German experience of the war without referring to it.

The *Great Disorder* is THE book on the economic and social history of the German hyperinflation. Feldman practically wove all of German society into his portrayal, fully utilizing the roughly 1,000 pages of double columned, densely written fine print. As a sort of *Gesamtgeschichte* ('total history'), it comes, as close to being a two-dimensional representation of Germany between 1914–1924 as any book can hope to accomplish. It won the Best Book award from the Central European History of the American Historical Association for 1995. No one can move forward on this time period without addressing this text.

Allianz and the German Insurance Business 1933–1945 won the prize from the German Studies Association and the Hagley Prize of the Business History Conference for the best book of 2002. In it, Feldman demonstrated how *Allianz* had transferred life insurance benefits to the Nazis from Jewish beneficiaries, unscrupulously lobbied the Nazi state not to be held liable and minimize the cost of damages incurred during the Great Pogrom. 'Since here one is dealing with the destruction of public property not worthy of protection', quoting *Allianz* executive and leader of the Reich Group for Insurance, Eduard Hilgard.[14] *Allianz* insured the concentration camps and organized tours to the camps; so they definitely knew what was happening! As Feldman wrote in regard to the Great Pogrom of 9–10 November 1938: 'It was a state-sanctioned exercise in collective moral turpitude on the part of everyone engaged in this enterprise of trying to cope with the results of the Pogrom and cover up responsibility and liability for the damages'.[15] No one can understand the Third Reich without confronting this text.

Feldman also authored the section on the Weimar period of a book on the 100-year history of Deutsche Bank (1995) with Lothar Gall, Harold James, Carl-Ludwig Holtfrerich and Hans Büschgen.[16] The Deutsche Bank book initiated a wave of corporate histories, often financed by businesses themselves (Hoechst, Dresdner Bank, BASF, Degussa, Schering, Allianz), which have documented the moral and ethical collapse of business during the Nazi years. The Deutsche Bank book pioneered the hiring of external experts to delve into their records in the interest of full disclosure of even the worst aspects of their corporate history. In this respect, too, did Feldman set high standards for commissioned business histories that moved beyond celebratory anniversary issues. Feldman did not pull his punches. While working on the Austrian Creditanstalt project he once told me: 'They won't like what they will have to hear.' Feldman made clear that those firms he researched (and many others) could not possibly portray themselves as mere victims of the Nazi regime. He accused Allianz executives of showing 'how successfully and easily the regime had undermined the most elementary principles of legal and business ethics and how readily the leadership of the insurance industry had succumbed to an often unprincipled opportunism.'[17] At the same time, he refused to countenance that the National Socialists were an instrument of big business. Feldman countered some sceptics that any commissioned history was doomed not to tell the full truth:

> I see no reason, however, why historians should not be compensated for their work as independent scholars, especially when their expertise has been built up over a long professional life, or why reasonable compensation will make them less honest. More importantly, I can imagine no sum worth my personal and scholarly reputation, and I think that the colleagues I work with in this field feel the same way… Yet part of that commitment is to be highly critical of those businessmen who through whatever combination of political short-sightedness, opportunism, and sheer greed nearly destroyed German capitalism and had co-responsibility for the wreckage experienced by concerns like Allianz in 1945. Finally, I think it worth noting that I am a Jew and there have been many times when I have found working on this book depressing and even intolerable… I do not regret having done so, but the research and writing of this book have been anything but conducive to the softening of my views and judgments.[18]

As stated earlier: 'untouchable'. Throughout his career, Feldman's works have set benchmarks for the profession.

Feldman also set remarkable standards for his prodigious productivity and the length of his individual volumes. Feldman probably would have had at least two more books plus innumerable articles published by the age of eighty; he had not slowed down. Moreover, his works regularly topped 750 pages; the *Great Disorder* and *Hugo Stinnes*[19] topped 1,000 pages. As a writer of a none-too-small volume myself, Gerry and I joked that if we were writing about heavy industry, it had to be a heavy book. He was simply indefatigable when visiting new archives to unearth new sources. According to his colleague at Berkeley, Martin Jay, 'Feldman was very much a real historian's historian. He had a tremendous respect for the archives and getting the truth revealed'.[20] Indeed, Feldman's approach to understanding German history emerged through the business archives. He probably visited almost every German business archive at one point or another in the attempt to understand what went wrong in Germany before 1945. Because of this attention to detail, particularly biographical information and sensitivity to phrasing by contemporaries themselves, his books hold up even if his own overall interpretation shifted over time.

Despite their considerable length, his major books read extremely well because of Gerry's gift for a sharp turn of phrase and the clarity of his writing. He remained mentally quick, funny, and as sharp as ever at seventy. He had an eye for the trenchant detail and telling quote. When discussing the different groups who supported the Hitler-Ludendorff Putsch of 9 November 1923 in the *Great Disorder*, he moved to student support: 'If this was the case among some workers, it was even more so among students, who were probably most enthusiastic about conquering Germany; and getting something to eat at the same time' because they might have regular meals in an army. Then quoting a Bavarian state commissioner of the time: 'The local authority believes that this is a not to be underestimated factor in the entire Hitler movement'.[21] The eye for detail and the empathy of a historian shines through this quote as one Berlin savings bank organized a meeting for 'honest buyers and sellers' during the period of hyperinflation so as to prevent the rise of 'profiteering'. Feldman noted how the 'situation was genuinely pathetic', then lets a contemporary set the scene:

> A walk through the small salesroom with its tables and glass cases is heart-rending. There lie spread out so many lovely things so pleasing to the eye... everything in short that once decorated a house is assembled here... There is some old piece, a picture, a porcelain dish, a vase, which appears to the loving but unskilled eye of the owner as a true rarity and who, if she must part with it, wants to receive as much as possible. One now has to tell her that it has neither material nor artistic value, and the sick, embittered souls are always inclined to take this as a personal affront and bad will... A look out the window – there slides by the restless life of the metropolis, the fine silk stockings and expensive furs, there sit autos with the fat figures of *Schieber*, and here inside, in the quiet room, an impoverished Germany quietly and painfully weeps in its silent misery.[22]

Feldman's prose is the voice of an empathetic historian with a deep respect for providing a space for hearing how contemporaries viewed their own situation, at their own time, in their own words. He could also cut through the bureaucratic euphemisms by using the bureaucratic language against itself to demonstrate its often horrible real world consequences. Due to 'correction of some damage reports', Allianz paid less than they promised, then figured out a way to make fictional payments to Jews who had the audacity to make claims, then sent around a standardized letter 'to the Jewish policyholder' that ostensibly paid them a sum of money 'due to the events of November 1938... without recognizing a legal obligation in view of the doubtfulness of the case', and then asserted that 'no further claims against us exist on the basis of the existing insurance policies as a result of the events of 8–10 November 1938'.[23] After Feldman's skilful setup, the document needed no further comment as it demonstrated its own terrible deviousness.

For a historian interested in economic and business history, Feldman did not write dryly, perhaps however, with a dry wit. The whole *Great Disorder* is framed by a cartoon from *Simplicissmus* portraying the loss of traditional, spiritual values by the German middle class who once read the classics around a *gemütlich* table scene, but who now danced to jazz with the books as mere scenery.[24] The *Great Disorder* begins with a novelist commenting that the 'constellations were certainly in a wild state' and an astrologist who correlated fluctuations of currency exchange rates with the planets.[25] Try to get an economic historian to write like that today! Although Feldman had no formal training in finance or economics, he skilfully guided readers through such complex discussions about different theories of inflation, always to show how these theories had political – and often moral and ethical implications. And although he stressed the importance of economy and business, he was no economic determinist. If anything, he stressed the importance of individual and group decision-making, the choices real life people made often under considerable duress – an approach with an implicit engagement for liberal democratic politics. For Feldman, one could learn a lot by examining how democracy could break down.

If one reads key passages about Feldman's philosophy of writing history in the preface and introduction to the *Great Disorder*, one can hear a deeply historicist mind at work. The dense level of detail, quotes, and anecdotes relayed in his books is an expression of how important Feldman felt that going back to the source for evidence, and piecing together the puzzle of the past in a sort of honest reconstruction process, could lead to a sort of objectivity – not as some Archimedean point of absolute truth outside of history itself, or one that led to only possible interpretation – but rather as a space for debate based on commonly held pieces of evidence:

I hold the view that the evidential rules and canons of historical scholarship exist as necessary and potent antidotes to human frailties. This is the reason why they should be treated as normative values and not simply as convenient instruments or rhetorical devices. In any case, I have tried to make this a work of continuing value for my fellow scholars and readers by providing material in the text and documentation that can be used to refute my arguments or open the way to alternative interpretations in our common search for the truth.[26] It is one reason why early works such as *Army, Industry, and Labor* or *Iron and Steel in the German Inflation*[27] hold up so well, not necessarily in the overarching interpretation that even Feldman moved beyond, but in their reconstructions. If accurately rendered, they are still useful to others decades later, perhaps even open to later opposing interpretations, but nonetheless still useful. Feldman stated at another point:

> Objectivity does not preclude engagement, but it does make possible mutually intelligible discussion and the effort to persuade and possibility of being persuaded on the basis of shared methods and standards. It prevents the degeneration of scholarship into a babble of self-serving discourses.
>
> The necessity of bringing contradictory modes of analysis and interpretation into confrontation and objectively testing them against one another as far as possible is of special relevance to this study.[28]

This approach made him sceptical of grand overarching theories as starting points, rather than beginning with archival records. His fellow historian and friend, Jürgen Kocka, termed this approach 'critical empiricism', which remained open to interpretation, debate about the meaning of evidence, and openly critical engagement. Feldman could be quite critical of business executives and their actions during the Third Reich yet still understand the dilemmas or stark choices they faced given their embeddedness in a historically very particular context. To paraphrase the late historian Tim Mason, 'if one must hate or criticize, then one must hate or criticize precisely'. The classic historians' virtue, understanding (*Verstehen*), underpinned Feldman's work.

This philosophical stance helps explain how Feldman became most (in) famous in the mid-1980s and embroiled in the so-called 'David Abraham Affair' with the publication of Abraham's *The Collapse of the Weimar Republic*.[29] This is not the time or place to rehash the debate, which can be found in published form in numerous articles and books. Feldman approved Abraham's book for publication even though he disagreed with the overall thesis. He was especially concerned about the over-stylized and rigid structures that were, in his opinion, not sufficiently sophisticated to capture history which is constant change. As well, he considered central pieces of evidence misleading, quotations wrongly rendered, and documents sloppily transcribed. Of course he considered these facts against all ethics and principles of what it meant to be a historian. It was less about pedantic accuracy (after all we all have made mistakes in our works and, in fact, Richard Evans pointed out in his review of the *Great Disorder* in the *New York Times* that a printer's error missed the true scale of the hyperinflation by missing three zeros) but more about the use of evidence in decisive parts of the overall argument.[30]

What was inexplicable from my perspective was that Gerry welcomed, warmly welcomed, people into the field. Gerry was no mere archive mole. He grew up in the Bronx and had an ordinary man's touch. As any number of people in *eabh* could relate, he made people feel comfortable, included in the conversation. He could talk about anything: literature, music, baseball, Wagnerian operas (a love in spite of the ideological baggage it brought to German history), movies, travel or food. He made people feel at home. He had an aura about him, a joy of life.

And this is what I will remember most, not the scholarship, not his books but the times I had dinner with him in small restaurants in Berlin, over a beer in Harvard Square (to paraphrase Heinrich Heine, if you are a German historian you are required to drink beer), or at his home with his wife, Norma. My own wife finally met this mysterious man in my life (we always somehow met in Germany, only twice in the United States) over dinner with Per Hansen and my doctoral advisor Jim Sheehan and his wife Peggy Anderson – by no means shabby historians themselves. Afterwards, my wife was amazed at how comfortable he made her feel. *Old School* in her words, he included her in the conversation and asked about her own research. He was easy to talk with, just a fun person to be around, no sign of pretension; his eyes twinkled. And anyone could recognize his look and the sound of his laugh around a dinner table. As my wife and I talked about the dinner on the ride home, we came to the conclusion that it was like having dinner with, well, Santa Claus. Put a beard on him and he really (really!) could pass for Santa. He was a person who exuded generosity, joy, and laughter; plainly just enjoyed a good conversation and a good joke. Please do not think me disrespectful in this context, but I used to jest about how German history used to end after the hyperinflation in 1924 for Gerry. Once over a beer with him, I presented him with this so-called theory, and after a good laugh (yes, many of you can hear it), he replied that he had now moved forward twenty years. He could take a joke. He just had a remarkable range of knowledge that fed into a deep desire to explore and exhaust a particular time period, one that he felt crucial for understanding modern German history (not only the Third Reich). And despite all of the scholarship and intellectual firepower of near fifty years, that is how I will always remember Gerry just discussing and laughing over a beer.

He will be sorely, no, terribly missed. Even now, after almost ten years have passed since he passed away, it is hard to believe that he is gone as present as he still is, as such a vibrant, alive person, in our memories, as a foundation of our future scholarship.

And in that sense he is not really gone. Thus rather than writing *in memoriam*, I write *in appreciation*!

Notes

1 Feldman, G. D. 2001. *Allianz and the German Insurance Business 1933–1945*. Cambridge: Cambridge University Press.
2 Feldman, G.D. and Seibel, W. eds. 2004. *Networks of Persecution. Business. Bureaucracy and the Organization of the Holocaust*. New York and Oxford: Berghahn.
3 Feldman, G.D., Rathkolb, O., Venus, T., Zimmerl, U., eds. 2006. *Österreichische Banken und Sparkassen im Nationalsozialismus und in der Nachkriegszeit*. Munich: C.H. Beck.
4 Feldman, G.D. 2008. *Finance and Modernization*. Oxford: Routledge Taylor & Francis Group.
5 Anderson, M.L., Brady, T.A., Connelly, J. 2007. *In Memoriam: Gerald D. Feldman*. [online] Available at: http://senate.universityofcalifornia.edu/inmemoriam/gerald feldman.html [Accessed 9 March 2016].
6 Feldman, G.D. 1966. *Army, Industry and Labor in Germany, 1914–1918*. 1st ed. Princeton: Princeton University Press.
7 Wehler, H.-U. 1994. *Deutsche Geschichte. Das Deutsche Kaiserreich 1871–1918* (*German History. Imperial Germany 1871–1918*). 7th ed. Göttingen: Vandenhoeck & Ruprecht.
8 Winkler, H.A. 1973. *Organisierter Kapitalismus: Voraussetzungen und Anfänge* (*Organised Capitalism: Preconditions and Initial Phase*). Göttingen: Vandenhoeck und Ruprecht.
9 Feldman, G.D. 1992. *Army, Industry, and Labor*. Providence and Oxford: Berg, pp. 14–15.
10 Ahrens, R., Frei, N., Osterloh, J. 2009. *Flick. Der Konzern, die Familie, die Macht* (*Flick. Corporate Group, Family, Power*). Munich: Karl Blessing Verlag.
11 Feldman, G.D. 2001. *Allianz and the German Insurance Business, 1933–1945*. New York and Cambridge: Cambridge University Press.
12 Feldman, G.D. 2001. *Allianz and the German Insurance Business, 1933–1945*. New York and Cambridge: Cambridge University Press, pp. 8–9.
13 Feldman, G.D. 1993. *The Great Disorder: Politics, Economics and Society in German Inflation, 1914–1924*. New York and Oxford: Oxford University Press.

14 Feldman, G.D. 2001. *Allianz and the German Insurance Business 1933–1945.* Cambridge: Cambridge University Press, p. 223.
15 Feldman, G.D. 2001. *Allianz and the German Insurance Business 1933–1945.* Cambridge: Cambridge University Press, p. 228.
16 Büschgen, H., Feldman, G.D., Gall, L., Holtfrerich, C.-L., James, H. 1995. *The Deutsche Bank, 1870–1995.* Munich: Weidenfeld & Nicolson.
17 Feldman, G.D. 2001. *Allianz and the German Insurance Business 1933–1945.* Cambridge: Cambridge University Press, p. 235.
18 Allianz 2010. Study on the History of Allianz. [online] Available at: www.allianz.com/en/press/news/company_news/history/news14.html/ [Accessed 15 May 2010].
19 Feldman, G.D. 1998.*Hugo Stinnes. Biographie eines Industriellen 1870.*1924. Munich: C.H. Beck.
20 Anderson, M.L., Brady, T.A., Connelly, J. 2007. *In Memoriam: Gerald D. Feldman.* [online] Available at: http://senate.universityofcalifornia.edu/inmemoriam/geraldfeldman.html [Accessed 9 March 2016].
21 Feldman, G.D. 1993. *The Great Disorder: Politics, Economics and Society in German Inflation, 1914–1924.* New York and Oxford: Oxford University Press, p. 779.
22 Feldman, G.D. 1993. *The Great Disorder: Politics, Economics and Society in German Inflation, 1914–1924.* New York and Oxford: Oxford University Press, pp. 555–556.
23 Feldman, G.D. 2001. *Allianz and the German Insurance Business 1933–1945.* Cambridge: Cambridge University Press, pp. 227–228.
24 Feldman, G.D. 1993. *The Great Disorder: Politics, Economics and Society in German Inflation, 1914–1924.* New York and Oxford: Oxford University Press, p. 858.
25 Feldman, G.D. 1993. *The Great Disorder: Politics, Economics and Society in German Inflation, 1914–1924.* New York and Oxford: Oxford University Press, p. 3.
26 Feldman, G.D. 1993. *The Great Disorder: Politics, Economics and Society in German Inflation, 1914–1924.* New York and Oxford: Oxford University Press, p. 8.
27 Feldman, G.D. 1977. *Iron and Steel in the German Inflation. 1916–1923.* Princeton: Princeton University Press.
28 Feldman, G.D. 1993. *The Great Disorder: Politics, Economics and Society in German Inflation, 1914–1924.* New York and Oxford: Oxford University Press, p. 10.
29 Abraham, D. 1986 *The Collapse of the Weimar Republic: Political Economy and Crisis.* 2nd ed. Teaneck: Holmes & Meier Pub.
30 Hayes, P. 1987. History in an Off Key: David Abraham's Second 'Collapse', *Business History Review*, 61(3) pp. 452–472.

2 Starting from scratch?

The beginnings of Banca Commerciale Italiana: 1893–1894

Peter Hertner

Some introductory thoughts

It is hardly surprising that the stories of banks mostly deal with monetary institutions, which can look back on a relatively long existence. A very trivial reason for this circumstance might be the fact that only successful, and thus 'long-living', banks get to celebrate anniversaries, which in return, usually lead to corresponding anniversary publications.[1] The manufacture of such a *Festschrift*, as long as it was not written by journalists but by historians, has the positive side effect that – next to the expected self-presentation of the banking establishment – historical sources of the bank's foundation and development are fitted together. In the most favourable cases those documents were collected and permanently preserved in archives particularly established for this purpose. Afterwards, these sources are made available for publications that satisfy scientific criteria. In this way financial historians, in particular, helped to preserve the long lasting influence of credit institutions in the historic memory.[2]

In this sense the foundation of Banca Commerciale Italiana, which took place in 1894 in Milan, can be seen as quite an emblematic event particularly as the bank would serve as the biggest Italian commercial bank for the next four centuries. Further, this exemplifies how much the foundation itself as well as the months which led up to it, were deeply embedded in the early 1890s. In addition, this example perfectly highlights how much the international financial world not only took notice of such an event, but was also involved directly with some of its most important key players. Thus, the following contribution is meant to present a case study of such. Both the foundation itself as well as the relationships which led to this result and which were also intended to be built for the future had long-term consequences. These consequences influenced the image which the newly founded banking institution could project of itself and which it reflected in its national and international environment.

Economy and finance in 1890s Italy

The Italy of the 1880s had seen a (albeit relatively modest for that time) move towards industrialisation, which was also massively supported by the state, particularly in the iron and steel industry, in fields of mechanical engineering, and in shipbuilding. It should be beyond dispute that this move was nurtured by the state and up to a certain point also supported by the inflow of foreign capital, even though varying views and different attempts at the quantifications of the actual dimension of this development still exist.[3] The following international financial crisis of the early 1890s, which occurred around the same time as the Baring-crisis, the well-known crisis involving the export of British capital to Argentina caused by the London Baring Bank, did not spare Italy. Neither did the homemade financial scandals. The breakdown of Banca Romana, one of the country's six issuing banks, in 1891, the weaknesses of the other issuance banks and the subsequent foundation of Banca d'Italia, which would then become by far the leading issuing bank of the country, can all be seen as inevitable implications of these crisis years. When at the end of 1893, respectively in the beginning of 1894, both of the leading commercial banks, Credito Mobiliare and Banca Generale, had to shut down their counters a provisional climax seemed to have been reached. With this loss the foundation for a new beginning in the financial sector could be established, so as to close the created gap within the commercial bank sector. At least that is how one could interpret the foundation or respectively re-foundation of two new banks mentioned above, which in 1894 led to the creation of the Banca Commerciale Italiana and the Banca di Genova, which was replaced by Credito Italiano in January 1895.[4]

German capital was involved in both reorganisations: while it maintained only a minority share in regard to Credito Italiano, it had a clear majority position in the foundation of Banca Commerciale, which we will now examine more closely. The involvement of German capital in both cases also has to be acknowledged in view of the growing commitment of German capital in Italy – as portfolio capital but also in the form of direct investments – ever since the mid-1880s, but which can only be mentioned incidentally here.[5] One could say that the starting point was the foundation of Società delle strade ferrate del Mediterraneo, the Mediterranean railways where German banks under the lead of the Disconto-Gesellschaft were involved with approximately 20 per cent of their capital resources. In the following years this foundation was succeeded by the issuance of three per cent of railway obligations with a nominal value of 1.3 million Lire, of which the 1888 founded Consortium for Italian Business (in which almost all German major banks were represented) took the main share.[6] When it came to a tariff war between France and Italy in 1888, the government in Berlin also decided that German capital had to be provided in the form of bonds to support the Crispi government financially, since Italian state revenues had been lost due to the trade crisis with France and as a result of recession.[7] Direct actions of this sort lasted until the fall of 1893, until presumably the Italian banking crisis interrupted the financial involvement of German banks in Italy.

The foundation of Banca Commerciale

In October 1894, in the presence of the Milan notary Biraghi, the Banca Commerciale Italiana was brought into being. The establishment of the bank was the result of a year-long conversation and negotiation between foreign banks. Although foreign banks were meant to become the initial founders of the bank, discussions also took place between the banks and the Italian government as well as within Italian financial circles. These months of discussion are described here in detail as this particular case sets a good example to elaborate further on the difficult time of change in Italian domestic politics, in economic and financial politics, and in the credit sector of the country during first half of the 1890s. The investigation is about the contradiction between these 'darkest years for the economy of the new kingdom', which is how Gino Luzzatto, probably the best-known economic historian of his time, described the era directly after World War II.[8] He also described the period immediately thereafter as the so-called *Giolitti-era.* This era lasted until the beginning of World War I and brought with it a decisive movement toward industrialisation throughout the country. It is only this contradiction, which can explain in lucid terms the conditions for the medium- and long-term success of Banca Commerciale.

But let us start with the prehistory of the said foundation. At the beginning of 1894 Otto Joel, who would influence the development of Banca Commerciale like no other for more than two decades (but who still served as general inspector of Banca Generale at this point) wrote to Arthur Salomonsohn, one of the directors of the Disconto-Gesellschaft in Berlin:[9]

> A country of 30 million and such extensive trade and partially well developed industry... can no longer be without a financially powerful credit institution and the newly founded Banca d'Italia has already an urgent need for a better nexus with the business world. In Italy itself, significant potential could be found, given the Italian mentality however, foreign participation would encourage confidence.[10]

Joel did have his reasons. At the end of November 1893, Società Generale di Credito Mobiliare Italiano, the most important commercial bank of the country had literally lost half of its deposits; they had decreas from 52.8 to 28.3 million Lire since May 1893.[11] On top of this, as already mentioned above, came the problem that all six issuing banks were also caught in a profound crisis, even though the law of 10 August 1893 had included a radical reconstruction of the whole banking sector as well as the establishment of a quasi-central issuing bank[12] – the future Banca d'Italia. No significant support for money- and credit-policy could be expected from the three remaining issuance banks during the more than year-long period of transition. Even after that time the new Banca d'Italia was mainly involved in the clearing and settlement of short- and medium-term illiquid liabilities of its predecessor institutions and thus temporarily limited in practicing macroeconomic functions. When his own institute, Banca Generale, was then forced to cease payment only ten days after Joel had written the above quoted letter to Arthur Salomonsohn, Otto Joel stated that 'a huge, an incurable misfortune had occurred.'[13] The profound disappointment, which Joel must have felt deeply in that moment, can also be derived from another letter written on the following day:

> Today I have to convince myself that I have sacrificed my best years to not only reach a negative result for myself, but also for so many interests of this country that I respect and love as my own home country.[14]

Who was this Otto Joel, who had just expressed his gratitude for receiving the *Commendatore della Corona d'Italia* from the former Prime Minister Giovanni Giolitti with the words, 'Even though I am of a foreign nationality, I have spent my whole working life here in Italy?'[15] Descending from a German-Jewish family and born in Danzig in 1856, he had come to Italy at the age of 15 but due to health reasons and (with the exception of three years which he apparently spent in a bank in Frankfurt for educational purposes) had lived permanently in Italy ever since. In 1886 he became associate director of the branch office of Banca Generale in Milan. In 1889 he became director of its Genoese branch office and in 1893 *Ispettore Generale* (chief of the internal audit department of the same bank). Until he acquired Italian citizenship in 1910, Joel had been a Prussian citizen. His perfect bilingualism, profound knowledge of the German as well as the Italian banking system, his empathic understanding for German as well as for Italian mentalities and behaviours, his work ethos and extraordinary negotiation skills made him the ideal partner and negotiator for representatives of both sides; German and Italian banks, industrialists and politicians.[16]

Consequently, it comes hardly as a surprise that Banca Generale had already sent Joel into German-speaking countries in order to make some preliminary enquiries and to undertake negotiations. He entered into discussions with Schweizerische Kreditanstalt in Zurich in July 1892.[17] At the end of September 1893 Joel even travelled as a representative of the Italian government to Berlin in order to receive a credit of 50 million Lire from the Reichsbank. The credit was meant to support and maintain the issuing bank, Banca Nazionale, as well as the two commercial banks, Banca Generale und Credito Mobiliare. The mission was successful. Reichsbank and Preußische Seehandlung agreed to grant the credit after the imperial government also supported the cause of pre-financing the banks of the so-called Consortium for Italian Business with an amount of 40 million marks, which then would be allocated for six months.[18]

In 1890/91 the project of establishing a bank in Genoa with a German investment of 15 million Lire was still received with 'a head shake'[19] within the financial circles of Berlin. In the fall of 1893, when the crisis of both Italian commercial banks had become obvious and their collapse could no longer be ruled out, the situation was judged differently. Now initiatives from different sides appeared in order to oppose the threat of a collapse of the Italian banking system. Presumably, on the occasion of Joel's visit to Berlin at the end of September 1893, there had already been considerations concerning the creation of a new bank with German capital or at the minimum a willingness to support the restructuring of one of the major banks. Even though there might not exist conclusive proof for these considerations, the *Frankfurter Allgemeine Zeitung*, which was usually well-informed, had also made the proposal of founding a bank with German investment in Italy. As a result, a well-aimed indiscretion cannot be ruled out with respect to this case.[20] Further proof that the inclusion of plans with a similar aim were brought into the ongoing discussion concerns a project of Count Fantoni, who represented the already mentioned Consortium for Italian Business in Rome. At the beginning of November 1893 he proposed to establish a trust for Italian pensions with 40 million marks capital, which was to bring a return of four and a half per cent up to double the level of its nominal capital in return for Italian state bonds. This would assist the national stock exchange rate and counter international speculation. Even though Fürstenberg from the Berliner Handelsgesellschaft and Steinthal from Deutsche Bank showed interest in this model, it was never initiated due to its corresponding financial risks.[21]

More specific and definite offers could be established from the beginning of December 1893. On 9 December, for example, Joel mentioned in a letter to Grillo, general director of Banca Nazionale nel Regno (the biggest predecessor bank of Banca d'Italia) that the 'most important German bank'[22] had contacted him with the offer to support Banca Generale in this difficult situation with a capital increase in order to further promote the political and economic relationships between Italy and Germany, as these were of 'vital interest' for both countries.[23] Further, Joel also informed his Genoese friend Edilio Raggio on the following day that there had been considerations of a German capital contribution (by the mentioned bank and its consortium) on a scale of up to 10 to 15 million Lire.[24] 'But we must sustain our own house after the collapse of our neighbour's house, Joel wrote to Herman Rosenberg, one of the owners of Berliner Handelsgesellschaft, on 13 December: 'but the storm was severe and I will never forget these days and nights.'[25]

Additionally, there were also attempts to get the already stranded Credito Mobiliare afloat again. Its director, Giacinto Frascara, had already been to Berlin at the beginning of November 1893 in order to, as Joel suspected, bring 'a bigger operation' (most likely a cash injection for his crisis-ridden bank) to a satisfactory conclusion.[26] Nevertheless, it became obvious that the initiative was without success. Subsequently, at the end of December, the new Crispi government also involved itself in these efforts. Treasurer Sonnino asked his colleague in the foreign ministry, Blanc, to promote negotiations between Credito Mobiliare, which was already in liquidation, and various Berlin banking institutions, Bleichröder in particular. Furthermore, he was also supposed to indicate that the Italian government 'while it acknowledges the private character of this matter, could not avoid acknowledging with satisfaction the assistance received in Italy in the form of German capital investment.'[27] However, the telegraphic answer of the Italian ambassador in Berlin, Lanza, was characterised by reserved scepticism,[28] while the banks themselves and as parties directly involved also saw this development with scepticism at that time. Gustav Mauthner, director of Österreichische Credit-Anstalt in Wien, indicated to Julius Schwabach, co-owner of the banking house Bleichröder, in the beginning of December 1893:

> The question of whether or not to support the foundation of an Italian bank had been discussed at our institution several times before and the director of our branch in Triest in particular supported the suggestion. We have not engaged in this business so far because we considered the Italian circumstances not to the best advantage; and current events have proved us to be right.[29]

At the end of January 1894 Mauthner commented to Schwabach:

> I too am relatively unenthusiastic about the foundation of an Italian bank. I do not believe the new institution would generate very good results in the first or second year. However, if we would plan with a very hard working management, I could envision a future for such a bank under patronage of another strong [foreign] banking institution.[30]

Nevertheless, it seemed, particularly at this critical juncture, as if considerations among the financial circles of the German capital regarding concrete measures to solve the Italian banking crisis had started to take shape. On 27 January 1894 there had been a meeting of the banks of the Consortium for Italian Business, as ambassador Lanza reported telegraphically the day afterwards from Berlin. Progress had been made and steps for the establishment of an Italian bank had been initiated. Nevertheless, the Berlin private banking houses, Mendelssohn and Warschauer, had definitely dropped out of the group.[31] On 24 January, Hermann Rosenberg (Berliner Handelsgesellschaft) had asked Joel to come to Berlin. The following day the same request was made by Arthur Salomonsohn of Disconto-Gesellschaft. Rosenberg had informed Joel on 24 January accordingly.[32] Joel himself did not seem to have reached a final position. It seemed as if he was torn between a purely Italian solution (even so in practical terms outruling the option of a reconstruction of Credito Mobiliare and Banca Generale) and a German or German-Italian-Swiss option. At least that was the impression that he tried to express to the Marchese Durazzo Pallavicini of Genoa in a letter from Berlin dated 12 February 1894, in which he characterised the position of the representative of the Basel Banking Association, which according to him would lead to the following development:

> The old can only be liquidated in the long run and thus, cannot serve as foundation for a credit institution, which needs to have new, fresh life and liquid assets. If you Italians are able to bring this institution into life … then we would not wish for anything better than to abstain.[33]

The topic of the insufficient supply of risk capital was mentioned in a conversation that the German ambassador had had a few months earlier with Earl Ruspoli, the mayor of Rome. Ruspoli apparently stated that: 'The country did have enough money, but no one had the courage to invest it. He himself had 200.000 Lire in the cabinet, however would rather risk to lose interests than the capital.'[34]

Still, it seems that there had not been a lack of plans to mobilise domestic capital in general at the beginning of 1894. Achille Villa, a private banker in Milan and well-acquainted with Joel because of their joint deals at Banca Generale and Ferrovie Meridionali, called Joel's attention to the initiative of Count Sanseverino Vimercati and other Milan financiers and industrialists, who were in favour of the establishment of a bank:

> Which could replace [Banca] Generale, whereupon they deemed it absolutely necessary that there was a credit institute directly in Milan, which also took care of the needs of our economy. Sanseverino Vimercati (who eventually would be elected president of the board of directors of the new Banca Commerciale not long after this) would, due to the close relationship that he maintained to Crispi, the new prime minister, surely achieve what others had not managed to accomplish before.[35]

While discussions in Berlin continued, the planned establishment of the bank was also discussed in several sessions of the financial commission of Schweizerische Kreditanstalt in Zurich. Even though people there still waited for the formal invitation from the Berlin consortium, some fundamental criteria, which were supposed to serve as guiding principles, were already determined at a session on 8 February 1894.

> The new bank has to be organised as independent as possible from the government so that foreign (non-Italian) elements form the majority in the board of directors and so that the bank's management is formed in a way that provides the most possible forms of guarantees. Involvement in industrial ventures and speculations should principally be avoided. Safeguarding the institution's own capital against exchange rate fluctuations will be considered *condition sin quo.* Finally, we would prefer to establish the bank in Milan only and postpone the establishment of any branches for the time being.[36]

A week later the Federal Foreign Office in Berlin summarised the interim results of the local negotiations for the German ambassador as follows:

> One could assume that the negotiations of local banking institutions with regard to the foundation of a bigger bank in Italy presumably lead to a more favourable result. A syndicate consisting of Bleichröder, Disconto-Gesellschaft, Deutsche Bank, Berliner Handelsgesellschaft, Bank für

> Handel und Industrie and Dresdener Bank has been formed and is currently working on the draft statutes of the newly founded institution. The head office of the bank is supposed to be in Milan. Branches in Turin, Genoa and Rome should be established and the core capital would amount to 50 Mill. Frcs, the exact amount of impayments still to be decided.[37]

A memorandum of the involved banks in Berlin addressed to the Federal Foreign Office, dated back to 15 February 1894, also included several additional issues, which obviously seemed of great importance:

1 In case of authorised capital of 50 million Lire, the capital stock of the new bank should amount to 20 million Lire for the time being.
2 In addition to the banking business the new credit institution shall also actively negotiate and contribute to the implementation of more extensive Italian financial activities in which the German-founder banks were to be involved, without the direct participation of the Italian bank itself.
3 If the Italian note issuing banks who, as creditors, would become responsible for an orderly and gradual liquidation of the now illiquid assets of Banca Generale and Credito Mobiliare, the new bank would constructively participate in this liquidation.
4 With a corresponding gold deposit, the new bank shall be entitled to borrow Italian valuta interest-free from Italian note issuing banks in an amount not exceeding the new bank's capital stock at the current exchange rate. The gold was to be withdrawn upon the return of the borrowed currency.[38]

The last of the mentioned requests; namely the deposit of gold with the Italian note issuing banks in exchange for currency and the corresponding re-exchange to gold at all times; was also characterised as 'really abnormal: of clearly colonialist design' by the expert Antonio Confalonieri. Confalonieri assumed that, in case this request was of a serious nature at all, it was mainly intended to serve as an object of exchange for a different goal, namely 'the exclusive access to the placement of the major issues of Italian government bonds.'[39] However, if one tries to empathise with the point of view from German as well as of Swiss banks (as shown in the outrageous requests from above) the request loses its apparent outrageousness. Only a few days later, on 21 February 1894, the legally mandated forced exchange of the Italian currency was reimposed (it was already in effect from 1861 until 1883) after the Lire in practice had already been traded with a discount at international markets for several years. If the possibility existed that the gold of the Banca d'Italia could fall into the hands of the Italian government, this probably seemed a possible threat for the gold of the German banks. Thus, German banks had done nothing more than to prepare an exclusion from the rules of the legally decreed forced exchange in this particular scenario.

Even though these claims might have been understandable when looking at them from the banks' point of view, they still remained unrealistic and politically impossible. Thus, they also stood as an impediment to the establishment of a bank in Italy. Therefore, it hardly comes as a surprise that the Federal Foreign Office declined to send this memorandum to the Italian government via the official diplomatic channel. While the ambassador in Rome was indeed officially instructed to support the wishes of the Berlin banks, the general opinion in Wilhelm Street was that the memorandum in its current form was not very adept and at times too harsh in its language:

> We cannot impose binding regulations for economic and financial politics on the Italian government. The question of the gold reserves is a purely technical problem and as such to be solved by the experts. To this end, Judiciary Council Winterfeldt, one of the owners of Berliner Handelsgesellschaft will travel to Rome within the next days.[40]

Winterfeldt indeed came to Rome at the beginning of March. However, concrete results of this journey only materialised very slowly, while instead it resulted in downright trench warfare (one could also call it a poker game) between the representative of the Berlin banks and the Italian government. On 12 March, ambassador von Bülow sent a message from Rome: 'Mr Winterfeldt travelled to Capri very quickly after having arrived in Rome, as he told me, in order to indicate how little interest German banks had in the foundation of an Italian bank.'[41]

On 26 March, von Bülow then reported to Berlin, that in a conversation between the two foreign ministers Blanc had 'apparently intentionally mentioned that the Parisian banks had made better offers than the Berlin *Haute Finance*, because they seemed to be much more convinced....'[42]

Another two days later, Winterfeldt had informed the ambassador in a short letter that he had to return to Berlin and only wanted to report 'that the local circumstances still seemed to be too insecure and involute to seriously approach German banks with plans to implement the project.' Regarding the question of the gold deposit, Banca d'Italia had not been willing to give binding guarantees. Since it was uncertain how long finance minister Sonnino would remain in office, it was also uncertain if regulations regarding this matter had any chance to be realised at all.[43]

All initiatives had obviously reached a dead point, and for weeks it seemed that Berlin would give preference to waiting.

In these circumstances it is not surprising at all that Joel, whose professional as well as personal existence were directly linked to the realisation or the failure of these plans, staggered; as he already had two months before. On the one hand, he had not completely lost hope that a joint credit institution could be built from the ruins of Banca Generale and Credito Mobiliare.[44] On the other hand, he also wrote to Arthur Salomonsohn, one of the directors of Disconto-Gesellschaft, on 8 April 1894: 'I personally take a clear wait-and-see approach, since I do not want to commit to one side or the other before I have not gained a better overall view of the circumstances.'[45]

Nevertheless, the hesitation of the banks in Berlin seemed to draw Joel's thoughts towards a more moderate solution. At the end of April, he wrote to Rosenberg, it had to be assumed, 'that a well managed [banking] house wouldn't need too much of any initial capital and might attract important national and international clients.'[46] Rosenberg seemed to encourage Joel in this direction as he wrote to him shortly afterwards with regard to such a smaller solution in the belief:

> That the first local institute would be able to trust us with its limited liability capital, namely because I would assume we are not talking about huge sums, but rather small amounts of approx. 500.000 Francs per individual. I believe that we (Berliner Handelsgesellschaft, P.H.) and Deutsche Bank would join such an endeavour if reassured by the personal commitment of certain individuals.[47]

Joel for his part envisioned a banking house with approximately two million Lire capital stock, carried by Berliner Handelsgesellschaft and Deutsche Bank, but most probably also by personal friends of the Frankfurt *Haute Banque*, in the event that such a smaller solution could be implemented.[48]

Only a few days later, Rosenberg was in a position to signal to Joel that Berlin had also taken another turn and was reconsidering the idea of a big bank.[49] In his response, Joel underlined that it seemed 'completely impossible' to him that the 'gold guarantee' which German and Swiss banks still insisted on, would ever be approved by the Italian government. Besides this, he believed that it would be difficult to establish the headquarters in a town in Northern Italy, particularly if one tried to conduct large-scale financial transactions with the Italian government at the same time.

> You know of my antipathy to Rome as a business city. Nonetheless I have come to the conclusion that in the particular Italian circumstances, continuous contact with leading personalities of the government and Banca d'Italia is absolutely essential in order to avoid being pushed back.[50]

There is nothing that one could add to this, particularly if German banks envisioned the main activity of the to-be-established credit institution as that of conducting financial operations with the Italian state. Joel certainly must have been right in recommending a head office in Rome.

It was also at the end of May 1894, when the name of Federico Weil, who had led the branch office of Credito Mobiliare until the previous year, came up in discussion for the first time. Like Joel, Weil was of German-Jewish descent, born in 1854 in Randegg in Southern Baden close to the Swiss border. He came to Italy aged thirteen and learned the banking business in several Milan banks. Furthermore, again like Joel, he was an *italiano d'elezione* – an Italian by choice.[51] Furthermore, Weil was a cousin of the well-known Milan banker Alberto Weill-Schott, who was also born in Randegg, and in whose bank Weil temporarily worked as authorised officer.[52] At the end of May, Federico Weil had apparently been in Berlin and had negotiated with Carl Fürstenberg, who was by all accounts the leading figure at the Berliner Handelsgesellschaft. One may assume that it was Fürstenberg, who wanted to have Weil as director of the to-be-established institution with Joel as his partner. He wanted the two men to cooperate well in the future.[53] While we do not know Joel's reaction to this decision, he presumably put a good face on the matter and loyally worked together with Weil from this point on. In any case, both complemented each other very well: Joel was highly communicative and principally represented the bank to the outside world. Weil preferred to work behind the scenes, but due to his long experience with the credit transactions of businesses as well as with the Milan stock exchange, he was just as irreplaceable for the bank.

Proof of the fact that finally serious steps were taken in Berlin can be found in the meeting of representatives from German, Swiss and Austrian banks in Milan in mid-June 1894.[54] Prior to this meeting there had been a telegram, initiated by Julius Schwabach, shareholder of the Bleichröder banking house, and sent from prime minister Crispi to the Italian ambassador in Berlin, Graf Lanza, in which the establishment of a German bank in Italy was welcomed with the utmost pleasure.[55] An example of the seriousness with which the project was received can be seen in Zurich, where a long discussion of the board of directors of Schweizerische Kreditanstalt took place on 21 June 1894. The result of this discussion was to participate in the bank-to-be with an amount of 500.000 CHF out of the required 20 million gold Lire.

> In general … we are of the opinion that the two directors-to-be; Mr Joel in particular, do not of sufficiently proof to be the leaders needed in order to establish a management that follows principles of high and solid business ethic… we therefore strictly recommend the election of a third person who qualifies in this regard for the board of directors.[56]

Thus, as soon as a suitable personality had been found, they would insist on the implementation of a third director for the bank.[57] In this context, one cannot help but wonder (without receiving a satisfying answer) where this negative judgment about the two directors, Joel in particular, had come from? Nevertheless, the following two decades should have proven the contrary.

Negotiations with the government in Rome, which were immediately initiated after the Milan meeting, still failed to deliver a concrete result. Prime Minister Crispi gave a rather cool welcome to the German bank representatives and further declined the request for a gold depot, which had been voiced several months earlier. Even more far-reaching ideas of a bank-to-be, which would have the exclusive right to provide the Italian treasury with foreign currency, did not meet with approval.[58] In light of this reluctant attitude in Rome, the German party had to abandon these requirements quickly; particularly as these requests had also been vehemently criticised throughout the Italian press.[59] In the end, the second round of negotiations failed as well. One of the alleged reasons was the failure to win a prominent Italian for the board of directors of the new bank.[60]

It may have been Joel who felt the deepest disappointment about this repeated failure and who subsequently wrote to a business acquaintance:

> Ignorance and selfish intrigues on the one hand, lack of knowledge about the circumstances of the country on the other hand, have brought failure to a project that seemed to be safe and would have been economically beneficial for the entire country.[61]

As it had been already considered before, now the smaller solution of a limited partnership with Joel and Weil at the top was favoured by the German party. In order to not lose the two German-Italian experts, at the end of June Winterfeldt required that the German banks should pay a monthly salary of 25,000 Lire to both Joel and Weil, starting on 1 July 1894. Further, if the planned limited partnership could not be achieved until the end of August, both had to receive another instalment of 25,000 Lire each.[62] But there seemed to be progress on other levels as well: Clemente Maraini, engineer from the Tessin, who had worked with the German group for quite some time and who was meant to become representative of the new Banca Commerciale in Rome in 1895, as experienced networker,[63] conducted preliminary negotiations with the above-mentioned Count Sanseverino Vimercati with the aim of recruiting him as president for the bank-to-be.[64] The same Maraini travelled to Germany in August in order to strengthen connections with bankers from Frankfurt and Berlin.[65]

The decisive breakthrough finally happened when, on 22 September, Steinthal from the board of directors of *Deutsche Bank* wrote to Weil that it had been decided in a meeting on the previous day, 'that the immediate foundation of the bank in Italy was confirmed.... The idea however, that you and Joe would be the directors was abandoned, mainly because of Swiss resistance.'[66] The latter institution had, as well as the representatives of the Austrian banks, also participated in the gathering. On the same day, in a letter to Joel, the Bleichröder banking house mentioned, that the new bank would be founded 'without consideration whether or not there would be Italian members on the supervisory board'. The draft of the statutes of the bank-to-be, which had already been prepared several months before, were changed accordingly and thus 'the regulation which opposed the purchase of Italian pensions or other state bonds through the bank was abandoned. A suitable limit for the future should be found through a decision of the supervisory board'.[67]

Insights about the next steps and the intentions of the German (or rather of the international) banking group can also be derived from a letter by Max Winterfeldt, dated back to 26 September, in which he emphasised that:

> It is in no way our intention to exclude the Italians from the bank or to be unfriendly towards the government. In truth our programme remains unchanged; namely to complement the board of directors with qualified Italians after the foundation of the bank. For the time being the board of directors will consist of seven Germans, three Swiss and four Austrians. Once the bank is set up, it will be our task to find the right persons in Italy that are suitable and willing to accept a mandate. We are happy to appoint any suitable candidate that might be found in the meantime; only we do not want to postpone the foundation (not even for 24 hours) due to any negotiations regarding the matter with the Italians. An unfriendly position towards the Italian government should be ruled out in any case since the primary aim of the creation of the bank is to create and strengthen good business between our group and the Italian state.[68]

At the same time, Winterfeldt also sent a copy of the newly elaborated statutes to Joel in order to emphasise that

> in paragraph two Rome is mentioned as the representation of the institution. However, in order to have our hands tied behind our backs we have added paragraph fifteen, stating that the board of directors will decide about the inauguration of the representation.[69]

Consequently, the earlier suggestions of Joel had been adopted; while the draft of the statutes, which had been agreed by the German banking group in mid-June, did not explicitly consider a branch office or representation in Rome at this point.[70]

Apart from that, the adopted statutes stated that the credit institution, which was now officially known as the Banca Commerciale Italiana, had to have a share capital of 20 million Lire with a nominal value of 500 Lire for each shareholder (art. 5). An increase of the capital stock up to 50 million Lire was possible without changing the statutes but only with the necessary vote in the general meeting (art. 8). Furthermore, the creation of a central authority with at least two equitable members was created as well as the establishment of an administrative board with at least 11 and a maximum of 25 members (art. 11 and 23). According to article 21:

> The administrative board had the possibility to entrust individual members or local committees... with the task of permanently monitoring the management of the head office as well as of its individual branch offices.[71]

However, such 'delegates of the board of directors' as they can also be found, for example, in French or Swiss corporate law, did not exist at the Banca Commerciale. Only in 1908 – after both had stood the test in the bank's management for over one and a half decades – the *direttori centrali* Joel and Weil were elected to those positions.[72]

Of great importance, especially for the first years of the bank, was the content of article 22, which stated: 'The members of the board of directors, who live abroad, form a committee, which can freely decide on its provisional seat.'

Like no other regulation, the establishment of the so-called *Auswärtigen Comités*, which met foremost in Berlin at first, but later also sometimes in Luzern, illustrated the influence the German, Swiss, and Austrian founding banks intended to exercise on their Milan foundation for the years to come.

Further to be mentioned is the particularly important article 4 of the statutes, in which the area of responsibility is defined – 'banking business of all kinds of both its own account as well as for third parties, including deposit-taking, the commodities business as well as the commissions business via the trade of goods' – but which also defined the limitations of those activities.

> For the acquisition on own account of goods, shares, fixed-interest values, and all those tradable obligations with more than nine months' maturity after the acquisition took place … the approval of the board of directors is mandatory. Apart from that, the value of assets which the bank bought with the consent of the board of directors for its own account of securities, along with the total amount of all commitments the bank had due to participation in consortia of all kinds as well as of security papers bought by the bank for its own account, can never exceed the 20 per cent of paid-up capital.[73]

This clause was surely meant to be a precaution, as during the establishment of this statute article, one doubtlessly had the negative example of Credito Mobiliare and Banca Generale, the two failed predecessors, in mind.[74] For the unhindered expansion of a universal bank; and despite all initial ambiguities this was where Banca Commerciale was heading at last; such a 20 per cent clause would quickly prove to be a millstone around its neck. Thus, it does not come as a surprise that with the dynamic growth of Banca Commerciale this tight regulation was loosened rather quickly.[75]

Further lessons, which had been drawn from the breakdown of the two predecessor banks and of the note issuing sector, can be found in the regulation at the end of article 4 of the Banca Commerciale statutes: 'The bank is only allowed to buy real estate in case of its own need for work space or if the acquisition is necessary to safeguard credits of the bank.' The effects of the Italian real estate crisis of the late 1880s and the early 1890s with its devastating consequences for the involved credit institutions had obviously been felt.

According to the discussion of the board of directors of Schweizerische Kreditanstalt at the end of September, the requirements of article 4 of Banca Commerciale statutes, which initially intended to prohibit transactions on its own account in securities in Italian currency, were adjusted at the instigation of the Berlin banks in favour of a larger sphere of action for Banca Commerciale.[76] Once more, Zurich asked the question of a 'third member of the board of directors as soon as a suitable person can be found'.[77] Even though,

Swiss banks had finally been promised this position at that time and despite the absence of any reason, it never came to the appointment of a person in practice.

For the notarial foundation of Banca Commercial Italiana in Milan on 10 October 1894,[78] Winterfeldt from the Berliner Handelsgesellschaft and Imelmann from the banking house Bleichröder represented the Berlin banks; Julius Blum came for the Österreichische Credit-Anstalt, while the Swiss credit institutions were represented by Johann Jakob Schuster-Burckhardt, the president of the Basel Banking Association. For the time being, the only Italian was Count Sanseverino Vimercati, senator of the kingdom, who held with 200 shares a comparatively small amount. Confalonieri assumed with near certainty that this was meant as compensation from the other founders,[79] as Sanseverino was meant to become the first president of the board of directors, and thus, in the end they were successful in finding a local notable person for this rather representative position.

The for-the-time-being nominal capital of 20 million Lire, divided into shares of 500 Lire (nominal value), was provided by the six German founding banks, namely Berliner Handelsgesellschaft, Deutsche Bank, Bank für Handel und Industrie, S. Bleichröder, Disconto-Gesellschaft and Dresdner Bank. With six equal parts they provided 76.86 per cent of the total capital: 13.4 per cent came from the Österreichische Credit-Anstalt (which was the exact amount each of the German banks had made available). Seven and a half per cent came, again in equal shares, from the three Swiss institutions: the Basel Banking Association, Union Financière de Genève and Schweizerische Kredit-Anstalt.

Immediately after the establishment, sub-participations were already granted, for example, from the Österreichische Credit-Anstalt to the Anglo-Österreichische Bank, Vienna, and to the Wiener Bankverein. As a result, the shares of the Credit-Anstalt were halved immediately. The two smaller Vienna banks are actually also recognised as founding banks of Banca Commerciale, perhaps not directly in the establishment process itself, but with regard to the 'syndicate-regulations', with which the vehemently stressed supremacy of the Credit-Anstalt is at least expressed externally. The German founders gave up shares from their shareholdings to the following banks in Germany: L. Behrens & Söhne, Hamburg, Gebrüder Bethmann, Frankfurt/Main, Commerz- and Disconto-Bank, Hamburg, Norddeutsche Bank, Hamburg, Sal.Oppenheim jr. & Cie., Köln, A. Schaaffhausen'scher Bankverein, Köln, Jacob S.H. Stern, Frankfurt/Main, and M.M. Warburg & Co., Hamburg. However, none of these participations could have been very comprehensive. In the case of Oppenheim we do know that it amounted to one per cent, which equalled 200.000 Lire.[80] Further, in the form in which it was offered in a letter to Oppenheim this participation of one per cent is quite revealing. Dated 6 October, and thus already sent before the actual date of establishment, it stated: 'Ihnen zugleich bei allen zukünftigen, von unserer Gemeinschaft abzuschließenden Italienischen Geschäften nach Massgabe dieses Consortial-Vertrages … reservirt bleiben soll. [that all future Italian business of our corporation should be reserved according to this Consortial contract. (translated by ed.]' Of particular importance later on for the capital increases of Banca Commerciale, was the following further condition, communicated to Oppenheim in the same letter:

> Sofern bei dem einen oder anderen späteren italienischen Geschäfte die Zuziehung einer nicht in Italien, Deutschland, Österreich-Ungarn oder der Schweiz domizilierenden Gruppe erforderlich werden sollte, werden alle Betheiligungen, mithin auch die Ihrige, pro rata der neuen Abgabe reduzirt. [In the event that the one or the other Italian business eventually requires the participation of a group not domiciled in Italy, Germany, Austria-Hungary or Switzerland, all shares, including yours, will be reduced on a pro rata basis per new submission. (translated by ed.)][81]

According to the already quoted 'syndicate-requirements' the founding banks had also

> In Italien an geeignete Firmen und Privatpersonen Betheiligungen bis zu 15 Prozent des Ganzen abzugeben, welche von der deutschen und österreichischen Gruppe aus deren Antheilen pro rata der respectiven Quoten zu bestreiten sind. [In Italy a total of 15 percent of the total is to be relinquished to suitable companies and private persons. These shall be met by the German and Austrian group from their respective pro rate quotas. (translated by ed.)]

As a matter of fact, right from the beginning of Banca Commerciale's activity, the Turin private banking group Marsaglia received 1,000, and three banks from the Swiss canton Tessin received 600 shares as sub-participations.[82] It is also informative that, according to the protocol of the meeting from the four representatives who had travelled from Berlin, Vienna and Basel to Milan, and which had taken place directly before the notarial establishment, one million Lire was meant to be the nominal maximum amount of 'syndicate' sub-participations to be granted to outsiders, meaning non-members of the board of directors.[83] Hence, it was obvious that founders planned to essentially stay amongst themselves and subsequently remain in command, at least in the early phase of the new bank.

During these weeks in October 1894 public opinion in Italy, which for months had voiced its approval for the restoration of Credito Mobiliare and Banca Generale or at least for a solution in which Italian capital was decisive, remained all in all positive towards the new foundation. *Il Sole*, one of Milan's leading economic newspapers, was able to conclude on 12 October: 'The foundation of the new Banca Commerciale Italiana is greeted with general and sincere satisfaction. Newspapers of the capital all seem satisfied.' The German consul in Milan was also able to report to Berlin on the same day, 'dass die hiesige Presse fortfährt, dem Unternehmen [der Banca Commerciale, P.H.] freundliche Haltung zu zeigen' [that the local press continues to show a good attitude towards the company (Banca Commerciale)].[84] However, such general courtesy did not exclude a differentiated attitude as the example of *Corriere della Sera* illustrates, which underlined in its edition of 21–22 October that 'foreign capital is and would be indispensable in the long run.' The article then addresses the establishment of Banca Commerciale concretely and poses the question, 'but what is the Italian contribution?', before it proceeds:

> Auslandskapital ist in Ordnung: aber Kapital, das für den Betrieb einer großen Bank bestimmt ist, dabei kann … nicht wünschen, dass es ausschließlich von ausländischen Elementen gebildet und vertreten wird. Die vielen Gründe aufzuzählen, die dafür sprechen, ist überflüssig. Wie kommt es also, dass außer einem früheren Präfekten – [hier wird eindeutig, und nicht sehr schmeichelhaft, auf Sanseverino Vimercati hingewiesen, P.H.] – dem, um es banktechnisch auszudrücken, in der Bilanz kein großes Gewicht zukommen dürfte, wir in der neuen Schöpfung kein einziges italienisches Element erkennen können? … man könnte den Eindruck gewinnen, dass die Italiener noch nicht genügend vorbereitet sind, um bei dem Werk, dass das Auslandskapital in Angriff nehmen möchte, mitwirken zu können. [Foreign capital is acceptable, however capital designated for the operation of a big bank should preferably not exclusively consist of and be represented by foreign elements. It is unnecessary to mention the various reasons here. Hence, how is it that apart from a previous prefect (this is clearly a – not very flattering – reference to Sanseveriono Vimercati, P.H.) – who, to say it in a technical way, will not have any significant impact on the balance sheet – it is not possible to recognise a single Italian element in this new creation? … One could get the impression that the Italians are not sufficiently prepared to contribute to this endeavour, which seeks to utilise foreign capital. (translated by ed.)]

For his part Otto Joel had already personally informed the German ambassador at the Quirinal, von Bülow, about the foundation of 'his' bank during a visit in Rome. In a letter from 25 November, also addressed to Bülow, he further added:

> Bei meinen offiziellen Besuchen bei S[einer] Excellenz Sonnino, dem Generaldirektor des Schatzamts, Comm.[endator] Stringher, u. der Generaldirektion der Banca d'Italia habe ich allerseits das freundlichste Entgegenkommen constatiren können, so dass zu hoffen ist, dass der neuen Bank ein Anschluss, soweit er ihr in ihrer unabhängigen Stellung erwünscht und nothwendig sein wird, nicht fehlen werde. Aus den industriellen und Handelskreisen wird ihr allgemein aufrichtiges Wohlwollen entgegengebracht, das der richtigen Erkenntniß entspringt, von wie hohem Werth eine starke, wohl organisirte Bank für die weitere ökonomische

> Entwicklung ist. [On the occasion of my official visit at his excellence Sonnino, Secretary General of the Treasury Department, Commendator Stringher and the General Directorate of Banca d'Italia, I have established mutual friendly goodwill, so we would expect the new bank will not lack support – as far as this will be needed and desired given its independent position. The bank is very well and genuinely received by the industrial and commercial circles. This goodwill arises from the realisation that a strong and well organised bank will be highly beneficial for economic development (translated by ed.)].[85]

The reactions of public opinion, but also – as shown in Joel's letter above – the attitude of the people directly involved in the establishment of the bank leave the impression that contemporaries were well aware of the meaning the foundation of a new commercial bank had at that time and how the gap, which the breakdown of Credito Mobiliare and Banca Generale had created, could finally be closed. Thus it was surely not a coincidence that only a few months after Banca Commerciale had been brought to life, its most important competitor for the foreseeable future, Credito Italiano, entered the stage.[86] In this case, the reconstruction of Banca di Genova had relied on a financial institution which had existed since 1870 but which principally had a local significance. As was the case with many of the other banks, the Banca die Genova had not managed to manoeuvre unscathed through the crises of the previous years: Out of a capital stock of 20 million Lire in 1889, the volume of Banca di Genova had been gradually reduced to three million Lire in June 1894. One month later, it had increased again to 5 million Lire. The decisive leap followed in December 1894, when the capital was increased to 20 million Lire, even though only 14 million Lire were initially deposited.

This substantial capital increase, even though to a much lesser extent than in the case of Banca Commerciale, was also carried by foreign capital: out of the nine million Lire of fresh capital, the Milan private bank of Swiss origin, Vonwiller & C., provided 3.5 million Lire and subsequently handed its own banking business including its staff over to the newly founded institution. The Berlin private banking house Robert Warschauer & Co. and the Bank Manzi & C. in Rome together added three million Lire to the capital injection, while the former shareholders of Banca die Genova contributed the remaining 2.5 million Lire.[87] Warschauer & Co. had participated in the establishment of the private bank Manzi in Rome in the summer of 1893, and thus held significant influence as a limited partner. In a notification to the Auswärtiges Amt in Berlin, Warschauer elaborated on its decision to participate:

> Wir sind bei dieser Unternehmung von der Überzeugung ausgegangen, dass das deutsche Kapital für die ökonomische Entwicklung Italiens ersprießlicher mitwirkt, wenn es dauernd daselbst im Umlaufe verbleibt, als durch zeitweise Übernahme von Staats-, Communal- und Eisenbahn-Anleihen behufs Einführung an den deutschen Börsen.[88] [With respect to

this business we have proceeded with the conviction that German capital can be employed effectively for the economic development of Italy, particularly when it alone remains in circulation; as opposed to being occasionally funded by state, municipal and railway shares for the purpose of introducing these to German stockmarkets. (translated by ed.)].

The participation of Warschauer and Manzi in Banca die Genova only originates from December 1894, but the corresponding negotiations, which initially aimed for a reconstruction of Banca Generale and only turned to Banca di Genova after a couple of weeks,[89] had already became known to the general public by mid-October, directly after the foundation of Banca Commerciale.[90] On 5 February 1895, the general meeting of Banca di Genova changed its name to Credito Italiano, by which, in practice, the establishment of the institution was made publically known and – in rivalry to Banca Commerciale – by which it claimed to act on a national level.[91] Only four out of the 15 members of the newly elected board of directors of Credito Italiano were foreigners: two representatives of Warschauer & Co., as well as one representative for the Nationalbank für Deutschland, Berlin, and the Basler Handelsbank. Thus, compared to Banca Commerciale – even after several Italian representatives were elected to its board of directors, starting in 1895–96 – Credito Italiano had much less foreign representation, while additionally the represented foreign banks were institutions from the second league.

Conclusion and outlook

This representation of circumstances that led to the establishment of Banca Commerciale – and marginally to the foundation of Credito Italiano – including the short characterisation of the involved protagonists, particularly of Otto Joel and Federico Weil,[92] and the at times quite detailed description of the negotiations between the founding banks themselves as well as the discussions with the Italian government, is further augmented by the dialogue between the founding banks and the experts hired for the future leadership of Banca Commerciale. Thus, a dense network of information, which allows for the following conclusions, has been created: firstly the involvement of especially German banks in both the foundations, particularly in the case of Banca Commerciale Italiana, did not occur out of nowhere, but was a consequence of the steadily growing participation of German capital in the financing of the Italian economy since the mid-1880s. In global terms one can ascribe the non-appearance of a crisis in Italy, at least until about 1890, as Fenoaltea did,[93] to the cyclical upturn of the 'Kuznets cycle' and the worldwide effect of British capital exports. However, the significance of such for a detailed analysis of the specific situation in Italy remains unclear. Secondly the initial objectives of German, Swiss, and Austrian banks to establish Banca Commerciale as an instrument for comprehensive capital transactions with Italian currency dissolved quickly, and they did so not only due to the above described opposition of the Italian government against all monopolistic claims by foreign investors during the summer of 1894. While the economic upswing in 1895–96 opened various new possibilities in industrial financing for the bank, a step-by-step sanitation of the national budget, initiated by the minister of finance Sonnino, reduced all preliminary hopes of business in the public finance sector. Even though it was not possible to foresee this development, both new credit institutions were guided towards the path of universal banks of the Middle-European, respectively the Scandinavian variety. While they willingly followed this path afterwards, it would lead to difficulties in certain industrial divisions, such as the iron and steel industry, a century later. Of course, there were connecting factors to the two predecessor banks, yet their destiny was to be avoided at all costs. Even when, starting in 1899, French banks as the powerful Banque de Paris et des Pays-Bas took part in Banca Commerciale – while Comptoir National d'Escompte and two Belgian banks participated in Credito Italiano[94] – the 'genetic code' of the two universal banks remained almost unchanged. Accordingly, both banks had a major influence on the financing of the first industrial breakthrough, even though it was mostly restricted to the Northeast of Italy at that time.

Despite the apparent process by which an increasingly differentiated internationalisation in ownership structures took place, as well as a simultaneous growth in the percentage of Italian shareholders, Banca Commerciale seemed to be an essentially 'German bank'. This was not merely public opinion, but also the perspective of British and French diplomats, at least until the breakout of World War I and in the months directly afterward.[95] However, figures proved the exact opposite: one year after its foundation, the German and Austrian founder banks still owned 74 per cent of Banca Commerciale's share capital, but six years later the overall share had been reduced to only about ten per cent, and it only amounted to 2.4 per cent in 1914. Meanwhile, Swiss and French shareholders respectively controlled 20.5 and 14 per cent of the capital of Banca Commerciale while 63 per cent of the total capital was owned by Italian shareholders. At least those are the figures, which were published on the occasion of the 25th anniversary of the bank in 1920[96] – one of the reasons being to underline the 'national' character of the bank shortly after the end of the war as well as to prove that the influence of the former enemy had been in fact of minor impact. Entirely in contrast to these share figures – and this had been, of course, a reason for constant argument – the distribution within the board of directors of Banca Commerciale until shortly after the breakout of World War I was as follows: 1896, two years after the foundation, out of the 21 members eight were Italian citizens, along with seven Germans, three Austrians and three Swiss representatives. In 1914 the board of directors had increased to 31 seats, comprising amongst others 15 Italians and seven Germans, whereas the two delegates of the board of directors, Otto Joel and Federico Weil, initially of German ancestry, both had acquired Italian citizenship.[97]

In 1914–15, in the period of Italy's neutrality at the beginning of World War I, which lasted until the end of May 1915, and in the first year of the

Italian entry into the war, the actual or – often – alleged influence of the German founder banks on Banca Commerciale was one of the leading themes in Italian domestic politics. The way in which this influenced foreign policy has been elaborated on in the above example. It was, as if the initial requirements and the complicated development of the founding process of the bank had become stuck in the collective memory of institutions and politics over the decades and could be utilised again whenever it was necessary. That the events of the years 1893 and 1894 had in fact to be reconstructed from structures and processes at that time and that the derived results could again be subject to quick change afterwards should be clear from this contribution.

Notes

1 Richard Tilly has already clearly stated this in a volume which was published by Gerald D. Feldman and others two decades ago:

> Individual banking histories have provided much valuable information on the social background and personalities of the commercial bankers themselves. They have also done well in the task of describing key transactions such as mergers and large-scale financial projects, accompanied by related contemporary assessments of their riskiness and profitability. It is true, to be sure, that these studies are marked by an obvious, if unfortunate, bias toward ultimately successful projects.

(Fase, M.M.G., Feldman, G.D., Pohl, M. eds. 1995. *How to Write the History of a Bank?* Aldershot: Ashgate, pp. 68–85)

2 An outstanding example of such a *Festschrift*, which still meets today's standards in all respects is the publication published on the occasion of 125th anniversary of Deutsche Bank. (Büschgen, H.E., Feldman, G.D., Gall, L., Holftrerich, C.-L., James, H. 1995. *Die Deutsche Bank 1870–1995*. Munich: Beck.)

3 Stefano Fenoaltea, to whom – among others – we owe the improved indices of industrial production in Italy between the agreement of the country dating back to 1860 and the outbreak of World War I, stressed, the significance of the 1880s for the dynamic development of 'social overhead capital' and the construction industry in Italian cities. In: Fenoaltea, S. 2006. *The Reinterpretation of Italian Economic History. From the Unification to the Great War*. Cambridge: Cambridge University Press, pp. 70–75.

4 Confalonieri, A. 1975. *Banca e industria in Italia, 1894–1906, Vol. 2: Il sistema bancario tra due crisi.* Milan: Banca Commerciale Italiana pp. 3–41.; Hertner, P. 1984. *Il capitale tedesco in Italia dall'Unità alla Prima Guerra Mondiale.* Bologna: Il Mulino, pp. 74–97; and the innovative and continuing and yet at all times balanced analysis by Brambilla, C. 2008. *Banche d'investimento in Europa. Tipologie e strutture operative prima del 1914*. Pisa: Liberiauniversitaria, in particular pp. 73ff.

5 Hertner (1984), pp. 74–89.

6 Anonymous. 1901. *Die Disconto-Gesellschaft 1851 bis 1901. Denkschrift zum 50jährigen Jubiläum*. Berlin: Kessinger Publishing, pp. 68–70.

7 Hertner, P. 1986. Die Deutsche Bank in Italien und ihre Beziehungen zum italienischen Kapitalmarkt bis zum Ausbruch des Ersten Weltkrieges. *Beiträge zu Wirtschafts- und Währungsfragen und zur Bankgeschichte*, 21, Mainz: v. Hase und Koehler, pp. 35–77 and in particular pp. 44–54.

8 Luzzatto, G. 1968. *L'economia italiana dal 1861 al 1894*. Turin: Einaudi, p. 177.

9 Arthur Salomonsohn was elected as one of the six proprietors of the business of the disconto company in 1896. Anonymous (1901), p. 22.

10 Archivio Storico Intesa Sanpaolo, 1894. *Patrimonio storico Banca Commerciale Italiana* [hereafter abbreviated: asi-bci]. PJ 2, p. 182. Milan. *Joel adressed to Salomonsohn* [text in German].
11 Pantaleoni, M. 1936. La caduta della Società Generale di Credito Mobiliare Italiano. *Studi storici di economia*. Bologna: N. Zanichellip, p. 225.
12 'Quasi-central', because Banco di Napoli and Banco di Sicilia were planned to co-exist as investment banks, even though their influence was highly reduced.
13 Asi-bci (1894), PJ 2, p. 192. *Joel addressed H. Rosenberg* [text in German].
14 Asi-bci (1894), PJ 2, p. 193. *Joel addressed to a certain Romanego* [text in Italian].
15 Asi-bci (1894), PJ 2, pp. 185f. *Joel addressed to Giolitti* [text in Italian].
16 Garruccio, R. 2002. *Minoranze in affari. La formazione di un banchiere: Otto Joel.* Soveria Mannelli: Rubbettino.
17 Asi-bci (1892), PJ 1, pp. 397f. *Joel addressed to Allievi* [text in Italian].
18 Political Archive of the Federal Foreign Office Berlin [hereafter abbreviated: PA AA] 1893. IA Italien 73 geheim (secret), vol. 8: *Records of the undersecretary of the Auswärtiges Amt* (Federal Foreign Office), von Rotenhan, 18 and 30 September 1893; letter of the president of the Reichsbank Koch, 18 September 1893; von Rotenhan addressed to Koch, 1 October 1893 and Historical Archive of Deutsche Bank, Frankfurt am Main [hereafter abbreviated: HADB] 1893. p. 2803: *Sessions of the consortiums for Italian business*, 29 September and 5 October 1893.
19 PA AA (1893), vol. 4: *Decree addressed to the imperial ambassador in Rome (Quirinal) Graf Solms* on 23 January 1891.
20 Compare the Italian press coverage to this suggestion: *L'Italie*, 4 October 1893. *La Perseveranza,* 3 October 1893 and *Fanfulla*, 3 October 1893.
21 HADB (1893/94), p. 2802: *Fürstenberg and Steinthal addressed to Fantoni*, 8 respectively 10 November 1893; Deutsche Bank addressed to Frascara (Credito Mobiliare), 23 November 1893; Archivio Sonnino, Montespertoli (Firenze): *Documenti-lettere, Ministero delle Finanze,* 1894, scatola 33, cartella 1 (Undated and unsigned memorandum, probably dated back to December 1893).
22 Which German credit institute was meant here remains unclear, but most probably either the Disconto-Gesellschaft or Deutsche Bank.
23 Asi-bci (1893), PJ 2, pp. 111f.
24 Asi-bci (1893), PJ 2, pp. 115f. *Joel addressed to E. Raggio.*
25 Asi-bci (1893), PJ 2, p. 129. *Joel addressed to Rosenberg* [text in German].
26 Asi-bci (1893), PJ 2, p. 38. *Joel addressed to Disconto-Gesellschaft.*
27 Archivio Sonnino (1893), scatola 33, cart. 1, n. 11–15. *Sonnino a Blanc* [text in Italian].
28 Archivio Sonnino (1893), scatola 33, cart. 1, n. 11–15. *Telegram from Lanza to the Italian Foreign Minisitry* [text in Italian].
29 Bleichröder-Archive, 1893. Box XXVI. *Mauthner addressed to Schwabach.* Kress Library of Business and Economics, Harvard Business School. Boston: Mass [text in German].
30 Bleichenröder Archive 1984. Box XXVI. *Mauthner addressed to Schwabach* [text in German].
31 Archivio Sonnino (1894), scatola 33, cart. 1. *Telegram from ambassador Lanza* [text in Italian].
32 Asi-bci (1983), PJ 17, fasc. 6 and 8.
33 Asi-bci (1894), *Joel Letter to Marchese Durazzo Pallavicini of Genoa*, from Berlin dated 12 February.
34 PA AA (1893). IA Italien 68, vol. 29. *Solms addressed to Reichskanzler Caprivi.*
35 Asi-bci (1894), PJ 17, fasc. 11 and 13. Villa addressed to Joel [original text in Italian]. Villa is also mentioned by C. Martignone 2001. *Imprenditori protestanti a Milano, 1850–1900.* Milan: Franco Angeli, p. 130.
36 Historical Archive of Credit Suisse, Zurich 1894. *Protocol of the finance commission*, 8 February 1894 (abstracts of this protocol have been generously provided to

me by the head office of the former Swiss Credit Association, which is today's Credit Suisse – P.H.) [text in German].

37 PA AA (1894). IA Italien 73 geheim, vol. 10. *Auswärtiges Amt addressed to Botschafter von Bülow* [text in German].

38 PA (1894). IA Italien 73 geheim, vol. 10. *Memorandum from 15 February 1894* [text in German].

39 Confalonieri (1975), p. 24 [text in Italian].

40 PA, AA (1894). IA Italien 73 geheim, vol. 10. *Auswärtiges Amt addressed to Ambassador von Bülow* [text in German].

41 I PA, AA (1894). *Von Bülow addressed to Auswärtiges Amt.* [original text in German].

42 PA, AA (1894). *Von Bülow addressed to Auswärtiges Amt* [text in German].

43 PA, AA (1894). *Winterfeldt addressed to von Bülow on 28 March 1894.* – This was after the recruitment of Sonnino, who rejected direct intervention in the companies and who wanted to restrict actions to restructure the state budget and to keep control of money circulation. Manacorda, G. 1993. *Dalla crisi alla crescita. Crisi economica e lotta politica in Itali 1892–1896*, Rome: Editori riuniti, particluarly p. 172.

44 Asi-bci (1894), PJ 2, p. 287f. *Joel addressed to a 'good friend'* [text in Italian].

45 Asi-bci (1894), PJ 2, fol. 295f. *Joel addressed to Salomonsohn* [text in German].

46 Asi-bci (1894). PJ 17, fasc. 21. *Joel addressed to Rosenberg* [text in German].

47 Asi-bci (1894). PJ 17, fasc. 22. *Rosenberg addressed to Joel* [text in German].

48 Asi-bci (1894). PJ 17, fasc. 27. *Joel addressed to Rosenberg* [text in German].

49 Asi-bci (1894). PJ 17, fasc. 31. *Rosenberg addressed to Joel* [text in German].

50 Asi-bci (1894). PJ 17, fasc. 32. *Joel addressed to Rosenberg* [text in German].

51 As phrased in Asi-bci (1894). *Verbali del consiglio d'amministrazione* [Protocols of the Board of directors, hereafter VCA], vol. 5, p. 141 (in commemoration of Federico Weil in the session on 23 October 1919).

52 HADB 1894, S 2804,*Federico Weil in a letter to Max Steinthal (Deutsche Bank)*; Piluso, G. 1999. *L'arte dei banchieri. Moneta e credito a Milano da Napoleone all'Unità*, Milan: Franco Angeli 1, pp. 105–107.

53 This can be derived from: Asi-bci (1894). PJ 17, fasc. 35. *Rosenberg's letter addressed to Joel.*

54 Asi-bci (1894). PJ 17, fasc. 41. *Salomonsohn adressed to Joel.* PA AA (1894), IA Italien 73 geheim, vol. 11. *Ambassador von Bülow adressed to Auswärtiges Amt.*

55 Crispi, F. 1913. *Questioni internazionali. Diario e documenti*, 2nd edn. Milan: Fratelli Treves, p. 186. Manacorda (1993), p. 176.

56 Credit Suisse, Historical Archive (1894). *Protocol of the Board of directors*, 21 June.

57 Credit Suisse, Historical Archive (1894). *Protocol of the Board of directors* [text in German].

58 PA AA (1894). IA Italien 73 geheim, vol. 11. *Schwabach adressed to Auswärtiges Amt* [text in German].

59 PA AA (1894). Report of the German consul in Milan. In: *Vossische Zeitung*, 27 June 1894.

60 PA AA (1894).

61 Asi-bci (1894). PJ Vol. 2, pp. 468f. *Joel addressed to K. Lupold* [text in German].

62 Asi-bci (1894). PJ 17, fasc. 50. *Winterfeldt adressed to Joel.*

63 Compare the letters of *Banca Commerciale* adressed to Banca d'Italia and other big companies and representative offices in Rome from 15 April 1895, announcing the appointment of Clemente Maraini to become representative of the bank in Rome. Asi-bci (1895), CpD Vol. 4, pp. 275ff.

64 Asi-bci (1894). PJ 2, pp. 477f. *Joel adressed to Winterfeldt.*

65 Asi-bci (1894). PJ 17, fasc. 61 and 62. C. *Maraini addressed to Joel.*

66 Asi-bci (1894). PJ 17, fasc. 71. *Steinthal addressed to Weil.* Also: Credit Suisse, Historical Archive (1894). *Protocol of the Board of directors* [text in German].
67 Asi-bci (1894). PJ 17, fasc. 72. *Bleichröder addressed to Joel* [text in German].
68 Asi-bci (1894). PJ 17, fasc. 76. *Winterfeldt addressed to Joel* [text in German].
69 Asi-bci (1894). In the official registered statutes which had been finally constituted for the establishment of the bank, article 2 stated that 'the bank has its registered office in Milan and will install a branch office or procuration in Rome. The bank may establish other branch offices or procurations in other cities of the kingdom of Italy.' (Supplemento al Foglio periodico della R. Prefettura di Milano. Annunzi legali, anno 1894, n. 88bis del 4/11/1894) [Translation taken from the Italian original text].
70 Asi-bci (1894). SR 1, fasc. 3. *Statutes derived from the decisions from 9* [crossed by hand and replaced with '15/16'] June 1894, Berlin: Otto von Holten.
71 This quote is taken from the statutes. Like all others it has been translated from the Italian original text.
72 Banca Commerciale Italiana, 1908. *Annual Report. Relazione del consiglio d'amministrazione for the o. and a.o. HV*, 31 March 1908, Milan: Banca Commeciale Italiana, p. 12.
73 See Art. 4 of the Statute Draft from 15/16 June 1894.
74 Pantaleoni (1936), pp. 229f. And Confalonieri (1975), pp. 296ff.
75 Confalonieri (1975), pp. 52ff.
76 See Art. 4 of the Statute Draft from 15/16 June 1894.
77 Credit Suisse, Historical Archive (1894). *Protocol of the Board of directors*, 28 September 1894.
78 Bollettino ufficiale delle società per azioni, vol. 12 (1894), fasc. 45, pp. 2ff.
79 Confalonieri (1975), p. 32, annotation 5.
80 It was also set in the 'Syndicats-Bestimmungen' from October 1894: '*Die genannten Firmen treten diesem Vertrage bei. Dieselben gelten als Mitglieder des Syndikats und sollen insbesondere berechtigt sein, bei einer etwaigen Emission den Prospect mit zu unterzeichnen*' [The aforementioned companies join this contract. These same count as members of the syndicate and shall in particular be entitled to sign the prospect at any possible emission. (Trans. ed.)]. Sal. Oppenheim jr. & Cie., Cologne, Hausarchiv, no. 155.
81 Sal. Oppenheim jr. & Cie., Cologne, Hausarchiv, no. 155. *The six founding banks in Berlin addressed to Oppenheim*, 6 October 1894.
82 Confalonieri (1975), p. 33.
83 Asi-bci (1894), SR 1, fasc. 3 – According to this document an attempt was made to dispense holdings of the syndicate not only to the yet-to-be elected executives of the board, but also to known and well-respected Italian citizens or firms who could be of use to the society.
84 PA AA (1894). IA Italien 73 geheim, vol. 12. *Report of the consul in Milan*, 12 October 1894.
85 PA AA (1894). *Joel adressed to von Bülow*, 25 November 1894.
86 Confalonieri (1975), pp. 185ff.
87 Archivio Storico Unicredit, Milano: *Banca di Genova/Credito Italiano, Verbali del Consiglio di Amministrazione* [Protocoll of the board of directors], vol. 14, pp. 85ff., Session of 12 December 1894 [text in German].
88 Bundesarchiv Berlin-Lichterfelde, AA 1638: R. Warschauer addressed to the Auswärtige Amt on 13 July 1893.
89 Compare: *Il Sole*, 22/23 October, 28 October, 29/30 October and 17 November 1894.
90 PA AA. IA Italien 73 geheim, vol. 12. *Report of the German consul in Milan*, 12 October 1894.
91 Doria, G. 1973. *Investimenti e sviluppo economico a Genova alla vigilia della Prima Guerra Mondiale, vol. 2*. Milan, pp. 171f.

92 During the years 1893–94 Federico Weil still called himself *Fritz* in correspondence with German bankers who used to address him as such. Compare: *Letters of Max Steinthal addressed to Weil*, 25 May and 5 June 1894. In: HADB, 1894, p. 2804.

93 Fenoaltea (2006), pp. 102ff.

94 Fenoaltea (2006), pp. 102ff.

95 See here three examples: With reference to British import licenses for the at this time still neutral Italy, the consul general wrote to the Foreign Office in Genoa on 31 October 1914: 'It is reported that the Banca Commerciale Italiana is practically a German concern …' National Archives, Kew, FO 368/1018. – Further, in a report of the British ambassador in Rome to the Foreign Office from 16 November 1914, Sir Renell Rodd concludes – among others – concerning a visit of Giuseppe Toeplitz, director of the Banca Commerciale to the British embassy that

> Its [i.e. of Banca Commerciale, P.H.] influence is now so great and it has been extended with such dexterity and skill by the clever experts at its head that it may be said to dominate nearly every commercial enterprise. While nominally an Italian institution it is really controlled by a small group of those international financiers who have believed in the rising star of Germany and therefore work for the King of Prussia.

To this a short hand-written note is added (dated to 27 November 1914) from a leading public officer at the Foreign Office to the report of the ambassador: 'It has always been understood that the Banca Commerciale is under the thumb of the big German banks and is run by them. But it must be admitted that the "Italian façade" is very cleverly constructed.' National Archives, Kew, FO 368/1016.

96 These numbers can be found in: Banca Commerciale Italiana, 1920. *La Banca Commerciale Italiana 1894–1919*. Milan: BCI – Tipografia Bertieri e Vanzetti, p. 100. Interestingly, even Toeplitz stated in his conversation with the British ambassador that the German share of joint-stock capital was 3 million Lire out of a total 156 million Lire – thus, denoted with two per cent.

97 Compare: Data of the printed annual reports (*Rapporti sull'esercizio*) of Banca Commerciale Italiana for the years 1896–1914.

3 Jewish financiers in the City of London

Reality and rhetoric, 1830–1914[1]

Ranald Michie

> London is now a truly competitive international financial centre and the people who work in the financial services industry operate in what is the nearest thing to a true meritocracy. Nationality and ethnic background are unimportant and employees are as likely to have been educated in Paris, Bombay or St Petersburg as in the UK.[2]

Introduction

The City of London has been one of the leading financial centres in the world for three centuries, sharing its position, successively, with Amsterdam, Paris, Berlin, New York and Tokyo. At times it occupied the premier position while at others it was in second or third place. Throughout that period and longer it owed part of its success to successive waves of immigrants, ranging from Italians in medieval times through French Huguenots in the early modern period to nationalities from all countries by the beginning of the twenty-first century. What these immigrants brought were skills, contacts and a determination to succeed which helped to maintain London as a dynamic financial centre and one possessed of the connections that were essential if it was to play an international role.[3] Considering the long association of Jews with both commerce and finance it was inevitable that they would number among those immigrants settling in London over the centuries. As Roth reflected in 1938, 'It is with the field of finance that Jewish economic achievement is usually associated.'[4] Consequently, important Jewish merchants and financiers were to be found in the City of London prior to their expulsion in 1290 and again after 1663, when the ban was finally repealed, as well as clandestinely in the intervening years.[5] As early as the late seventeenth century the Jew, Sir Solomon de Medina was playing a key role in the interplay between London and Amsterdam as financial centres, and he was among the first of many who made a major contribution to the City of London as a financial centre in subsequent centuries.[6] In the centuries that were to follow, other Jews made an important contribution to the City of London as with Samson Gideon in the eighteenth, Nathan Rothschild in the nineteenth and Sigmund Warburg in the twentieth. Through the likes of these, the City of London became strongly identified with Jewish financiers who were able to exercise enormous power there. To J.A. Hobson, writing in 1902, these Jewish financiers epitomised the capitalist system and all that was wrong with it:

> These great businesses – banking, broking, bill discounting, loan floating, company-promoting – form the central ganglion of international capitalism. United by the strongest bonds of organisation, always in closest and quickest touch with one another, situated in the very heart of the business capital of every state, controlled, so far as Europe is concerned, chiefly by men of a single and peculiar race, they are in a unique position to manipulate the policy of nations. No great quick direction of capital is possible save by their consent and through their agency. Does any one seriously suppose that a great war could be undertaken by any European State, or a great State loan subscribed, if the house of Rothschild and its connexions set their face against it?[7]

A degree of popular antagonism towards these Jewish financiers in the City was only to be expected in a Christian society with its suspicion of all whose livelihood was derived from lending money at interest. Even without Jews the City of London attracted hostility as it was so strongly associated with capitalism, and its profit-making imperative, as well as the intermediary role it played in both trade and finance, as that was seen as essentially parasitic.[8] As Dallas Brett noted in his 1945 diatribe against usury, 'the City of London is the very citadel of world usury'.[9] Jews were footloose financiers undermining national interests and thus existed in direct opposition to the interests of the nation state and the concerns of the native population. They were there to be tolerated as long as they were of value but were liable to expulsion or worse when they no longer served their purpose, as with Shylock in Shakespeare's play, *The Merchant of Venice*.[10] However, it might have been expected that these attacks would have abated over the course of the nineteenth century as many of the most prominent British Jews, such as the Rothschilds, became increasingly anglicised, though retaining their Jewish faith. Others converted to Christianity, intermarried with the native population, and became confidants of the ruling elite. With Benjamin Disraeli, Britain even had a prime minister of Jewish origin. Nevertheless, the degree of hostility towards Jews in the City appeared to increase in virulence over the course of the century, reaching a peak in the years before the First World War. Why this should be, has never been either investigated or explained for, it cannot be simply the product of anti-Semitic sentiments of long-standing duration. That was the conclusion reached by the respected financial journalist, Hartley Withers, in 1916. 'Much of the prejudice against financiers is based on, or connected with, anti-Semitic feelings, that miserable relic of medieval barbarism.'[11] Such a view explains a constant and underlying antagonism towards Jews but not its depth and breadth in the late Victorian and Edwardian age. For that the interaction between what Jews were doing in the City needs to be matched to changing perceptions over the course of the long nineteenth century. Was the perceived power and influence of Jewish financiers supported by the reality of the situation? If not, why was the rhetoric of antagonism towards Jews in the City so strong?

Reality

Over many centuries London received a small but steady stream of Jewish immigrants. Most were engaged in trade, especially dealing in precious stones and metals, but there was a gradual shift into finance both among the newcomers and within the families who settled in London. Some areas of finance were closely related to trade, as shown by the bullion dealers, Mocatta and Goldsmid. Moses Mocatta was a merchant and diamond dealer in London in the late seventeenth century. His sons became major dealers in silver in the early eighteenth century and by the late eighteenth century the family were leading bullion dealers in the City, being joined by another London Jew, Asher Goldsmid. However, other Jews moved into pure finance ranging from money lending through stock and bill broking to handling government loans. John King's father was a Jewish street trader in the mid eighteenth century whereas he became a very successful money lender in the late eighteenth century. The fathers of both Abraham Goldsmid and Henry Raphael were Jewish merchants in London but their sons became bankers and stockbrokers in the course of the eighteenth century. Similarly, Samson Gideon and Joseph Salvador came from Jewish mercantile families but moved into handling government loans during that century. Given the emerging opportunities in London in finance from the late seventeenth century onwards, those with expertise and connections in allied areas found it relatively easy to respond and Jews were numbered among these. The most successful of these Jewish financiers had also succeeded in integrating into the top echelons of British society through their children. In the mid eighteenth century Samson Gideon had married a Christian, brought up his children as Anglicans, and bought estates in Kent and Lincolnshire. The result was that one of his daughters married Viscount Gage while his son became Baron Eardley.[12]

There was then an additional influx of Jews in the late eighteenth and early nineteenth century as the French Revolution in 1789 sparked decades of disruption and warfare across continental Europe. That did not finally end until the defeat of Napoleon at the Battle of Waterloo in 1815. It was at this time that Nathan Rothschild arrived in London from Frankfurt as part of a family dispersal that linked that city with other European financial centres.[13] As a result the City of London possessed a significant group of Jewish financiers by the 1820s ranging from those running an extensive international business to those operating at the domestic level as various forms of brokers and money lenders. However, even in the areas of finance where they were prominent, Jews were never dominant. The City of London attracted numerous non-Jews from Continental Europe as well as drawing upon the native population for talent. There were also areas of financial activity in which Jews were largely absent such as domestic banking and insurance, though a few notable exceptions existed.[14] London's Jewish community was a relatively small one, numbering around 20,000 in total by the early nineteenth century, and most were not engaged in financial activities, even at the lowest level. Most London Jews were poor and continued to live in the East End where they were engaged in such occupations as tailors, jewellers, watchmakers, street traders and second-hand dealers. It was only a few who succeeded in international trade and finance, and many of these had come from mercantile and banking families abroad. They had been attracted to London because of the unrivalled opportunities it increasingly offered. And once successful there they moved their residence out of the City and settled in the West End. These successful Jews also intermarried, so cementing business relationships with family ties. In 1806 a daughter of Levi Barent Cohen, a very successful London merchant, married Nathan Rothschild. In 1812 another daughter married the stockbroker Moses Montefiore, whose uncle was Moses Mocatta, the bullion dealer. Though there were differences between Sephardic Jews from the Mediterranean and Ashkenazi Jews from Central and Eastern Europe, these were overcome by the needs of business and the possession of wealth. Nevertheless, considerable rivalry existed between different Jewish financiers as they competed for business while none could afford to confine their operations to dealings with fellow Jewish firms. The result of this was a changing balance within London's Jewish community as a small number grew away from its roots in the East End of London and established a new and respectable identity for themselves in the West End, where they intermingled with many non-Jews.[15]

By the 1820s there thus existed in London a numerically small Jewish elite that was increasingly integrated into both the commercial and financial activities that took place in the City and the upper layers of London society. This elite group was then joined by a small but steady trickle of Jews into London attracted by the openings it continued to offer for those engaged in trade and finance. Carl Joachim Hambro, whose father was a Jewish merchant in Copenhagen, moved to London in 1832 and opened a merchant bank there in 1839. Henri Bischoffsheim, whose father was a Jewish banker in Amsterdam, came to London in 1849, where he settled and established his own merchant bank, Bischoffsheim and Goldschmidt. The City's drawing power even attracted the Sassoons from Bombay in 1858. There was also internal migration within Britain with Samuel Montagu coming from Liverpool, where his father was a Jewish watchmaker and silversmith. He moved to London in 1847, becoming a bullion dealer and foreign exchange broker in association with his brother.[16] The result was that by the 1850s Jewish financiers had become accepted within the City, and their importance valued because of their expertise and connections in a few selected areas, especially international finance. The Rothschilds, in particular, were singled out as being the leaders within this elite group, as they were the wealthiest, the most successful and the most influential. According to Morrier Evans, in his 1852 description of the City, Jewish financiers were both feared because of their 'aptitude for business' and admired for their 'honesty'.[17]

By then the success of this Jewish elite was being translated into an even wider acceptance as the fortunes they had accumulated allowed them to buy their way into the very top of British society. The degree of acceptance can be judged from the removal of laws restricting their freedoms. During the early 1830s various legal prohibitions on the positions that Jews could occupy were ended, while in 1846 Parliament repealed the law preventing Jews owning land. Eventually, after a long battle, Lionel Rothschild was allowed in 1858 to take up his seat as an elected Member of Parliament while still being a practising Jew. It was at this time that Jewish financiers established their credentials among the land-owning aristocracy by purchasing country estates. Beginning in 1842 the Rothschilds began buying landed estates, acquiring a number in Buckinghamshire and Hertfordshire by the 1870s. Eventually they accumulated a total of 30,000 acres. They were not the only Jewish financiers to do so from the mid nineteenth century onwards as the Hambros, Montagus, Sassoons and Bischoffsheims followed suit. As a result, according to Alderman:

> By the 1870s families such as the Sassoons and the Rothschilds moved easily within the highest echelons of London society; they formed an Anglo-Jewish aristocracy, interlocked by ties of marriage and by mutual recognition of communal as well as national obligations.[18]

By 1880, as many as 5,000, or twenty-five per cent, of London's Jews were living in the West End and other suburban areas. This was indicative of both their material progress and social advancement. Success in commerce and finance as bankers, brokers and merchants had provided Jews with the means to transcend long-standing hostility and integrate into London society, which was much more fluid and open than that found in smaller towns and the countryside. Many of their children had also moved into the professions as well as academic and political life, leaving behind the occupations of their parents. Several had also converted to Christianity. Such a transition received public recognition in 1885 when Nathaniel Rothschild was made a peer. He was first among a succession of successful Jewish financiers who were honoured in this way in the late nineteenth century, such as Sydney Stern (Lord Wandsworth) and Henry de Worms (Lord Pirbright) in 1895 and then Samuel Montagu (Lord Swaythling) in 1907. It appeared that the Jewish financial elite had come of age translating success in business into social and political acceptability.[19]

Contributing to this acceptance was the nature of the business that they did. By 1880 most Jewish financiers were engaged in complex international transactions ranging from issuing loans in London on behalf of foreign governments, as with the Rothschilds, to operations in securities and foreign exchange between the financial centres of the world, which was a speciality of Samuel Montagu. Obtaining the trust of those with whom they were dealing was a key element in their success, whether they were dealing with the agents of indebted foreign governments or other bankers and brokers in the City or abroad, as business of this kind involved both co-operation and competition. A reputation for expertise and honesty was a vital ingredient in maintaining this trust and so was jealously guarded by long established Jewish financiers in the City. Some had even made it into the mainstream of British banking with Felix Schuster being the most important, though his father, a German Jewish merchant banker, had converted to Christianity. Felix had become a partner in Schuster, Son and Co. in 1879 and then a director of the Union Bank of London when it took over the family bank in 1888. Eventually Schuster became Governor of the Union Bank in 1895 as it became one of the major forces in British joint-stock banking, merging with Smith, Payne and Smith in 1902. He was regularly consulted by British governments on financial matters and became a baronet in 1906. Even the more recently arrived Jewish financiers from abroad usually came with well-established reputations gained in other financial centres. The Franco-Prussian war of 1870/1, for example, drove a number of Parisian bankers to relocate to London. One was Ernest Cassel, whose father was a German Jewish banker. He left Paris for London in 1871, where he started work with Bischoffsheim and Goldsmidt, and then established himself as an independent international financier. Another was Baron Emile D'Erlanger, whose family were French bankers in Paris but of German Jewish origins. He came to London at this time and set up the merchant bank, Erlanger and Co.

Despite these more recent arrivals, London's Jewish community remained tiny, which also made acceptance relatively easy, as Jews could not be construed as posing a threat to society. In a study conducted in 1883 Joseph Jacobs concluded that the number of Jews in London was around 46,000 of whom only 5,000 were in business, including those in the City. Furthermore, there were only 1,500 really wealthy Jewish families living in the West End. By examining London trade directories for 1883, and trying to identify Jewish names, he was able to conclude that 'the Jewish tailor, both as master and as workman, is by far the commonest figure among the occupations of the Jews of London.' When comparing the number of Jews with the total in each of a wide range of financial and commercial activities, Jacobs noted that in only a small number of specialised areas were Jews dominant, such as the trade in cane, cigars, coconuts, diamonds, esparto grass, feathers, hair, oranges, sponges and piece goods.[20]

The working population of the City of London in 1881 is estimated at around 300,000, which would suggest that Jews comprised less than two per cent of the total, based on Jacobs' figure of 5,000. Among certain groups the proportion that was Jewish was clearly higher, with merchant banking being an area that contained a number of prominent Jewish firms. However, in stock broking Jacobs estimated that only five per cent of the membership of the London Stock Exchange was Jewish. Overall, the proportion of Jews in financial activities was probably very low, given the importance of the joint-stock

Table 3.1 Areas of business in which Jews are important, 1883

Business	*Number of firms*	*Number Jewish*	*Proportion Jewish*
Birmingham merchants	23	4	17%
Bristol merchants	23	6	28%
Brokers	1,881	75	4%
Stockbrokers	2,826	141	5%
Cane importers	7	3	42%
Cigar manufacturing	300	66	22%
Coconut merchants	3	3	100%
Curiosity dealers	47	16	35%
Diamond cutters	52	10	10%
Diamond merchants	183	34	62%
Esparto merchants	5	3	60%
Fancy trade	270	40	15%
Horsehair merchants	40	10	25%
General merchants	2,700	135	5%
Money changers	7	3	42%
Orange merchants	8	6	75%
Ostrich feather dealers	23	13	57%
Piece merchants	25	17	68%
Rag merchants	141	28	20%
Sponge importers	8	5	62%
Sponge merchants	49	13	27%
Total	8,621	631	7%

Source: Jacobs J. 1891. *Studies in Jewish Statistics: Social, Vital and Anthropometric*. London: D. Nutt, p. 40.

banks where few Jews were to be found. The relative importance of Jews in finance in the City probably changed little in the period between then and the First World War. So despite the attractions that the City of London exerted on Jewish financiers from abroad in those years, they were only one of the many groups who arrived in the City at this time, attracted by the global importance of its money and capital markets.[21]

One of the Jews who did come to the City at this time was Saemy Japhet. He was already an established German banker and broker from Frankfurt when he opened a branch of his German business in London in 1896. In 1900 he made it the base for his international operations, which he believed greatly benefited the business that he did, as he reflected in his reminiscences: 'Now my head office was in London … business developed splendidly and we were busier than ever.' His firm became one the leading dealers in securities between London, continental Europe and New York, especially in arbitrage, which involved the simultaneous sale and purchase of the same securities in different markets. 'We were recognised as one of the leading arbitrage and commission houses,' according to Japhet, who gave the credit to the skills of his key employee, another Jew called Lowenstein. To Japhet achieving success in the City before the First World War was all about hard work, good organisation, and establishing connections, and nothing at all about being Jewish:

> The City of London has no room for sentimentality. It only respects serious and genuine efforts and also results but it demands that everything else – organization, volume of business and proper limitation of commitments must be in harmony. Besides, all this must be covered by adequate capital.

He benefited from the patronage of Ernest Cassel but being a Jew did not save his connection with Goldman Sachs, the Jewish investment bankers in New York, when the non-Jewish merchant bank, Kleinworts, offered them better access to London and Paris than Japhet was able to. The stockbrokers, Helbert Wagg, had found that being of Jewish origin did not help them retain orders from Rothschild in the early twentieth century when the non-Jewish brokers, Panmure Gordon, offered the merchant bank access to the Far Eastern connection it had built up if it switched business to them. As a result Helbert Wagg resigned from the Stock Exchange in 1912 and set themselves up as a merchant bank in competition with the likes of the Rothschilds.[22]

Representative of the way the City drew in Jews from home and abroad was its position in the world's precious stones and metal industry. During the 1880s and 1890s diamond and gold discoveries in South Africa transformed this industry and London became the centre for both buying and selling mining finance. The opportunities it offered attracted both established Jewish firms in London, like Raphaels and Erlangers, as well as creating openings for others. One was Barney Barnato, whose father was a Jewish shopkeeper in London. Along with his brother and cousins he became a very successful diamond merchant and financier in the late nineteenth century. Arriving from Germany was Alfred Beit, who was the son of a Hamburg merchant of Jewish origin, though now Lutheran. He became a diamond merchant in South Africa but made London his head office in 1889, setting up Werner, Beit and Co. in 1890. He both traded in diamonds and financed diamond mines. The City of London was constantly creating new opportunities for entrepreneurial financiers, among whom were several Jews.[23]

Nevertheless, the way the City of London was changing from the late nineteenth century onwards was eroding the advantages that Jewish financiers possessed, as Joseph Jacobs was perceptive enough to detect at the time. Writing in the Jewish Encyclopaedia, which was published between 1901 and 1906, he concluded that the reason that Jews had taken an early lead in international finance in the nineteenth century was because they had family connections in all the major European financial centres. This was not exclusive to the Rothschilds but included the likes of the Bischoffsheims, Seligmans and Lazards. However, by the late nineteenth century these advantages were steadily eroded as alternative networks were developed by the large banks, aided by the worldwide revolution in communications delivered by the telegraph from 1850 onwards. Between 1860 and 1913 the number of foreign banks with London branches rose from three to seventy-one, while there was also a group of British overseas banks with London head offices but branches spread around the world. These were only the most visible manifestations of the links that existed between banks in the City of London and their overseas counterparts. The most common was a correspondent connection in which a bank that had a London office acted on behalf of those that did not. By 1912 a total of 1,211 banks from around the world had a presence in London through these correspondent links.[24] Though London's Jewish financiers did participate in these correspondent networks, the real growth was occurring in the international business being done in London by the branches of such banks as Deutsche Bank, Société Générale, Credit Suisse and Credito Italiano.

This forced Jewish financiers to concentrate on those areas where individual enterprise still had a role to play, as in handling loans and dealing in diamonds, gold, foreign exchange and securities. Important as these were, the conclusion that Jacobs drew was that the Jewish influence in international finance had peaked around 1850 and then declined steadily thereafter as corporate banking replaced private.[25] Ferguson suggests that the Rothschilds managed to maintain their dominant position until 1880 but even they declined thereafter. However, this appears unlikely given that the direction of British overseas investment shifted from Europe to the USA and the Empire and away from government to railways, neither of which were particular strengths of the firm. Paris rather than London was the centre of the European government bond market from the late nineteenth century onwards.[26] Generally it

Table 3.2 The City of London and international banking networks

	1890	*1912*
Foreign banks known in London	237	1,211
Links to London banks via		
Foreign banks with branches in London	21 (7.1%)	673 (32.9%)
London commercial banks	172 (58.3%)	587 (28.7%)
London merchant banks	69 (23.4%)	670 (32.7%)
Total links to London banks	295	2,046

Source: *The Bankers' Almanac*, 1890 and 1913.

can be seen that even within merchant banking the Jewish firms in London faced strong competition from non-Jewish firms that were willing to operate on lower margins, take more risks, or were better connected, especially to the increasingly important financial centre of New York. In terms of trade finance, Rothschilds lost out steadily to the likes of Kleinworts and Schroders, neither of which was Jewish, though both were of German origin. In the issue of corporate stocks and bonds J.S. Morgan (later Morgan Grenfell) was a major force with its New York connection to J.P. Morgan.[27]

To an even greater extent than in the 1870s this cosmopolitan Jewish elite had become well integrated into London society by the Edwardian era. This was not just at the highest reaches, populated by the likes of the Rothschilds, but extended down into the upper middle classes, especially those with City connections. This was especially true for the children of Jewish financiers. Through attending the same schools and universities, frequenting the same social and sporting events, holidaying in the same locations at home and abroad, and enjoying the same pleasures and outlook on life, a high degree of bonding took place extending to lifelong friendships and intermarriage. Among the few from outside who penetrated this social group were actresses, valued as mistresses and even wives on a few occasions. The prospect of impending war with Germany was no impediment to acceptance among those who were German Jews, for hostility only came once the war actually started and especially in the aftermath of the sinking of the Lusitania in May 1915.[28] Race, religion and nationality were no longer barriers to integration for those lay people with class, wealth and inclination.[29]

Table 3.3 Leading merchant banks in London, 1914

Name	*Capital (in million £)*	*Acceptances (in million £)*
Rothschilds (Jewish)	6.37	1.31
Barings	1.02	3.72
Brandts	1.0	0.72
Brown, Shipley	0.78	5.1
Anthony Gibbs	1.22	1.17
Hambros (Jewish origin)	1.0	1.34
Huths	0.75	3.3
Kleinworts	4.42	8.5
Lazards (Jewish origin)	1.0	–
Schroders	3.54	5.82
Morgan Grenfell	1.0	–
Seligmans (Jewish)	3.0	–

Source: Ferguson, N. 1998. *The World's Banker: The History of the House of Rothschild.* London: Weidenfeld & Nicholson, p. 808.

Rhetoric

The story of Jewish financiers in the City of London from the mid nineteenth century until the First World War can be summarised as growing respectability, increasing integration and relative decline. By the Edwardian era they had amassed great wealth and had gained entry into the highest levels of British society but their financial power waned in the face of new ways of doing business and the aggression of younger rivals. Judging from references to Jews in the fictional literature of early and mid-Victorian Britain, the public were aware of both the respectability and integration but were too impressed by the conspicuous wealth to note any signs of decline.[30] As early as 1831 Thomas Peacock, in *Crotchet Castle*, showed that the public were aware of the transition that Jews had been making within British society. In the novel the reader is introduced to Ebenezer MacCrotchet, who had been born in London of a Scottish father and a Jewish mother. Ebenezer's maternal grandfather had been a City merchant and it was this business that he inherited, using it to create a fortune.

> Mr MacCrotchet had derived from his mother the instinct, and his father the rational principle of enriching himself at the expense of the rest of mankind, by all the recognised modes of accumulation on the windy side of the law. With this fortune he had become a respectable member of society through buying a country estate, marriage to an English Christian, losing his Scottish accent, and changing his name.[31]

This bears a remarkable similarity to the life-cycle of Samson Gideon.

By the early 1840s there appeared to be a greater acceptability of those Jewish financiers who retained their faith, judging from Disraeli's popular novels. In his 1844 novel *Coningsby*, Disraeli introduced a character based on the Rothschilds, namely the Jewish financier Sidonia. Sidonia was not only rich, powerful and successful but was also respected for his intelligence and integrity. He is referred to as 'lord and master of the money-market of the world' and this was a mantle that had descended from father to son. When Sidonia entertained it was a lavish and well-attended event that:

> exceeded in splendour and luxury every entertainment that had yet been given. The highest rank, even Princes of the blood, beauty, fashion, fame, all assembled in a magnificent and illuminated palace, resounding with exquisite melody.[32]

Though Jews continued to be regarded by some as little better than 'fishwomen, chickweed-boys, scavengers' carts and letter carriers', as in the 1854 novel by Mrs Gore, *The Money Lender*, the same author also reveals that it was Jewish financiers who were the 'real masters of the world, the moneymongers of its various exchanges'.[33] As Jewish bankers made the transition from money-lending to international finance they gained respect in society and achieved social advancement. Such a view of Jewish financiers was also found in Charles Lever's novel, *That Boy of Norcott's*, which appeared in 1869. They were credited with 'immense wealth' and power which 'unthroned dynasties, and controlled the fate of nations with a word'. The riches and position they acquired as a result meant that the daughter of a Jewish financier could marry the son of a knight so restoring his family's fortune that had been dissipated through gambling and lavish living.[34]

However, the 1870s did appear to witness something of a reversal in the rhetoric if the novels of Trollope can be taken as representative. In the *The Way We Live Now* the reader is introduced to the banker and company promoter, Augustus Melmotte. His origins were shadowy but he was thought to be both foreign and Jewish. Melmotte was involved in promoting the South Central Pacific and Mexican Railway, which was considered to be 'built upon the sands'. Its only purpose was to allow the promoters to make money by continually buying and selling the shares. When the company failed, Melmotte was exposed as a crook. 'Melmotte had committed various forgeries … his speculations had gone so much against him as to leave him a ruined man, and, in short, … the great Melmotte bubble was on the very point of bursting'. Faced with the prospect of prison, Melmotte committed suicide by taking prussic acid.[35] Suicide was also the fate that awaited another Jewish financier in Trollope's 1876 novel, *The Prime Minster*. The City financier, Ferdinand Lopez, was both 'a nasty foreigner, and probably of Jewish descent' and 'one of those fabulously rich fellows out of the city'. That latter reputation allowed him to cross all social barriers, including becoming a friend of the Prime Minister's wife and marrying the daughter of a wealthy man from a landed aristocratic family. What ruined him in the eyes of society was that he turned out to be little better than a gambler, and an unsuccessful one at that 'My business is precarious … I buy and sell on speculation…. I am a good deal at present in the South American trade.' Facing bankruptcy, disgrace and prison for forgery he committed suicide by stepping in front of a train. When the truth came out he was revealed to be 'as vile a scoundrel as ever was made by the love of money'.[36] Despite the disparaging comments about certain Jewish financiers Trollope readily admits that they were not typical. Both Melmotte and Lopez were seen as on the fringes of the City whereas Ezekiel Brehgert was in the mainstream. 'The man was absolutely a Jew; not a Jew that had been, as to whom there might possibly be a doubt whether he or his father or his grandfather had been the last Jew of the family, but a Jew that was.' Despite being a Jewish banker Breghert was accepted in the highest reaches of society. 'Mr Brehgert was considered to be a very good man of business, and was now regarded as being, in a commercial point of view, the leading member of the great financial firm of which he was second partner.'[37] This suggests that by the 1870s the public were able to differentiate between those Jewish financiers who conducted a safe and respectable business and those whose activities were risky and dubious. The former was associated with long established British Jewish bankers, like the Rothschilds, while the latter took the shape of more recent arrivals from the Continent.

By the mid-1890s that relatively mature and even benign perception of Jewish financiers had given way to open hostility, which continued unabated until the First World War. This can be seen in Headon Hill's 1896 novel, *Guilty Gold*. The plot concerned the promotion of a South African gold mine, the Golden Kloof Mining Company. This was a completely fraudulent affair as the promoters knew there was no gold to be found on the land they had acquired. One of the main culprits was Israel Levi, a City bullion dealer. Levi is referred to as 'an oily little Jew of obsequious manners and an unwholesome appearance….' He supplied samples of gold-bearing ore that were meant to have been found on the farm. '"I faked 'em expreshly for the Golden Kloof," bleated the cringing Hebrew.' The other Jew involved was Gus Eppstein, who was an outside broker in the City. He operated an establishment that was simply a gambling den where the public could bet on the rise or fall of share prices as they clustered around the ticker tape machine, relaying prices from the Stock Exchange. He also persuaded gullible investors to buy the shares in worthless companies, operating under the name Sydney Engledue.[38] Indicative of the fact that *Guilty Gold* was no isolated attack on Jewish financiers other novels appeared in the 1890s expressing much the same views. One was Francis Gribble's *The Lower Life*, which also appeared in 1896. This featured Benjamin Cohen, a 'self-made man whose sudden fame had sprung up like a mushroom in the City of London, who touched no enterprise that he did not profit from, and whose marvellous Asbestos Companies were the financial topic of the hour'. In contrast others saw him as an 'ignorant, unmannerly vulgarian, who doubtless knew no better use for gold than to squander it on racehorses, and loose women, and champagne, and vainglorious display….' Cohen's latest venture was an Australian gold mine. On the receipt of a private telegram saying that no ore had been discovered, he sold all his shares at a large profit before the news became known, leaving the investing public to take the loss.[39] Jews like Benjy Cohen were seen to thrive in the City because they possessed no moral scruples about the way they made money. In the 1899 novel by Frederic, *The Market-Place*, the tables were turned and it was Jewish financiers who were punished for their greed. In the expectation that they would be able to buy the shares of a newly promoted company at the issue price, a group of the Jewish financiers sold prior to the allotment. However, they were not allocated any shares and were then forced to pay an exorbitant price to obtain them or face expulsion from the Stock Exchange. Despite the fact that it was fellow stockbrokers that were the victims, little sympathy was expressed for them as Jewish financiers were so disliked in the City. 'They get hold of most of the things that are going, because they're eternally on the move. It's their hellish industry and activity that gives them such a pull, and makes most people afraid of them.'[40]

From 1900 until the First World War the crooked Jewish financier then became a standard feature in popular novels. In the 1904 novel by Thorne and Custance, *Sharks*, Professor Pentique was an American 'of continental Jewish extraction, plump and with an intelligent, hairless face' whose inventions formed the basis of fraudulent companies whose shares were sold to investors.[41] A joint stock company with an equally far-fetched scheme featured in the novel, *The Yellow God*, by H. Rider Haggard, which appeared in 1909. The intention was to develop the Sahara Desert by flooding it but the whole scheme was completely fraudulent. The promoters expected to become rich by gradually unloading shares on an unsuspecting public, duped into believing the feasibility of the project through heavy advertising and persuaded that the shares had value by the creation of a false market. Again, Jewish City financiers were prominent. 'To describe them is unnecessary, for they have no part in our story, being only financiers of a certain class, remarkable for the riches they had acquired by means that for the most part would not bear examination.'[42] Jews were regularly portrayed as having a natural aptitude to financial work of all kinds and at all levels, as E. Phillips Oppenheim observed in his 1904 novel, *Anna, The Adventuress*.[43] From that position it was an easy step to attribute to them all that was considered reprehensible about the City of London, as Oppenheim did in two novels that appeared in 1912. In *Havoc*, there was a description of the stockbroker Alfred Morrison, who was 'a Jew to his finger-tips, notwithstanding his altered name … glossy and immaculately dressed, with a flower in his buttonhole, boots that were a trifle too shiny, hat and coat, gloves and manner, all imitation but all very near the real thing.' He had lost £40,000 speculating and then left his partner to face the consequences.[44] In *A Millionaire of Yesterday* there was a very unflattering portrayal of Hiram Da Souza, a Jewish company promoter. He was both foreign and Jewish and would stop at nothing to achieve success, including lies, blackmail and deception.[45]

Also from 1912 was Grace Pettman's novel, *A Study in Gold*. This featured the financier Caleb Otto-Smith who was 'the most successful company promoter and financier of the day'. With his wealth he had bought a country estate and built a large mansion, called Castle Royal. Despite his wealth Otto-Smith remained ostracised from English landed society, because he was foreign and Jewish and had made his money in the City. He stood apart from 'the rich Jewish community which is such a power in the financial circles in England', because on his arrival in Britain as a refugee from Russia he had ceased to be a practising Jew and had anglicised his name. This did not mean that Otto-Smith was shunned by society as a whole. 'Caleb Otto-Smith was a man flattered and fawned on by many, because of his gold, and the financial power behind his name in City circles.' This included the possibility of marriage to any of the available daughters of impoverished aristocrats. 'Men of his type who had accumulated wealth usually sought in marriage a girl of rank, who had the entrée of the very highest society, and was willing to exchange the prestige of her title and ancestry for a share of the millionaire's gold.' Among the possibilities was Lady Beatrix Urbeville, whose father, the Marquess of Limehouse, was close to bankruptcy. 'Most of these girls had been trained by ambitious mothers to believe that the chief end of their lives was to make a brilliant match; possibly not one among them would have refused to bestow her aristocratic hand upon the grey-haired unprepossessing financier who had come to England as an alien, a young Polish Jew, a well-nigh penniless exile.' As it was, his schemes finally ended in failure, impoverishing the investors who had bought shares. 'The bubble had burst. The companies floated by Otto-Smith were hopelessly bankrupt; his affairs had been placed in the hands of the official receiver, and a warrant was out for the great financier's arrest for conspiracy and fraud.' Otto-Smith fled but was apprehended aboard an American liner bound for New York, through the use of wireless-telegraphy. He was extradited to Britain, made to stand trial and then sent to prison.[46]

By this time Jewish financiers were not only regarded as crooks; they were also seen wielding immense power, as in Joseph Hocking's *God and Mammon*, also dating from 1912. In the City Jews were a large and powerful group and used their knowledge and influence for their own advantage, whatever the cost to others, though some were worse than others. 'You may be right about Jews; there are doubtless many straight, honourable men among them; but there's nothing under heaven worse than the shady members of the Semite race.'[47] A similar verdict emerges from Gilbert Parker's 1913 novel, *The Judgement House*. The financier, Wallstein, was vilified by the press as 'the Jew mining magnate, who didn't care a damn what happened to England so long as his own nest was well lined…. He was spoken of as a cruel, tyrannical, greedy German Jew, whose soul was in his own pocket and his hand in the pockets of the world.' This was despite the fact that 'he was none of these things, save he was of German birth.'[48] Among novelists of this era it was Hilaire Belloc who was most consistent in identifying the influence of the Jewish financier in the City of London. Over the course of four novels written between 1904 and 1910 he introduced the reader to a Jewish merchant banker loosely modelled on the Rothschild family but containing elements of the activities of Sir Ernest Cassel. In the 1904 novel, *Emmanuel Burden*, the financier, I.Z. Barnett, is introduced. I.Z. Barnett's father had been a Jewish banker in Frankfurt, where his elder brother remained after he had come to London. His first venture in London was the Haymarket Bank, which attracted depositors by offering to pay a very high annual rate of interest. This interest was paid out of the new deposits, and once the flow stopped when the fraudulent basis of the scheme was exposed in the press, the bank collapsed and the depositors lost all their money.[49] Barnett escaped prosecution and censure, becoming a successful promoter of foreign companies in the City, such as the Anatolian Railway. This made him a rich man.

Another venture was the M'Korio Delta Development Company. He had come across the tiny British colony of M'Korio when cruising off the coast of West Africa. It consisted mainly of fever-ridden swamps but he saw the possibility of combining personal profit and social and political advancement with imperial expansion if it could be converted into an economically successful corner of the British Empire. What he wanted was 'true political power, a thing to him worth all the effort of life'.[50] I.Z Barnett and the M'Korio Delta Development Company next featured in Belloc's 1908 novel, *Mr Clutterbuck's Election*. By then Barnett had an established reputation in the City as the founder of the Anglo-Moravian Bank, while the M'Korio Delta Development Company had been sold to the British government, though it had never paid a dividend in 17 years. The result was that Barnett had become both very wealthy and very well connected politically, being rewarded with the title Lord Lambeth. Eventually he became the Duke of Battersea with a house in London and an estate in Scotland. With his wealth and political connections the Duke of Battersea was now a very powerful figure in British society, though still referred to by many as the *Peabody Yid*.[51] By the 1909 novel, *A Change in the Cabinet*, Lord Battersea had become a powerful and respected member of the House of Lords.[52] However, a change was seen to be taking place in the 1910 novel, *Pongo and the Bull*:

> The Duke of Battersea, the chief and most respected of British financiers, was now a very old man. His landing in this country as plain Mr. Barnett, the early prejudice against him on the failure of the Haymarket Bank, his resurrection with the making of M'Korio were things of a generation ago – forgotten today. Some still remembered the Lord Lambeth of the beginning of the century and his active philanthropic work, notably the five per cent model dwellings that had gained him first in the street, later with the rich, the rough but loving title of the Peabody Yid.

With the government finances in disarray he was the obvious person to be asked by the Prime Minister to assist. This then revealed his true nature as he lectured the Prime Minister on the poor state of national finances and the difficulties there would be in raising a new loan. This greatly annoyed the Prime Minister who

> thought he detected a little note of sneering patronage, and he looked up with one of those rare glances of decision and anger which, seeing what his position was, had never failed when he used them to check a veiled opponent. It had no more effect upon the Duke of Battersea than the cries of the newspaperman outside. The Great Leader continued his tale, his lecture, undisturbed; still bringing down his fat hand at each conclusion of each objection, crushing an invisible something beneath that fat hand and brushing it away. He was particular and even detailed in his history of the fall of British credit.

Once conversation turned to business Battersea's tone changed. 'His mouth was not insolent, still less his words, but his tone was masterful, and he meant it to be. It was the Duke of Battersea's way of doing that particular kind of business.' The result was to antagonise the Prime Minister, but Battersea did not notice. His 'race' or 'breed' meant that he was not attuned to the Prime

Minister's body language. Also, Battersea was keen to secure the commission to issue the loan:

> his old usurer's heart continued to be glad within him. Things had not gone in the old supreme way well with him and his for a long time past – but he had got that Indian Loan! ...The German branch had underwritten the Romanian fiasco, and the French branch had made a hopeless muddle of the Garonne Canal. The New York house had only just been saved by an amalgamation, and his worthless nephew there was on a salary.

After this interview the PM was determined that the loan would not be handled by Battersea. He had tasted

> in his heart things that Englishmen of his generation had never yet tasted, and the bitterness of a certain cup. Leaders of every other people in Christendom save his had drunk deep of that cup at one time or another. He was being bullied: his country was being bullied by the money-lenders.... He had never thought of England save as the ally and even contemptuous ally of the forces that were now opposed to him. He had watched with indifference the intermarriage of the great families with these swine.

The British government's need to borrow was seen to have put it in the power of these Jewish bankers, whose interests were solely in making money. Battersea 'did not understand blood which was not his own, nor what sympathies might arise between men of one race and one society'. Faced with this the Prime Minister turned instead to G. Quinlan Smith, a very wealthy US financier with offices in both Wall Street and the City. He, like Battersea, was also well connected to the upper reaches of London society and was disliked by the Duke of Battersea who saw him as a serious rival. 'The Duke detested Yankees; they had not the English way of doing business; there was something too smart about them altogether.' He had now overtaken Battersea in terms of financial power. 'What he actually owned was enough to make him the equal, and now the superior, of the great banking houses which the European gentry had long since learnt to fear.' This was in contrast to the Duke of Battersea whose 'luck had now run steadily against him for quite fifteen years. In the last ten years it had run badly against him'. George Quinlan Smith appears to have modelled on the New York investment banker, J. Pierpoint Morgan, and his firm, Smith, Fischer and Company, on Morgan Grenfell. He agreed to handle the loan, though the Duke of Battersea fought hard to retain it. Despite the decline of his business and his age Battersea remained a well-informed and powerful international banker. 'There are those who think that the work of great financiers is done for them by others; they are mistaken. But the Duke of Battersea was an exceptionally industrious old man.' In the end he lost because the Prime Minister preferred to deal with an American banker than a European Jew. This defeat annoyed him. He 'could not forgive the house of Smith, Fischer and Co., and their commission rankled in his mind for three long years, at the close of which I am exceedingly glad to say the Duke of Battersea, having lost a good deal more money, died'. In the shape of a US investment banker Hilaire Belloc had conjured up a rival to the European Jewish financiers who were seen to dominate the City of London and exert a malign influence over British social and political life, though that day was still some way in the future. As *Pongo and the Bull* was set in 1924, or some nine years after *A Change in the Cabinet*, which was set in 1915, it appears that Belloc did not expect an immediate change in the power that Jewish financiers were believed to possess.[53]

Explanation

Judging from the portrayal of Jewish financiers in fiction, a major change seems to have taken place between the 1870s and the 1890s. In the middle years of the century Jewish financiers were seen to be gaining in respectability and acceptability, though never escaping the connections between their religion and the world of money, which was an anathema to many. In contrast, by the end of the century and in the period before the First World War, Jewish financiers were associated both with the worst practices found in the City and distrusted because of the immense power that they wielded. To an extent this can be attributed to the fact that those Jews who were successful in the City were spectacularly so. According to Rubinstein's calculations between 1858 and 1939, 43 Jews died millionaires and another 48 half millionaires. Of these Jewish (half-) millionaires the majority had made their fortunes in the City, with 46 being bankers, 6 stockbrokers and 15 merchants, trading in such commodities as diamonds, petroleum, timber, textiles and tobacco.[54] Though these were a small minority of the very wealthy in Britain there is always a tendency to exaggerate their significance, as Jacobs, observed in 1891. 'It is to the twenty millionaires or so who have "made their heap" on change that the general impression of Jewish riches is due.'[55] However, this stereotype of the wealthy Jewish banker manipulating international finance for selfish ends was hardly new and so cannot explain the intensity of antagonism that existed in the 20 years before the First World War.[56]

Another possibility exists with the dubious activities of particular Jewish financiers, as these could easily provoke a public outburst against their co-religionists. There were Jewish financiers operating over these years whose business practices were widely regarded as fraudulent and they did incur the public wrath of those investors who lost money in their schemes. One of those was Albert Grant. He had been born Abraham Gotheimer in Dublin in 1831, but operated from the City of London as a company promoter in the 1860s and 1870s. He was associated with the most infamous mining swindle of all times, the Emma silver mine, which turned out to be worthless after being floated as a company and sold to British investors in 1871.[57] His activities may account for the negative rhetoric associated with Jewish financiers in the 1870s, as found in the works of Trollope. It was not until the 1890s that another prominent Jewish financier appeared, namely Barney Barnato. He was born Barnett Isaacs Barnato in London where his father was a Jewish shopkeeper. Along with his brother and cousins he became a very successful diamond merchant and financier in the late nineteenth century, acquiring a reputation for dubious dealing in the process. He was involved in the promotion of South African diamond and gold mining companies in the 1880s and 1890s, a number of which proved successful in the long run. However, in 1894 he set up the Barnato Bank, Mining and Estates Company that collapsed in 1896, and he committed suicide the following year by jumping overboard while on his way from South Africa to England. He was one among a number of City financiers who were involved in the gold mining boom of the mid-1890s. A number of these were Jews either from Britain, such as Lionel Phillips and the Joels, or Germany, such as Sigismund Neumann and Maximilian Michaelis, but many were not, though believed to be because of their 'foreign' names. When this speculative boom collapsed it was only to be expected that investors would search for scapegoats who could be blamed for their losses, and Jewish financiers were an obvious target.

This hostility might have been expected to disappear as the memory of the event faded, and those mining companies that were successful rose in value and paid dividends. The successful prosecution of Whitaker Wright, an English nonconformist, who promoted West Australian gold mining companies, also revealed that the main culprits were not Jewish financiers of German origin.[58] However, it did not, and further hostility was fuelled by the Marconi Scandal of 1910. Involved were Godfrey Isaacs, managing director of the Marconi Company, his brother Rufus Isaacs, solicitor general, Herbert Samuel MP, postmaster general, and Gerald Montagu, a City banker. They were accused in the press of insider trading using knowledge gained from their position in government. They were all Jews. Then in 1912 Herbert Samuel, Sir Stuart Samuel and Sir Felix Schuster were accused of a plot to manipulate the silver market. Again, they were all Jews. In both cases the evidence against the men was circumstantial and, even if it had taken place, such activities were neither criminal nor rare. Such stories were more likely to be driven by political rivalries and concerns about rising German military power, so fuelling popular suspicion of those with German names. However, this seems far too weak a reason to explain why Jewish financiers in the City were so targeted in the Edwardian era.[59] Instead, a more plausible explanation is found not in the City, and the activities of Jewish financiers there, whether real or perceived, but in the changing composition of the Jewish population in London. The overall composition of the Jewish community in London changed dramatically in the 35 years before the First World War for causes entirely unrelated to the City and the needs of finance. With the persecution of Jews in the Russian Empire from 1881 onwards there was a mass exodus and though most went to the USA, especially New York, London received a substantial influx as a result.

Between 100,000 and 150,000 Jewish migrants arrived in England between then and the First World War with the great majority settling in the East End of London. Such were their numbers, and their alien language and dress that they were seen as a threat to British society in a way that the small number of long-settled Jews had not been. This was especially true in London, where so many of them lived. In 1900, for example, Russell and Lewis wrote a book entitled *The Jew in London: A Study of Racial Character and Present-Day Conditions* to document and assess the problem. Eventually in 1905 the Aliens Act was passed, which restricted immigration from 1906 onwards. By then a number of anti-Semitic stereotypes had been revived and gained popularity, including that of the Jewish financier.[60]

In reality very few of these recent arrivals of Jews from the Russian Empire possessed the skills, language and connection that would give them entry into the City of London. They were coming from peasant communities in Poland and European Russia and had little knowledge and expertise in finance of any kind, let alone international banking and broking, as was required in the City. Their almost negligible impact can be gauged from membership of the London Stock Exchange in 1914. In that year a total of 218 members and 31 clerks had been foreign born. Of those 153 were German and a further 20 were from Austria, 18 from the Netherlands and seven from Switzerland, and that group comprised 90% of the total. Among clerks a similar picture emerges with 27, or 88%, being from these four countries. In contrast, only one member and one clerk had been born in Russia.[61] Those foreigners who came to the City of London before 1914 were drawn there because of the opportunities it offered them to further their existing business, whether financial or mercantile, rather than because of persecution in their own countries. Among those were a number of German, not Russian, Jews whose background, wealth and connections gained them easy entry into the upper levels of British society. Unfortunately for them they were associated in the public mind with the influx of poor Jews who crammed themselves into the east end of London and appeared to constitute a threat to British society. It is this which explains the huge variance between the reality of Jewish financiers in the City before 1914 and the rhetoric that was to be found in the popular novels of the age.

Conclusion

Mass immigration has implications for those from the same racial or religious backgrounds, who have been long settled and become assimilated into society. It creates antagonism that spreads all the way to the wealthiest even though they commanded the respect of their peer group and were close personal friends of the most powerful in the land. The arrival of a mass of foreign Jews was perceived as a threat to British society and this fear led to Jewish financiers being targeted, even though they were engaged in a business that was vital for the continuing success of the City of London as a financial centre. This antagonism built upon the long-standing suspicion of Jews as moneylenders and usurers in a Christian community. However, in a period of limited government intervention such perception appeared to have no effect. Steps were taken to restrict the flow of poor Jews from Eastern Europe after 1906 but the City of London continued to provide an attractive base for Jewish financiers, whether home grown or newly arrived. The conclusion that can be drawn is that perception of Jewish power and influence in the City was completely out of proportion with the reality. Jews were always a tiny minority in the City and clustered in niche areas, where they did face strong competition. Their influence was also in decline as international financial transactions increasingly flowed through inter-bank networks and organised markets. Finance also became increasingly global, so moving beyond the European nexus, which was the strength possessed by Jewish bankers. However, this did not mean Jews were not important in the City. They brought expertise and connections. Without them London would have been a less successful financial centre, especially in the conduct of global business. It is important not to overemphasise the power and influence of Jewish financiers in the City and see them as some kind of international conspiracy. Conversely, they should not be written out of the history of the City as their contribution was greater than their actual numbers would suggest.

Notes

1 This paper incorporates material from my book: Michie, R.C. 2009. *Guilty Money: The City of London in Victorian and Edwardian Culture.* London: Pickering and Chatto. It was while working on that book that I had a number of conversations with Gerry Feldman on the question of Jewish financiers. His informed views encouraged me to plan a paper specifically on the subject of Jewish financiers in the City of London in the century before 1914. It is a personal regret that I was not able to send this completed paper to Gerry to read as it would have been much better for his input.

2 Anon. 2006. The New City, *The Financial Times*, 27–30 March.

3 See Cassis, Y. 2006. *Capitals of Capital: A History of International Financial Centres, 1780–2005.* Cambridge: Cambridge University Press. And Michie, R.C. 2006. *The Global Securities Market: A History.* Oxford: Oxford University Press.

4 Roth, C. 1938. *The Jewish Contribution to Civilization.* London: Macmillan, p. 227.

5 Jacobs, J. 1896. *Jewish Ideals and Other Essays.* London: David Nutt, pp. 171, 178–9; Hyamson, A.M. and Silberman, A.M., eds.1938. *Valentine's Jewish Encyclopaedia.* London, Amsterdam: Shapiro, Vallentine & Co, pp. 391–3. (Entry by Cecil Roth.)

6 Rabinowicz, O.K. 1974. *Sir Solomon de Medina.* London: Jewish Historical Society of England, pp. 23, 26, 33.

7 Hobson, J.A. 1902. *Imperialism: A Study.* Revised edition 1938. London: George Allen Unwin Ltd, pp. 56–7; cf, pp. 46, 61.

8 Rubinstein, W.D. 1993. *Capitalism, Culture and Decline in Britain, 1750–1990.* London: Routledge, p. 52.

9 Dallas Brett, R. 1945. *Usury in Britain.* London: St. Botolph Publishing Co, p. 139; cf. p. 120.

10 Rosenberg, E. 1961. *From Shylock to Svengali: Jewish Stereotypes in English Fiction.* London: Peter Owen, pp. 14, 27, 33–5, 140, 168–9, 297, 344.

11 Withers, H. 1916. *International Finance*. London: Murray, p. 111.
12 See Samson Gideon, Abraham Goldsmid, John King, Moses Mocatta, Henry Raphael, Joseph Salvador in *Oxford Dictionary of National Biography*, 2016. [online] Available at: www.oxforddnb.com [Accessed 28 March 2016].
13 Ferguson, N. 1998. *The World's Banker: The History of the House of Rothschild*. London: Weidenfeld & Nicholson, pp. 51–2.
14 Pollins, H. 1982. *Economic History of the Jews in England*. London: Fairleigh Dickinson, pp. 43–8, 56–8, 60, 108–9.
15 Cottrell, P.L. 1985. The Business Man and Financier, in S. and V.D. Lipman, 1985. *The Century of Moses Montefiore*. Oxford: Oxford University Press, pp. 24–6, 30–1, 40; Hyamson and Silberman, eds. (1938), pp. 391–3; Ferguson (1998), pp. 19, 55, 62; Brook, S. 1989. *The Club: The Jews of Modern Britain*. London: Constable, p. 16; Parkes, J. 1955. The History of the Anglo-Jewish Community, in M. Freedman, ed. *A Minority in Britain: Social Studies of the Anglo-Jewish Community*. London: Valentine, Mitchell & Co, p. 42.
16 Pollins (1982), pp. 111–12; Aris, S. 1970. *The Jews in Business*. London: Cape, p. 49. See Henri Bischoffsheim, Carl Joachim Hambro, Samuel Montagu in *Oxford Dictionary of National Biography*, 2016. [online] Available at: www.oxforddnb.com [Accessed 28 March 2016].
17 Morrier Evans, D. 1852. *The City; or The Physiology of London Business*. London: Baily Bros, pp. 4, 17, 47, 101–4, 128, 170.
18 Alderman, G. 2008. *Controversy and Crisis: Studies in the History of Jews in Modern Britain*. Boston: Academic Studies Press, pp. 232–6; Lipman, V.D. 1986. The Victorian Jewish Background, in A. and R. Cowen, *Victorian Jews through British Eyes*. Oxford: Oxford University Press, pp. xi–xiv; Kessler, D. 1996. *The Rothschilds and Disraeli in Buckinghamshire*. Aylesbury: Rothschild Waddesdon, pp. 20–2, 27–8; Ferguson (1998), pp. 55, 194, 304, 323–5, 341, 527–8; Hyamson and Silberman, eds. (1938), pp. 391–3; see Hambro, Bischoffsheim in Oxford Dictionary of National Biography, 2016. [online] Available at: www.oxforddnb.com [Accessed 28 March 2016].
19 Lipman, V.D. 1954. *Social History of the Jews in England, 1850–1950*. London: Watts & Co, pp. 9, 17, 27, 29, 54, 65, 68, 70, 99, 100; Alderman, G. 1998. *Modern British Jewry*. 2nd ed. London Clarendon Press, pp. 3, 7, 13, 15, 103–4, 117–9; Ferguson (1998), pp. 528, 589, 600, 774–8; see Cassel in *Oxford Dictionary of National Biography*, 2016. [online] Available at: www.oxforddnb.com [Accessed 28 March 2016].
20 Jacobs, J. 1891. *Studies in Jewish Statistics: Social, Vital and Anthropometric*. London: D. Nutt, pp. 10–14, 37, 40.
21 Michie, R.C. 1992. *The City of London: Continuity and Change since 1850*. London: Macmillan, p. 14; see Michie, R.C. 2006.The City of London as a European Financial Centre in the Twentieth Century, in *Europaische Finanzplätze im Wettbewerb* 45, Stuttgart: Bankhistorisches Archiv-Beiheft; and Michie, R.C. 2007. The City of London as a Global Financial Centre, 1880–1939: Finance, Foreign Exchange and the First World War, in P.L. Cottrell, E. Lange and U. Olsson, eds. 2007. *Centres and Peripheries in Banking: The Historical Development of Financial Markets*.Aldershot: Ashgate.
22 Japhet, S. 1931. *Recollections from my Business Life*. London: printed for private circulation, pp. 100–5; see Saemy Japhet, Alfred Wagg in *Oxford Dictionary of National Biography*, 2016. [online] Available at: www.oxforddnb.com [Accessed 28 March 2016]; Michie, R.C. 1999. *The London Stock Exchange: A History*. Oxford: Oxford University Press.
23 Gutwein, D. 1992. *The Divided Elite: Economics, Politics and Anglo-Jewry, 1882–1917*. Leiden: Brill, pp. 112–14; Aris (1970), p. 53; see Barnato, Beit, Erlanger, Raphael, Randlords in *Oxford Dictionary of National Biography*, 2016. [online] Available at: www.oxforddnb.com [Accessed 28 March 2016].

24 Anon. *The Banking Almanac Directory, Year Book, and Diary for 1845(–1919), 1860 and 1913.* London: R. Groombridge; Waterlow & Sons; Jones, G. 1993. *British Multinational Banking, 1830–1990*. Oxford: Oxford University Press. pp. 414–15.

25 Jacobs, J. (n.d.). *The Stock Exchange.* (n.p.); Hyamson and Silberman, eds. (1938), 1901–6; Jacobs, J. 1919. *Jewish Contributions to Civilization: An Estimate.* Philadelphia: Jewish Publication Society of America, pp. 228–9, 235, 239, 241–2, 245.

26 Ferguson (1998), pp. 589, 600, 805–10, 814, 817; Michie, R.C. 2002. One World or Many Worlds? Markets, Banks, and Communications, 1850s–1990s, in T. de Graaf, J. Jonker and J.J. Mabron, eds. 2002. *European Banking Overseas, 19th–20th Centuries.* Amsterdam: ABN Amro Historical Archives, p. 244.

27 See Cassis (2006).

28 The boat was torpedoed by a German U-boat and killed 1,198 people. The sinking turned public opinion against Germany and convinced the USA to enter the First World War. (Editor's annotation.)

29 For a sense of the social life enjoyed by the City elite in late Victorian and Edwardian London see two books by Nicholson, S. 1994. *A Victorian Household.* Stroud: Sutton; and Nicholson, S. 1999. *An Edwardian Bachelor.* London: Victorian Society.

30 For more on the use of fiction as historical sources see O'Gorman, F. ed. 2007. *Victorian Literature and Finance.* Oxford: Oxford University Press.

31 Peacock, T.L. 1831. *Crotchet Castle.* London: Folio Society, pp. 127–8.

32 Disraeli, B. 1844. *Coningsby.* London, pp. 230–2, 235–8, 237–8, 242, 278, 357–8. See also the subsequent novel Disraeli, B. 1847. *Tancded* or *The New Crusade.* London, pp. 112, 114–15, 124–6, 165, 212, 254, 282.

33 Mrs (Catherine Grace Frances) Gore, 1854. *The Money Lender.* London, pp. 16–17, 23, 31, 38, 46, 95, 98, 113, 134–9, 153, 162–3, 167–8, 181–90, 208–9, 226–7, 242.

34 Lever, C. 1869. *That Boy of Norcott's.* London, pp. 172, 192, 196–7, 222, 313–7.

35 Trollope, A. 1874–75. *The Way We Live Now, Volume 1.* London: xxx, pp. 30–4, 48–9, 84, 268–9, 349.

36 Trollope, A. 1876. *The Prime Minister, Volume 1.*London, pp. 1–15, 21, 26–9, 31, 117, 120, 128–9, 155, 173, 185, 191, 194, 222, 228–9, 230–8, 244; Trollope, A. 1876. *The Prime Minister, Volume 2.*London, 4–7, 31–2, 39–40, 51, 56, 73, 111, 194, 274–5, 320–1, 352, 379.

37 Trollope (1874–75), Volume 2, 26–7, 89, 91–2, 99, 140, 294, 304, 307, 319, 361.

38 Hill, H. 1896. *Guilty Gold: A Romance of Financial Fraud and City Crime.* London: C. Arthur Pearson, pp. 15–16, 27–33, 40–1, 207–9, 346–7.

39 Gribble, F. 1896. *The Lower Life.* London: A. D. Innes & Co., pp. 1–2, 6, 8, 10, 14, 16, 20–1, 25, 30–1, 61, 131–3, 149, 152, 176, 190–1, 238. 278–80, 285, 288–9, 294, 303, 307–11.

40 Frederic, H. 1899. *The Market-Place.* London, pp. 6–11, 20–2, 26–7, 36, 44, 48–9, 81–2, 157, 181–4, 187, 197, 202–3, 205, 214, 217–19, 236, 240, 282–5, 293–4, 296, 306, 308–9, 312, 358–9.

41 Thorne, G. and Custance, L. 1904. *Sharks: A Fantastic Novel for Business Men and their Families.* London: Greening & Co., pp. 2–15, 20–3, 30–3, 50–5, 144–5, 156–7, 180–1, 188–9, 226–9, 232–5, 278–9, 298–9, 340–5.

42 Haggard, H. 1909. *The Yellow God: An Idol of Africa.* London: Cassell & Co., pp. 1–18, 20, 22, 33–4, 40, 42, 48, 51–2, 86, 89, 116.

43 Oppenheim, E. 1904. *Anna, The Adventuress.* London: Ward, Lock & Co., pp. 8, 26–7, 56, 63–4, 72, 94, 110, 139.

44 Oppenheim, E. 1912. *Havoc.* London: Hodder & Stoughton, pp. 62–8, 74, 98–9, 105, 116, 118, 236, 289–90, 314–5, 320–1, 329–330, 342–5.

45 Oppenheim, E. 1912. *A Millionaire of Yesterday.* London: Ward, Lock & Co., pp. 60–67, 72, 90–1, 102, 114–5, 121–3, 134, 146, 170–2, 261–4, 273, 278, 296–300, 302, 314.

46 Pettman, G. 1912. *A Study in Gold*. London: S.W. Partridge & Co., pp. 101, 104, 115–7, 121–3, 126–8, 130, 132, 137, 146–150, 157, 165, 171, 201, 204–5, 207–8.
47 Hocking, J. 1912. *God and Mammon*. London: Ward, Lock & Co., pp. 212, 214–6, 219, 232–3, 245, 257, 263–5, 267–8, 275.
48 Parker, G. 1913. *The Judgement House*. London, pp. 39–43, 52, 66, 86, 117, 259–60, 269, 310–11, 470–2.
49 The basis of this story was another English non-conformist, Jabez Balfour and the Liberator Building Society. After his extradition from the USA he was prosecuted by the Jewish barrister Rufus Isaacs on behalf of the crown. On conviction he committed suicide. See Jabez Balfour, Rufus Isaacs in *Oxford Dictionary of National Biography*, 2016. [online] Available at: www.oxforddnb.com [Accessed 28 March 2016].
50 Belloc, H. and Burden, E., 1904. Merchant, of Thames St, in *The City of London, Exporter of Hardware: A Record of his Lineage, Speculations, Last Days, and Death.* London, pp. 54–61, 65–76, 82–91, 104, 113, 119, 121–2, 158, 170–1, 196–7, 206–7, 212, 223.
51 Belloc, H. 1908. *Mr Clutterbuck's Election*. London: T. Nelson & Sons, pp. 1–3, 11–13, 16–18, 20–4, 31–46, 52–62, 87–8, 120, 152, 180–1, 193–8, 216–220, 272–6.
52 Belloc, B. 1909. *A Change in the Cabinet*, London: Methuen & Co., pp. 33, 89, 232–3.
53 Belloc, H. 1910. *Pongo and the Bull*. London, pp. 3, 13–14, 33, 41–3, 71–80, 88, 94, 102–3, 178–9, 237, 305.
54 Rubinstein, W. 1971. Jews among top British Wealth Holders, 1857–1969: Decline of the Golden Age. *Jewish Social Studies*, 33, pp. 76–83.
55 Jacobs (1891), p. 31.
56 Aris (1970), p. 51.
57 Pollins (1982), pp. 112, 168. For an overview of fraudulent City financiers of this period see Robb, G. 1992. *White-Collar Crime in Modern England: Financial Fraud and Business Morality, 1845–1929*. Cambridge: Cambridge University Press.
58 Pollins (1982), pp. 168–9; See Barnato, Wright, Isaacs, Randlords in *Oxford Dictionary of National Biography*, 2016. [online] Available at: www.oxforddnb.com [Accessed 28 March 2016].
59 Holmes, C. 1979. *Anti-Semitism in British Society, 1876–1939*. New York: Edward Arnold Publishers, pp. 65–6, 77–9, 80–2, 108–9, 117; Baker, W.J. 1970. *A History of the Marconi Company*. London: Methuen, p. 17; Camplin, J. 1978. *The Rise of the Plutocrats: Wealth and Power in Edwardian England*. London: Constable, pp. 46, 49, 55, 156. See Isaacs, Samuel Montagu, Felix Schuster in *Oxford Dictionary of National Biography*, 2016. [online] Available at: www.oxforddnb.com [Accessed 28 March 2016].
60 Russell, C. and Lewis, H.S. 1900. *The Jew in London: A Study of Racial Character and Present-day Conditions*. London: Fisher Unwin, p. 12; Gartner, L.P. 1960. Notes on the Statistics of Jewish Immigration to England 1870–1914. *Jewish Social Studies*, 22, p. 99; Garrard, J.A.1971. *The English and Immigration, 1880–1910*. Oxford: Oxford University Press, p. 213; Alderman (2008), pp. 230–1, 237; Lipman (1986), pp. xii, xiv, xvi, xix.
61 Michie (1999), p. 144.

4 The financial culture of the Habsburg Monarchy at the end of the 19th century[1]

Dieter Stiefel

In 1881 the German-Austrian statistician and economist Karl Theodor von Inama-Sternegg[2] wrote that the specific imprint of the modern economy was due, beside steam power, to the loan system: Never before have loans codetermined all conditions of trade and production, never have they had so many and such refined forms, never has their use been so widespread and so regulated, never were such large sectors of the population so fully under their spell.[3]

> Everyone lends with one hand and borrows with the other. Thus, loans accompany commodities at all stages of production and use. Progress in agriculture, large factories and transport infrastructure would not have been possible without them. Our metropolises owe their incomparable public infrastructures, their monumental constructions, their canals and plumbing networks to the loan system. It is this that built palaces for state schools, put increasingly powerful tools at the disposal of works for the public benefit.... Welfare and education, freedom and power, all material needs of the middle classes have found in the loan system an indispensable condition for their realisation.[4]

Much more than today, in the second half of the nineteenth century people were aware that they lived in the 'era of loans'. In 1869, one of the large construction enterprises of that time, which still exists today, wrote, in the prospectus of its formation, about the 'unified strength of capital, loans and technology', expressing that it was precisely the combination of these three strengths which promoted industrialisation.

In the pre-modern era, loans were usually a social aid within a community, a village, a class and a family. They were secured through the social bond, through reciprocity and were meant to solve a financial difficulty. Accordingly, one was not allowed to make any profit from the distress of another person, and the church was consistently against charging interests on loans. Beside these social loans, there was soon another type, which was granted to people who were outside one's social conditions. Inama-Sternegg has called these loans 'unsocial', since they were granted to a 'stranger' and could therefore be issued only with high interest rates and special guarantees such as pledges. Because of its stringent conditions, this type of loan was also referred to as *Wucherkredit* (predatory lending). The particularly strict law of obligations was also directed to this unsocial loan form, which could even provide for the slavery of a defaulting debtor. He who sought a loan outside his social connections had no credit worthiness, and had to obtain it first. Only his pledges could give him credit worthiness and, in the worst case, he himself was the pledge…. He who wished to receive this type of loan had to accept being told that he wanted to live beyond his means and that he played an audacious game with property, freedom and honour.[5]

At the beginning of the modern age, the economy expanded and so did the monetary system. Money proved to have the power to free man from his traditional limits and help him to overcome all obstacles to his development.

> It increased the need for as well as the production of goods and thus made enjoyment no less boundless than acquisition…. Money has made men much richer but also much poorer. Excess and penury no longer alternate as often as they did before, but they still exist to an even larger extent next to each other and need an equalisation.[6]

Capital owners and spenders of capital were no longer identical, and loans helped to overcome the difference. The constant expansion of production simultaneously created the necessary basis for loans, namely the increased expectation of future profit. 'If financial difficulty was the mother of loans in the barter economy, surplus became the father of loans in the monetary economic system.' Without a loan system there would not be a modern economy. However, despite this positive view, Inama-Sternegg could not conceal 'an uncanny terror' that the whole daring construction built on credit might one day collapse and the national economic welfare be buried under its ruins.

> Greed, a profligate life-style appears as the builders, paper-based money as the building blocks; uncertain earning prospects and the profit of speculations are the beams and props; banknotes and cheques, bills of exchange and warrants the clamps and rivets; and the stock exchange, with its arbitrage business transactions industriously supplies the accessory services and continues to build relentlessly, without plan or aim, scaffolding or foundations. In the hands of the wealthy, loans become the most efficient means of selfish exploitation of the widespread national economic welfare… who has nothing but his job knocks in vain at its door; the fruits which grow on the fertile soil of the loan system remain inaccessible to him; the loan system increasingly takes away from him even the fruits of his work, putting them in the lap of movable property.[7]

The transition from a barter economy to a monetary economic system and a loan system was however, despite all risks, regarded as a civilising process.

'Who can deny that the loan system has become an essential, perhaps *the* essential foundation of modern economic life, world trade and world industry?'[8] The entire business was based on loans, which were the vital nerve of trade and growth 'and to the same extent as this was limited, production also had to suffer and the economic decline would have the same pace as the fall of the loan system'.[9] In a comparison with the human body, money was described as blood and loans as the nervous system. People regarded themselves, however, as being still at the beginning of the era of loans, which meant that many teething troubles were yet to come and the credit system was not yet correctly understood by many. Some argued that the payment moral was clearly closely linked to the level of economic activity. Whilst a businessman generally met his obligations in times of economic boom, during an economic recession he was incorrect, unpunctual, and imprecise, he did not meet his obligations in the manner agreed and tried to postpone payments using all possible excuses and expedients, 'in short, it leads to a whole series of inadmissible, unvirtuous acts and commercial vices'.[10] Conversely, when loans were regarded as proof of the trust a businessman should be given, the motto applied: 'He who meets his obligations with repeated delay is not worthy of the credit he receives.'[11]

This touched upon a topic, which was the object of many meetings of the Austrian chambers of commerce and of small and medium enterprises from the 1870s onwards. In countries such as Germany and Austria, which were relatively short of capital, many enterprises, especially in small business, were largely built on foreign capital. 'Loans, which should only represent a complement of an enterprise's operating capital, never the latter itself, are misinterpreted to the effect that the exploitation of loans fills the entire lack of operating capital.'[12] This happened by means of a radical exploitation of the supplier credit by the wholesalers and producers. Both of these regarded it rightly as peculiar that raw materials, for example in the textile industry, as long as they were raw materials, were traded only against cash payments, 'but as soon as they are processed, refined and their value increases, they appear, as a consequence of the addition of human labour, virtually discredited, as if they had lost value; because from this moment onwards they are sold or lent on deferred terms'.[13]

Whereas in England, then the most industrialised country, payment terms were a maximum of one month, in Austria the producer not only had to wait until the merchandise had reached the re-seller, but often until the latter had sold the product to the final consumer and had himself been paid. The supplier, the creditor of the goods, had therefore increasingly become the banker of his customers. 'One of the main causes of our economic inferiority towards the other cultural states consists in the unhealthy credit relations in our business and particularly in the excessively long credit terms which are granted almost without exception in more and more sectors',[14] complained an Austrian producer. Above all, businessmen outside the main urban centres argued that they could pay their suppliers only as soon as they could also record receipt of payment. This was precise proof that the person concerned did not do business by his own means, and, rather, considered the operating capital lent to him in the form of goods as his own fixed capital and did not have the power to return it.[15] Payments in cash (*Bar-Cassa*) meant in many cases a payment within three months; a term of payment of six months was perfectly common and people even feared 'that we will soon also have to speak of a twelve months' loan as the longest and, to an extent, rightly deployed form of loan'.[16] Suppliers and wholesale trade thus assumed an unregulated lending function and were very closely linked to the fate of their customers. As a consequence, the distinction between equity capital and debt capital faded.

> We have reached the point that today's lender is dependent on the mercy or ruthlessness of his debtor. To an extent, the creditor participates in the success of the business of his debtor in the manner of a dormant partner who, if his debtor does well, has the chance to be paid; however, in the other, not uncommon, case, the creditor has to pay with his own means for his debtor's default and other sins and deal with it by himself.[17]

In some German towns, individual associations for the request of cash payments were founded.[18] Austria also tried to establish such an association.[19] These associations, however, did not last long, since they tackled the problem from the wrong side, namely from the debtor's side, and it was the latter which had the least interest in the abolition of loans. More serious were the attempts at reform, which came from the various chambers of commerce and aimed to establish cash payments as a general rule for the retail business and the three-month bill of exchange for intermediary trade and the manufacturers.[20] 'No peasant will ever lend his cow for free for years and a true peasant will not by any means accept such business but keep his cow for himself. What a cow is for a peasant, the operating capital is for traders and manufacturers.'[21]

The reform attempts also aimed to secure that the loan system should not be carried by the producer or trade but rather by special banks. However, in such a relatively backward country as Austria at that time, the loan system was not developed enough by far to be able to fulfil this function. 'Large banks offer their services only to rich industrialists and the well-established wholesalers, whereas the largest majority of small traders, especially those in the province, remain virtually excluded from bank transactions.'[22] Banks themselves dealt almost exclusively with big clients, and credit cooperatives and mutual savings bank had yet to be developed. Furthermore, many debtors would not have passed the credit worthiness assessment by a credit institute. In order to manage the increase in production, a loan structure necessarily developed in the Austrian economy spanning from the producer to the wholesaler and the manufacturers and from small traders to the final consumer. For tailors, for example, it was common that customers would pay only towards the end of the year.[23]

Customer credit was to an extent the most important instrument of sales policy of the nineteenth century, in spite of the numerous objections against it. For trade or the manufacturers there were

> even some strong reasons for keeping and preserving the current loan system. Many have the strong, and yet completely wrong conviction that they are much better off with it than if they bought only with cash. They argue that thanks to loans they obtain a larger number of customers and keep them in the long term and above all they are attracted by the high profit, which the practice of buying on credit brings to them, at least on paper. Daily experience teaches, however, that heavy borrowers are neither good nor lasting customers; as regards the large profit thanks to loans, it becomes in effect a source of damage because of the enormous expenses related to interest rates ... even more, though, as a result of the strong losses with dubious and wholly non-collectable receivables.[24]

All the efforts of producers and wholesalers to limit, through the chambers of commerce, the abuse of the excessively long credit terms failed because of the fully grounded objections of their customers.

> Shop owners, craftsmen, etc. argue that they are unable to adjust the invoices earlier than half a year, or often a one-year term because they are allowed to send the bill to their customers only at the end of the year, after which they have to wait another three to six months or longer to be paid. As a result, they lack the cash to meet their obligations.[25]

The lenders who wanted to stay completely outside this system simultaneously stayed outside the market.[26] As a result, everyone was indebted to everyone else. Such an economic structure was alone for this reason particularly exposed to crises, without taking into consideration that a large part of the profit could be lost as a result of the interest difference. The so-called 'heavy hand', the reluctance to pay, seemed to be a recurrent situation in the Austrian economy. 'The intermediary trader tolerated it with the retail seller and compensated it by behaving towards the producer in the same manner, as a variation of the motto – tit for tat'.[27] Constantly criticised was also the increasing competition, which aimed to force suppliers to extreme tolerance with regard to collecting their receivables. 'As a result of the ambition to improve the already very small profit margin by means of an increased turnover', producers turned to

> weaker firms against their better judgement with the aim of persuading young people who have achieved a good reputation thanks to their knowledge of goods, often only as a result of their familiarity with provincial buyers, to become independent and to establish themselves by means of the credit which they promised to grant them.[28]

In addition to the decreasing profit margin as a result of the 'immense competition' there was also the increased risk due to the granting of loans. This much criticised competition made it 'necessary' for them to do business while accepting a significantly higher degree of risk than was compatible with strictly solid business principles.[29] Also, the argument that it was better that what was produced was not sold than that which was sold was not paid for was without merit.[30]

The lack of capital and the resulting lack of payment morals are probably detectable in most of the countries at the beginning of industrialisation. This became even more problematic as a result of the widespread principle of business secrecy. Around 1870, the majority of enterprises in the Austrian Monarchy were family firms, which were run according to the organisational principle of the whole house. This organisational model saw the *pater familias* as the leader, who regarded his house as his area of exclusive competence, in which public authorities did not have any role. In the pre-industrial era, commercial know-how was considered secret knowledge, an 'art to become rich', which was not, of course, shared outside one's own house, let alone published. People tried to preserve a wall of business secrecy in the industrial age. 'In the case of old businessmen it can be observed that they, on the grounds of the experiences of the older school, want to keep virtually everything that happens in the business, or that has to do with it, secret.'[31] The principle of business secrecy was, however, in contradiction with the information need of the modern economy. Everyone who wanted to request a loan had to accept that information would be sought about him.[32] A company about which, in the extreme case, there was absolutely no information, was per se completely unworthy of credit. If one knew nothing about a company, it was also impossible to become a stakeholder in it by means of loans. However, the principle of business secrecy was often exploited in order to 'keep the others uninformed on certain aspects about which they would have had the right to request elucidation.'[33]

The increasing need for information in the economy was already met in the mid nineteenth century by means of private credit agencies (*Auskunfteien*), which first emerged in England, France and the USA. In the mid-1860s, they also appeared in Germany and soon afterwards in Austria. In the 1880s, there were already eight credit agencies in Vienna. The biggest ones were the branches of a German office and those of a Budapest office. They published credit worthiness books, which contained names and addresses of firms with the addition of numbers representing a graded evaluation of credit worthiness.[34] There were also already information offices active in the private sector both in Austria and abroad, but they often offered little guarantee for the correctness and objectivity of their reports, 'so that our businessmen in most cases are at a loss with the question of the granting of loans'. An uncertain report could hardly help prevent uncertain lending. Most private offices were also in material terms insufficiently equipped, so that it was impossible for them to establish a vast information network. In these information offices it was possible to buy tokens in advance for each of which a single piece of information was given.

However, since private information offices were in fierce competition with each other, these tokens were often so cheap that one could not expect a scrupulous information service. Many organisations only imitated externally serious organisations for creditor protection, without having their capacity. One should not, however, collect credit information where it is cheapest but where it is most reliable.[35]

Finally, the renowned Viennese *Creditoren-Verein von 1870* (Creditors' Association of the year 1870)[36] also attempted to create a credit agency on a reliable basis. The creation of an information association was not, however, easy and would take decades. It was not until 1884 that the *Creditoren-Verein* submitted the statutes of the Vindobona Information Association for the Protection and Promotion of Austrian Trade and Industry to the competent imperial authority in Lower Austria (k.k.niederösterreichischen Statthalterei). The document read:

> One of the most important factors for the proliferation of trade and commerce, ... lies in the collection of reliable information on the conditions and the assets of those business partners with whom credit transactions are closed. Unfortunately, according to the unanimous judgement of the competent circles in this matter, our Austrian fatherland has remained behind all those countries which, like Germany, France, England, America and others, take special care of trade and industry and, as a result, enjoy a florid development of these conditions.[37]

In Austria's general business life, the granting of loans was the norm and therefore inevitable. 'However, the information network which has established itself in our country is in serious disorder. A unifying point is missing for obtaining reliable information about the credit worthiness of principals, so that it becomes virtually impossible to receive unvarnished, objective references from good sources.'

The imperial authority in Lower Austria, however, rejected the proposal of establishing an information association, since it regarded it as being against the law. An appeal with the higher authority, the imperial Ministry of the Interior, was unsuccessful, because the activity of credit agencies in Vienna was regarded as an interference with the area of competence of the police. When eventually charges were filed against an office, which periodically published black lists under the heading customer control, a raid against information offices ensued. All information offices were closed, with the exception of the German branch of a large credit agency.[38] The owner of one of the private agencies, however, had the courage to take legal action and filed a complaint with the higher administrative court. This decided that information offices did not need any official authorisation and like any other business enterprise could be freely run.[39] The *Creditoren-Verein* reacted immediately with an appeal to the imperial Ministry of the Interior. The appeal was successful, and the Ministry took back its objections – 'quite an exception in such questions'.[40] This paved the way for the establishment of the information association and its creation appeared to be all the more urgent since the freedom of trade in this field led to the expectation of a chaotic proliferation of private offices. On 16th April 1885, the *Vindobona* was founded. A secretary was employed and correspondents were appointed for the most important regions with the task of collecting information on site. Close cooperation with the *Creditoren-Verein* was also decided upon in order to benefit from the latter's vast information material. The *Creditoren-Verein* also put its monthly journal at the disposal of *Vindobona* for its notifications. After its first year in operation, the association already counted 232 members and in its first six months of activity it dealt with over 7,000 requests.[41] By 1893, the number of members increased to 1,359, who received 140,000 reports, with 160,000 investigations conducted on site.[42]

Within the information association *Vindobona*, a complaints department was also created, where wilful debtors were reported. It was a well-known fact

> that many people virtually make a profession of wilful mobbing, they even wish to be sued in order to receive, by means of a futile objection, the approval to defer payments indefinitely and be exempted from receiving annoying reminders as long as the lawsuit is pending, and during this time exploit loans from another source since their behaviour is not yet known in wide circles.[43]

As early as 1887, internal black lists were proposed in order to keep the 'buccaneers of credit' on file. The 'lazy, reluctant payers and victimisers' were always the same people; at most they increased in number or changed the name of their company or their domicile; only their victims changed, necessarily, from time to time. 'This category of customers, who become rich with all sorts of wilful victimisations, procrastinations, deductions, deferrals and even "out of court compositions" at the expense of honest businessmen, are the cancer of business.'[44] This cancer 'must be operated and eradicated', and this was only possible with the internal circulation of lists, which deprived those people of credit. However, the experience of black lists was much debated, and even the *Creditoren-Verein* had to admit that although the specialised press loudly heralded black lists, 'the impossibility for a serious organization to compile these lists has been known for a long time'.[45] It was mainly small associations that had committed to such lists. Also, and in addition to the fact that the publication of such lists was not permitted by law and they were therefore only for private use, black lists were rejected as misleading because a firm could still not be regarded as unworthy of credit even if for some reason it had not made a payment.[46]

The utmost discretion was a fundamental tenet, and special attention was paid to it. Information associations repeatedly reminded their 'gentlemen members'[47] that information should not be passed on to third parties. This concerned, in the first place, the free riders, who wanted to benefit from the extensive work for the compilation of information for free. Such episodes, wrote the information association, 'sap the will to work and undermine the whole enterprise'.[48] Secondly, information on credit worthiness was confidential and only meant for members. Therefore, individual firms, which contravened this principle and passed on information to others could be excluded from the association without hesitation.[49] In 1893, the *Creditoren-Verein* had to dismiss its inspector responsible for Vienna, since he had been bribed and had given away information for a price far below the official tariff.[50] Of course, there were also, repeatedly, complaints from firms about which unfavourable information had been circulated. In 1890, it happened that a furious businessman appeared in the office of the *Vindobona* and requested the cancellation of the negative credit information published about him, of which he had been informed through the indiscretion of a member. The information association refused to do so with good reason, and the person concerned published a counter statement in a Viennese newspaper. There was brief unrest among the members, which came to an end when the firm concerned filed for bankruptcy. Now the accused dared to maintain that the negative report of the *Vindobona* had caused his collapse. This left the information association indifferent, since its negative report could in no way be the cause of the fact that his liabilities exceeded his assets many times over. For the *Vindobona* the problem of this case was rather that some of its members had not drawn the right conclusions from the information. Rather, this case demonstrates that people, despite the decidedly negative report of the *Vindobona*, did not refrain from lending over and over again, until reality ultimately taught them that working with precarious firms is not actually business but rather a lottery which gives a 25% profit in the best case, but in many cases losses.[51]

The reports of the information association were given either orally or in written form upon presentation of a membership card.[52] After the association joined the telephone network in 1890, it was decided that information should not be given over the telephone in order to avoid complications.[53] This measure was necessary since allegations of insolvency could not only result in defamation[54] but also damage the interests of a company, which had a guarantee at the credit agency.[55] Rumours about insolvency, whose fabrication mostly 'went back to the stock exchange', could be very damaging. Especially in economically difficult times, 'the lightest suspicion is enough to cause the most severe measures on the part of credit issuing banks and firms. Under such circumstances, the circulation of malicious or superficial insolvency rumours must appear all the more criminal, and one cannot deplore severely and emphatically enough those who cause this.' This is where comfort ceased, 'because where the honour of businessmen must be protected, every other consideration disappears....'[56] Part of the problem was also the sensationalism of the press, which, with its inflated reports about insolvency waves, made confidential restructuring negotiations public and, in doing so, could impair them. 'No entrepreneur can be sure of his life any more', wrote the *Creditoren-Verein*, if the 'blade of the newspaper guillotine falls on him. If a newspaper announces to the world that a company is insolvent, that company is indeed already insolvent, because today no entrepreneur would be able to withstand the rush of furious creditors driven by panic.' Whether a company wanted to make its insolvency public or not, should be left to it and no newspaper had the right to declare it insolvent. 'Such newspaper reports are also a bad service for creditors who would be rather inclined to agree on restructuring proceedings regarding debtors, as long as the latter's difficulties remain secret.'[57]

A special function within the information association emerged with the appointment of a travel inspector who spent most of the year travelling. In cases in which contradictions about the situation of a company became manifest, a travel inspector was sent directly to the company in order to check the actual state of things. He was also responsible for supervising correspondents, since he performed his tasks fully independently, summarising them in detailed reports, which would then be compared with those written by the correspondents. In addition, he also drafted general descriptive reports from the various provinces of the Monarchy. The regional sphere of activity of the *Creditoren-Verein* encompassed a very unevenly developed territory within the Austro-Hungarian Monarchy. Highly developed regions, such as the areas around Vienna or Prague, were like islands of modernisation amidst a largely agrarian and industrially backward territory. Although this area was an important and well-protected market, a financial culture had also developed there which was in sharp contrast with that of the economic centres.

A travel inspector reported from Lemberg[58] in 1890 that the credit conditions had slightly improved and the market had been cleared at least of notorious fraudsters. In public places, people even talked about 'these Viennese having founded a business police whose detectives travel across the province looking for suspicious business enterprises'.[59] In those territories were a large number of women-owned firms, whose husbands had already been insolvent once or twice. Also, most business operations were deliberately not registered. 'Officially, they choose not to be registered because of high taxation, but in reality they do so in order to avoid that their legal position, the way they should sign, their marriage, etc. should become of public knowledge.' It was quite common to register one first name with the trade authority, another first name with the police and to have a third one on the company's name plate. And even with family names there are differences; apart from nicknames, it happens that women sometimes use their own, at other times their husband's surname, depending on whether he, she or both have already been insolvent, or whether they are married, or divorced, legally or only according to ritual customs; also, the name of the company often depends on whether the husband is of age and has already complied with military service. For these reasons, it was immensely difficult to gather information about such firms, and an intention to mislead could be detected everywhere.

However, the travel inspector observed that:

> It is impossible to do without this small businessman who is so deleterious for his creditors; for he is the main mediator of consumption, a

> consumption which cannot be underestimated. It is impossible for us to imagine the minimal organisation, the frugality of these pariahs. In doorways, small, dark and dirty archways, improvised wooden shacks and dirty flats, goods lie chaotically, about whose conditions the producer would be horrified. The whole family, husband, wife and children, the *commis*, search for customers, lure, hassle and persuade them. They inexhaustibly bargain and negotiate – until the customers buy, with or without profit, in cash or on credit: one way or the other, consumption triumphs.... It will take years before the conditions in these areas are adapted to Western European standards; until then, one has to accept the traditional economy.[60]

Even more surreal was trade at the annual markets with the so-called peasant's goods, which were exhibited by the city tradesmen. A trade, which was at any rate 'more lively than healthy', in the words of the travel inspector. These markets manifested the consumption capacity of the Galician population for all sorts of

> junk and other goods, whose origin is God knows where! It is incredible how many things are sold there: the most unimpressive things, the smallest residues, all sorts of leftovers from all corners of the world are sold here; I have seen even food rests being sold by weight. A second country with a comparable purchasing capacity for such wastes of production no longer exists and this one deserves from the economic point of view the interest of producers.[61]

From Stryj,[62] the travel inspector could only report that the consumption conditions looked bad and credit conditions possibly even worse.

> With the exception of a few companies, which are therefore doubly valuable, this place must, with regard to credit conditions, be considered corrupt and foul. The dumping of goods, distress sales, compensation proceedings are the order of the day. 'The end justifies the means, a man with a caftan told me in a confidential tone, and explained this old, familiar expression with another similar, and yet very appropriate common place, as bad examples spoil good customs', while he pointed at some experienced show-offs in silk caftans and sable fur hats who strutted in the full awareness of their success. 'The honest, yet poor, man is considered stupid, he is pitied, and yet the blessing comes from above.' He says, 'they make it too easy for people; the corruption of these areas is nourished less by compensation than by the new and simplistic practice of borrowing money'. And to a question concerning conscience and honour he replied: 'honour does not exist here, people here calculate in numbers and are ready to be arrested for a profit of a couple of hundred florins; thus also did the others who today, their heads held high, have become major players.'[63]

The further he travelled in Bukowina,[64] the more the travel inspector came to realise that credit transactions in the retail trade in those areas were linked to such high risk, that one would generally not recommend them. 'The last mediating hand in commodity transactions is recruited almost exclusively from people … who actually do not own any capital, since those who have money trade products in agricultural countries, such as Bukowina, Galicia, Hungary, etc. or they lend money, lease farms and *propinations*, take active part in public works, deforestation, restructure insolvent firms, buy bankruptcy assets, are appointed as liquidator, etc.'[65] One should make no mistake about the qualities of character and solidity of a retail firm:

> they have the same value as the motto faithful, hard-working, honourable in the domestic workers' books … where, by a good, honest man one usually means a good family man, by honourable a religious, pious man who is determined to keep up his image of honourable man by means of an outer formality and ostentatious devotion to ritual practices, which does not prevent him from cheating hitherto unknown creditors, dumping goods, filing for bankruptcy, being arrested, etc. he still remains in the local mentality a good, honourable man! In the battle of competition these people are ready to use all possible means. Nothing is inappropriate for them in order to make the direct rival harmless; anonymous denunciations, here called *Pasquilles*, are well known; unlike foreign creditors, local creditors rarely lose their money, because people will need them as creditors again.[66]

Similarly, from Siebenbürgen[67] the travel inspector could mainly report that loans in the retail trade were one of the saddest phenomena of economic life and represented one of the most frequent causes of insolvency. This is because many of those independent businessmen lacked not only the means but also the ability to run a business properly.

> As a sign of gratitude for the fact that an all too liberal loan system has called into existence a proletariat of trade, the latter does whatever is in his power in order to victimise the lender and to deprive him of his money by deceiving him; then, the better local customers, hit hard by the liberal loan system, sing in chorus: 'These Germans asked for it, why did they lend money', and both the authorities and the employees applaud. How often, during an inspection, must one hear from them: 'why this circumspection, why this scrupulous research, it is useless! We no longer take cases of bankruptcy, criminal charges, etc. very seriously'; on the contrary, one often hears how gentlemen poke fun by saying that 'German gentlemen do their very best in order to bring some money to the country, why should we not support them in this laudable undertaking!'[68]

Notes

1 This topic is part of the project on the history of bankruptcy, with which I have dealt for over a decade. Stiefel, D. 2008. *Im Labor der Niederlagen, Konkurspolitik im internationalen Vergleich*. Vienna: Böhlau Verlag. Grazter, K., Stiefe, D. eds. 2008. *History of Insolvency and Bankruptcy from an International Perspective*. Huddinge: Södertörn Academic Studies. Stiefel, D. 1997. Geschäftsgeheimnis. Zu den Anfangsschwierigkeiten der Informationsgesellschaft in Österreich im 19. Jahrhundert, in H. Matis ed. 1997. *Historische Betriebsanalyse und Unternehmer*. Vienna: Veröffentlichungen der Österreichischen Gesellschaft für Unternehmensgeschichte, vol 19; Stiefel, D. 1996. Zahlungsmoral. Aus der Praxis des Geschäftslebens im 19. Jahrhundert, in G.E. Tichy, H. Matis, F. Scheuch eds. 1996. *Wege zur Ganzheit*, Vienna: Duncker & Humbolt; Stiefel, D. 1995. Insolvenzen: Ein Spiegel der Wirtschaft? in *125 Jahre Kreditschutzverband von 1870*, Vienna.

2 Karl Theodor von Inama-Sternegg was born in Augsburg in 1843 and died in Innsbruck in 1908. He studied in Munich, was professor at the University of Innsbruck from 1868 and in Vienna from 1881. In 1884, he became president of the Statistische Zentralkommission (Central Commission for Statistics) and introduced the use of counting machines for the 1890 census. Beside his statistic publications (Österreichische Statistik, Statistisches Handbuch) he also wrote a three-volume history of German economy: Inama-Sternegg, K.-T. 1879–1901. *Deutsche Wirtschaftsgeschichte* Band 1: *Bis zum Schluß der Karolingerperiode*. Band 2: *Im 10.–12. Jahrhundert*. Band 3: *In den letzten Jahrhunderten des Mittelalters*. Leipzig: Duncker & Humbolt.

3 Inama-Sternegg, K.-T. 1881. Das Zeitalter des Credits. *Wochenschrift des Creditoren-Vereins von 1870*, p.183.

4 Matis. H., Stiefel, D. 1994. *Mit der vereinigten Kraft des Capitals, des Credits und der Technik – Die Geschichte des österreichischen Bauwesens am Beispiel der Allgemeinen Baugesellschaft – A.Porr Aktiengesellschaft*, 2 vol., Vienna: Böhlau Verlag.

5 Inama-Sternegg (1881), p.187.

6 Inama-Sternegg (1881), p.192.

7 Inama-Sternegg (1881), p.184.

8 Neustadtl, S. 1879. Die Reformbestrebungen auf dem Gebiete des kaufmännischen Zahlungs- und Kreditwesens, speech at *Wiener kaufmännischer Verein*, 24 January 1879. *Wochenschrift des Creditoren Vereins von 1870*, p. 75.

9 Anon. 1870. Die schwarzen Listen, *Wochenschrift des Creditvereins von 1870*, p.64.

10 Neustadtl (1879), p.75.

11 Anon. 1893. *Wochenschrift des Creditvereins von 1893*, p.159.

12 Neustadtl (1879), p.76.

13 Neustadtl (1879), p.76.

14 Anon. 1880. Die kaufmännische Creditgebahrung. *Wochenschrift des Creditvereins 1880*, p.154.

15 Neustadtl (1879), p.79.

16 Anon. 1880. Die kaufmännische Creditgebahrung. *Wochenschrift des Creditvereins 1880*, p.154.

17 Neustadtl (1879), p.76.

18 For example, the Free Association for Cash Payment in Munich (*Münchner freie Vereinigung für Baarzahlung*).

19 On the initiative of the member of the Reichsrat Neuber, a commission was created in 1885 at the Trade Association of Lower Austria to ‘discuss the question of the foundation of an association for the promotion of cash payments’. Is it not known whether such an association was created in the end. Anon. 1885. *Wochenschrift des Creditvereins 1885*, p.26.

20 Such a question was raised by the Trade Association of Lower Austria as early as 1876. Similarly, in 1877 the Chambers of Commerce of both Darmstadt and Düsseldorf attempted to pass decisions for a regulation of the commercial payment and loan system.
21 Neustadtl (1879), p.80.
22 Anon. 1894. Unsere Creditverhältnisse, *Wochenschrift des Creditvereins 1894*, p.70.
23 Versammlung der Wiener Schneidergenossenschaft, 1883. Zur Reform des Zahlungswesens. *Wochenschrift 1883*, p.162.
24 Die gewerblichen Creditverhältnisse, *Wochenschrift 1883*, p.83.
25 Jahresbericht der Düsseldorfer Handelskammer 1882, *Wochenschrift 1883*, p.183.
26 Fürstenthal, L. 1935. Kreditgewährung und Kreditschutz. *Mitteilungen des Creditoren-Vereins von 1870*, p.3.
27 Steiner, S. 1890. Ein Wort gegen die sogenannte 'schwere Hand', in *Mitteilungen der 'Vindobona',* Wochenschrift 1890, p.68.
28 Neustadtl (1879), p.87.
29 Anon. Die Sicherung des geschäftlichen Kredits, *Wochenschrift 1904*, p.140.
30 Auspitzer, J. Die Baarzahlung, *Wochenschrift 1890*, p.27.
31 Anon. 1937. Mehr Öffentlichkeit im Geschäftsleben. *Mitteilungen des Creditoren-Vereins*, 14 August 1937, p.2.
32 *Wochenschrift 1892*, p.172.
33 Mehr Öffentlichkeit im Geschäftsleben, *Mitteilungen*, p.2.
34 Byck, T. 1928. Das kaufmännische Auskunftswesen in Österreich, *Mitteilungen*, p.2.
35 Der vorbeugende Gläubigerschutz und seine Abwege, *Mitteilungen 5 November 1927*.
36 The foundation of the *Creditoren Verein* was a reaction to the law on bankruptcy of 1868, which left the economy very dissatisfied. In order to compensate for the disadvantages of this law, the association 'for the protection of creditors against fraudulent exploitation of insolvency and for the prevention of special benefits' was founded in 1870. The representatives of private economy had come together precisely in order to correct the malfunctioning of the State's bankruptcy law by means of a common action. The organization of creditors was an instrument of legal enforcement.
37 Informationsverein, *Wochenschrift 1884*, pp.93–4.
38 Byck (1928), p.2.
39 Das Informationswesen, *Wochenschrift 1885*, p.31.
40 Anon. 1885. *Vindobona* Informationsverein zur Wahrung und Förderung des Handels und der Industrie Österreichs, *Wochenschrift 1885*, p.42.
41 Anon. 1886. Erster Jahresbericht des Vereins Vindobona, *Wochenschrift 1886*, p.34.
42 Mitteilungen der Vindobona, *Wochenschrift 1894*, p.11.
43 Vindobona, *Wochenschrift 1885*, p.178.
44 Die schwarzen Listen, Mitteilungen der Vindobona, *Wochenschrift 1889*, p.64.
45 Unsere Auskunftsabteilung, *Mitteilungen* 17 September 1927, p.1.
46 Der vorbeugende Gläubigerschutz und seine Abwege, *Mitteilungen* 5 November 1927.
47 At that time, the association only had male members, since women were not allowed to have leading positions in registered companies.
48 Mitteilungen der Vindobona, *Wochenschrift 1893*, p. 36 und 1894, p.54.
49 These cases were published weekly in *Wochenschrift des Creditoren-Vereins.* For example: 1892, p.68 and 1893, p.107.
50 *Wochenschrift 1893*, p.160.
51 Anon. 1890. Die Insolvenz Arpad Laskai in Kronstadt, *Mitteilungen der Vindobona, Wochenschrift 1890*, p.176.

52 Oral information was given immediately; written information was sent within the same day by post. *Wochenschrift 1892*, p.160.
53 Mitteilungen der Vindobona, *Wochenschrift 1890*, p.36.
54 This was confirmed by a decision of the Supreme Court in Vienna. *Wochenschrift 1913*, pp.205–6.
55 Haftung für Kreditauskunft, *Wochenschrift 1914*, p.110.
56 Insolvenzgerüchte, *Wochenschrift 1885*, p.2.
57 Die Zeitungsguillotine, *Mitteilungen* 12 November 1927, p.3.
58 At that time in the Austrian province of Galicia, today it is part of Ukraine.
59 Anon. 1890. Bericht aus Lemberg, *Mitteilungen der Vindobona, Wochenschrift 1890*, p.111.
60 Anon. (1890). Bericht aus Lemberg, p.112.
61 Anon. 1890. Bericht aus Tarnopol. *Mitteilungen der Vindobona, Wochenschrift 1890*, p.136.
62 At that time in the Austrian province of Galicia, today in Ukraine.
63 Anon. 1890. Bericht aus Stryj. *Mitteilungen der Vindobona, Wochenschrift 1890*, p.64.
64 The crown land of Bukowina was administered from Galicia. Its northern part now belongs to Ukraine, its southern part to Romania.
65 Anon. 1890. Bericht aus Radautz. *Mitteilungen der Vindobona, Wochenschrift 1890*, p.80. By propination, (from Lat. 'to drink to someone'), people in Eastern Europe meant landowners' monopoly over profits from alcohol.
66 Anon. (1890). Bericht aus Radautz, p.80.
67 Transylvania (*Siebenbürgen*) is part of Romania today.
68 Anon. 1891. Bericht aus Siebenbürgen. *Mitteilungen der Vindobona. Wochenschrift 1891*, p.60.

5 French banks and public opinion

The public's negative perception of the French banking establishment (from the 1800s to the 1950s)

Hubert Bonin

'At every moment', said Honoré de Balzac, 'the living groan under the oppression of the moneyed'.[1]

Right from the inception of the money market, the role of financial intermediation by bankers has evoked much resentment and ire against their entire industry. These 'manipulators of money' have been accused of 'selling time' by deducting the amount accrued for interest on debt,[2] of forcing debtors into idleness by charging usurious rates of interest, and even of gambling away public money on leveraged speculations. Burnings and even (during the French Revolution) the guillotine have routinely purged cities and even entire nations of such money-manipulators. Even as recently as the 1930s, Vincent Auriol had this to say about them, just when he became minister of Finance in 1936 of Léon Blum's Popular Front government: 'I shall shut the banks and imprison the bankers'. Still today, academics and students fear that French universities will be sold to enterprises and banks, and most of all the risk to their strategic and financial autonomy by opening the doors to the influence of 'big business'.[3]

It is no wonder that certain agents and parties of the social system have had and continue to have what may be best called 'schizophrenic' relations with the banking establishment[4] – within a general and permanent trend towards various types of global resentment against capital, capitalism, capitalist firms and capitalists.[5] While banks and the business of banking in general have been perceived as indispensable aids to the economic growth of nations, they have also been roundly criticized and blamed for the shocking failures of many corporate borrowers. They have been accused of deliberately causing the recurring financial crunches which have invariably led to a tightening of the credit market and, via a 'Darwinian' process of elimination, to the eradication of 'bad investments' and the liquidation of mismanaged, fragile or speculative enterprises. Economists have called them 'crises of convenience', because they conveniently cleansed the market of its mismanaged enterprises. Such terms and suspicions have grown and fed aspersions of 'guilty money'[6] and even outright cries of 'conspiracy'[7] – the feeling that certain large, sinister networks were seeking to control the economic, and thereby the political life of the nation. This has fuelled a hundred conspiracy theories, in particular, the idea that the Diaspora (especially originating from Central and Eastern Europe)[8] had established dubious international and transatlantic networks. Another line of analysis might be found in the eternal struggle by the adepts of 'meritocracy' against those who epitomized 'the moneyed class' against mere 'smart and virtuous' people – and bankers have ever been targets for such social(-ist) resentment.

Perhaps a quick overview of the history of banking in the past century-and-a-half may help unearth some explanations regarding this generally negative impression of banks and bankers. At first glance it is evident that banks have played a key role in giving rise to industrial society – and therein lies the double edge: this very power has also inspired a sense of awe and fear. Over the years, the public had begun to identify the banking economy with the string of economic crises (bankruptcies, affairs and wheeler-dealings). These seemed to follow one after the other in almost routine fashion. The final straw was provided by the barely covered anti-Semitism, which, combined with this fear and revulsion, burst out into an outright rejection of banks and bankers in the years 1880 to 1900. Even during the *Belle Époque*,[9] the banking establishment's role in building the nation's economy was contested because it was felt that they had been more concerned with their international, rather than national, activities. This French cosmopolitanism was contrasted with the attitude of the German banking establishment which was thought to have been much more helpful to the enterprises within their own country. A number of studies and widely circulated pamphlets, which appeared throughout the years immediately before, during and after the First World War, attested to the patriotism of the 'German model'.

Then, as in England, the inter-war years saw the eruption of a lively debate regarding the role that could and should be played by bankers in regional development. A large section of public opinion felt that the domination and influence wielded by the large credit institutions should give way to a shorter money circuit which would help the larger medium-sized enterprises take full advantage of the second industrial revolution. The whole thing boiled down to the question of the survival of the local and regional banks in the face of the large Parisian predators. The debate took on added vehemence with the outbreak of the banking crisis in the years 1930 to 1936. Additionally, its focus shifted to *Les Deux Cents Familles* (The Two Hundred Families); referring to the 200 biggest shareholders of the Banque de France during the inter-war period and the only vote-givers at the yearly general assembly of its shareholders, and their supposed role in formulating the policies of Banque de France. In the eyes of the public, bankers joined the disreputable ranks of the big iron and steel barons and the large trusts, prompting the Finance Minister into launching a more stringent governmental control system. Bankers, even more than businessmen who can rely on fixed or productive capital and innovative assets, and not only on trust,[10] tangible assets and immaterial skills, have traditionally taken into account the psychology of public opinion to resist crises of confidence, risks of citizen illegitimacy, and moreover risks of nationalization (in the 1940s and in the 1980s). More recently, a few US experts denounced the 'bankocracy' of having seized the reins of financial power and (under-) regulation since the 1980s and through the present mood, which follows 'America's long love–hate relationship with money and banks'.[11] Europe and France do not escape this present outburst of anti-banking protests[12] because immoral uses of money and banking have revived the perennial issues of the mythology of money,[13] and thus psychological or public opinion issues are also at stake in parallel with mere financial or lending topics.

Reviving past perceptions of French bankers will therefore fuel arguments about the issue of the commitment of banks to society.[14] This chapter will thus focus on the perception of modern banks and bankers by some segments of French opinion, following an empirical approach based on literature (later also movies), pamphlets, and academic references. We are fully aware that it is impossible to gauge in a systematic manner the deep-rootedness of such bank phobia among the economic and social elite and moreover across the population itself. We recognize the limits of our literary analysis in advance, which ought to open doors to statistical studies spanning different periods, taking into account also paintings, novels.

The crystallization of the anti-bank lobby (from the mid-19th century to 1914)

While an anti-bank lobby grew out of the anti-capitalist and anti-proprietorship philosophies, in the eyes of the people, bankers turned into yet another incarnation of the *gros*[15] (lit. big bullies), who, while not actually snatching away work from the 'little ones', made off with the fruit of their labour and their savings. This hostility towards the banking establishment took shape very gradually. It was only when its role as promoter of the industrial revolution and the establishment of the industrialized society became more evident that the resentment took on a more concrete and aggressive form.

The fear of bankers' power

The Hugolian word *formidable,* which originally meant something striking that because of its power, induced a sense of fear, is an apt adjective for these bankers who had begun to assume *formidable* proportions from as early as the third decade of the 19th century (1830–1850). Having amassed great wealth and disposable capital by financing trade and overseas merchants, they began to make their presence felt in the emerging world of large-scale (of those times) business and took their place beside the big iron and steel barons and other captains of industry. Simultaneously, their power grew when they began to climb up the grand stairway of high society and formed large, yet close-knit networks forged by family ties and *mariages de convenance.* By 1805 Napoleon had already raised some of them into the peerage (Mallet, etc.) and their rapid ascent was furthered by the purchase of grand residences, wine *châteaux* in Gironde and manors in the forests of *Île-de-France*. Their subsequent, inevitable entry into ministerial posts and parliamentary seats (e.g. Casimir Perier, Fould[16]) was clear proof that power through money had now infiltrated the corridors of real power.

Stendhal's incomplete novel, *Lucien Leuwen*, is all about a Leuwen who rose through the ranks to become a Minister. Many scholars have already dealt with the power and influence wielded by bankers in the novels of Balzac and Zola. Memorable fictitious characters like Gundermann – 'who obstinately continued to build his tower of millions … till it came to dominate the entire planet' – Saccard, Nucingen, Hemerlingue and Haverkamp were based on actual people such as Rothschild and Pereire. They are clear indications and reminders that, despite their restricted readership these novels reflected the widespread uneasiness felt by many regarding the extent of the power banks had. Just when the industrial society was attaining its apogee, the reputation of family bankers of *Haute Banque*, especially the Rothschilds,[17] reached a nadir – in the minds of the common people, they had grown tentacled power-networks. By the end of the century, the image of the octopus had caught the public's imagination, in France, as well as abroad.[18]

Their control over the credit market gave rise to much hostility from debtors struggling under the yoke of high interest rates. This hostility drew fuel from religious dogma, for instance, in the tradition of religious mendicant orders, which called it usury. The *Cahiers de doléances* had denounced usury[19] in 1789. Business loans had not yet attained social acceptability – perhaps because, for the middle class, the act of borrowing was, and would be for a long time to come, a last ignoble recourse. Interestingly enough, this adjective was often used by farmers who were themselves quite happy to benefit from the mutual agricultural credit which had come into effect by the laws of 1894–1899. Even the revolutionary *Commune de Paris* (March–May 1871) proclaimed in its *Declaration to the People of France* of 19 April 1871: 'This is the end … of exploitation, of speculation, of monopolies.'

The nexus between banking and politics

The power of these bankers was also evident in the ease with which they could penetrate the highest echelons of political power. They had no hesitation in making full use of their immense wealth to spin their web around the political corridors at the heart of the nation's Financial Department. The undemocratic pockets within the political establishment made it possible to form elitist cliques made up of capitalists seeking licenses for their projects and politicians who were willing to furnish them in return for a slice of the profits. No wonder that the big banking houses and corporations were thought to have played a major role in the creation of the money and credit markets in which the sluice gates were controlled by a small number of power-brokers – heads of the major banking houses, captains of industry, developers of railroads and ports and sometimes even media moguls. People started to be aware of the 'interlocking' between bankers and financiers on one side, and business on the other side (their membership of boards or financial stakes). The caricatures of the day bear evidence of how the public viewed the July Monarchy that found itself so often compromised by collusion between political power, corporate executives and parliamentarians. The Second Empire's reputation for wheeler-dealing was supported not only by the public opinion of the day, but also by the republican opposition, which was quick to pounce upon any misdeed thought to have been the result of the influence of money or of the industry. One example of such influential people would be Rouher – a hero of Émile Zola's series of novels *La fortune des Rougon* – and especially of the novel *Son Excellence Eugène Rougon*. Furthermore, the model for the Duke of Mora, minister of State, in *Les drames de l'argent* and especially Morny were severely castigated for directing money towards the Bonapartists and covering corruption of the regime (*La Fête impériale* and its lavish style of life).

The subsequent scandals, which erupted under the Third Republic further degraded public opinion towards the money market. Especially as a large number of small investors was directly affected by the collapse of several banks and enterprises. Numerous books and novels, such as the historian Jean-Yves Mollier's *Le scandale de Panama*,[20] Maupassant's novel *Bel Ami* (1885), Maurice Barres' *Leurs Figures* and a story set in 1909 by Jules Romains,[21] in which the financier Haverkamp merrily waltzes through a string of shady land transactions – itself reminiscent of Zola's character Saccard in the novel *L'Argent* (1891)[22] and especially his novel *La Curée* (1871) – reveal the extent of the corruption. In practically every such romanticized story, the plot revolved around a conspiracy between finance, its slimy tentacles slithering into the corridors of political power and the press[23] – in short, the entire business and political community. The same theme reappears in Daudet (1878)[24] and Claretie[25] (1882), which goes to show just how deep rooted these Machiavellian ideas were in the literature of those times, and by extension, in the minds of the public. In Claretie's novel, the hero Émile Guillemard carries the same Christian name as one of the Pereire brothers, and like them, 'became one of the kings of Paris' by being an intermediate broker and having his own share portfolio, mainly in the distribution company L'Alimentation générale. He fell afoul of Rodillon, a banker in the 'classical' sense (the bank dedicated to general interest) and 'one of the bigwigs of the stock market and a founder of and shareholder in radical newpapers'.[26]

All through the *Belle Époque*, pamphleteers,[27] the mainstream press and even the more elitist leftist popular journals such as the *L'Assiette au beurre*, carried article after article detailing the misdemeanours committed by these 'money manipulators' as though they were some sort of serialized soap operas. Phrases like 'the aristocracy of the safe' and 'financial feudalism' gave body to the suspicions and vivid fantasies regarding the power and influence of financiers and their disastrous effects on the nation's economy:

> This high gentry, this financial aristocracy, which lusts after all the privileges which belonged to the old nobility, this league of the big and rich against the small and the poor, this vast syndicate of anti-nationalism, egoism and greed … worshippers of Mammon, Mrs. Grigou, Gobseck, Vautour.[28]

The running battle (1907–1908) between the anti-bank journalist Lysis[29] and the bankers' advocate Testis, also reads very much like a serial story. It helped consolidate the public's opinion, even among the intelligentsia, that money power was manipulating the government. That there was 'widespread domination by a financial oligarchy which controlled even the press and the government,[30] that four or five banks … have such a vast, well-connected network that they control even the national savings'.

They would short-circuit the democratically elected powers and by inserting their own delegates at the power centre – such as Finance Minister Maurice Rouvier, who was President of the Council and also a banker – be able to negate the effects of parliamentary alternation: 'What the big banking houses required of the Finance Minister is that he should in no way oppose the issue of this or that foreign fund in France.'[31] And novelist Anatole France[32] made it all too clear in his novel *L'Île aux pingouins*:

> The Isle of Penguins was a democratic state: several financial companies had greater power than some of the ministers of the Republic. These civil servants were more like petty lords, remotely governed and coerced either through intimidation or corruption by these large corporations which sought favours even at the expense of the nation's interests.

The power of the bankers reached its zenith when it allowed them to manipulate people, marriages and sentiments. Here we begin to edge towards hardboiled crime fiction, but this itself became a literary tradition, like for example, when a girl was seen to have only barter value (beauty, fecundity, dowry) as in the case of the superintendent of a big rural landlord who gave his daughter in marriage to Leclerc, a trading officer-cum-banker, a governor of Banque de France, a banker of warehouse wines.[33] It was the same story in *Le Père Goriot* (1835) and the fate of the two Goriot daughters, Mrs de Respaud and de Nucingen, the latter marrying the equivalent of a Rothschild. Morality was at stake in a few novels, and finance seemed to short-circuit human values.[34]

Looking at bankers as traders and confidence tricksters

The anguish of seeing one's hard-earned money, the savings of a lifetime, go up in a puff of smoke, has understandably been a recurring theme in literature as well as in the mainstream press. Who can forget the character of Robert Macaire, the charlatan trader who conned shareholders all through the 101 instalments, which appeared in *Le Charivari* from 1836 to 1838, or Hugo's portrait of Rothschild in not-very-inspired verse?

> This passing dandy
> Made his fortune while you were sweating blood;
> He went a bear and rode up a bull
> That our fall may be deeper still and full.
> Circling our dead, like a vulture foul,
> With grasping claws, always on the prowl…
> With our money he built his palace of gold,
> Our loss and sorrow his pleasures mould.

The inevitable turbulence which shook the Paris Stock Exchange during the transition between the first and second banking revolutions – when the system had not yet had time to stabilize itself and no adequate auto-regulatory mechanisms within the money market had been formed – gave the impression that bankruptcies were threatening people's savings, hampering a growth which was already taking a beating from the Great Depression, and especially, giving a free reign to speculative bankers and financiers. What shook the public most was speculation – the risks involved in constructing huge financial support structures for the development of vast, and as-yet untapped resources (mines, ore deposits, waterways, railways, metallurgical factories). They feared most for the future of their savings were they to be invested in the financial market or placed in bank deposits – they were afraid of becoming what Guilleminault called *gogos*,[35] a word that emerged in the 19th century. These worries led to a resurgence of hostility towards the banking establishment, which had seen an economic upswing in the years 1820–1840, due to the fact that banks were perceived as playing a key role in the life of the Paris financial centre, either through introductions on the primary market, or through trading on the secondary market.

Several popular novels of the time had characters based on some of these real-life money-manipulators. The banker-financier Eugène Bontoux – the key figure of the crash of Union Générale Bank in 1882 – appeared as Mr Bozan in *Les Drames de l'argent*. The novel *Le Million* portrayed typical middle-class men who found themselves both fearing and fascinated by the lure of easy money:

> The uncle [Ducrey] … reminisced about his old adventures at the stock market. In a hoarse, shaky voice punctuated by shrill laughter, he talked of the killings he had made. His eyes shone with an almost sensual pleasure… Ah! The thrill of playing for money, of striving for money, of fighting for the first million![36] To stake on money! The thought sent shivers of anticipation and fear down Ribeyre's spine [the nephew, a trader who was soon to lose everything at the stock market] …. A fever gripped him.[37]

Alexandre Dumas junior is an example of a prominent novelist to draw attention to links between banking, speculation, and finance.[38]

Comedy itself was called to denounce speculators, implying that financial drama could reach humane tragedy and that classical familial and tribal struggles could occur between new Atrides disguised as financiers[39] to convince the audience of the immorality of financial practices. And though *Les affaires sont les affaires*[40] – in the proverbial words of Octave Mirbeau – the Egyptian exploits of the banker Soubeyran and of his Land Mortgage Bank,[41] the meltdown of the Comptoir d'Escompte de Paris[42] in 1889 and the stock market crash of 1889–1891 raised severe doubts regarding the reliability of the Paris Stock Exchange – and Feydeau remained as one key observer of this financial society.[43]

As is well known – thanks to the pioneering book by Alphonse Toussenel[44] written in 1847 – the psychological tensions caused by the shake-up of the money market and the collapse of several banks, at a time when savings were being transplanted away from land and metal towards retail share and stock-holding, led to intense bouts of anti-Semitism.[45] These outbursts were supported and mediated by a certain section of the press, a number of pamphleteers and some novelists. The novel *Les Drames de l'argent*[46] refers to a 'Semitic conspiracy' led by the banker Hemerlingue[47] against Bozan-Bontoux that resulted in the collapse of his Société Universelle and the disintegration of his family – a clear case of unhealthy money versus family values. Ypsoloni 'came to know of the incredible collapse of Société Universelle, of Bozan du Breuil's ruin and of the disasters which had overtaken so many great businesses due to Semitic conspiracies',[48] that:

> they had been long preparing Bozan's ruin before actually striking him down with a sudden, stunning blow [...]. The word was spread that Bozan de Breuil had lost his way in dangerous speculations, that he had gambled with his shareholders' funds, and that one fine morning, the company's books had been seized.[49]

The prolific novelist Navery – forgotten today, who wrote scores of novels during the 1870s – also subscribed to the widespread belief of those times that it was a Rothschild-led conspiracy of the big banking houses which caused the collapse of Banque de l'union Générale, the ruin of its promoter Eugène Bontoux, and the bankruptcies of 1882. It was done, they said, to stop the intrusion of a modern rival and the establishment of a network of banks and depositors close to Catholic interests:[50]

> The Jewish tribe which felled Bozan de Breuil and caused his ruin in a single day, would never allow him to rise again. It needed this victim not only because the rapid rise of this financier offended it, but because by thus destroying such wealth, it wanted to send the message to all Catholics who may be thinking of uniting themselves against Jewish bankers that

> any such attempt would not only fail, but might well prove to be dangerous to them.[51]

Actually, Catholic banks such as Crédit Industriel et Commercial were doing very well, while the quarrel between the Pereire and the Rothschild in the years 1850–1860 – mentioned in *L'Argent* by Zola – was very much between coreligionists. Unfortunately, even as eminent an author as Daudet could not resist perpetuating these fantastic rumours regarding the machinations of the Jewish banking establishment. In his *Le Nabab* (1877),[52] the hero, Jansoulet (based on François Bravay), rose from poverty to wealth by devious transactions in Tunisia and returned to France as a financier – with the support of the character of Duke de Mora, inspired by Rouher – during the Second Empire. Daudet named Jansoulet's enemy Hemmerlingue – 'with whom Jansoulet was engaged in a ferocious money battle' – that is a deliberately Franco-Germanic name which brought to mind the battle between Rothschild and Pereire. It is true that the collapse of several banks in the 1880s (such as Union Générale, Comptoir d'escompte de Paris, Société de Banque et de Dépôts, Hentsch, etc.), and especially, the 'scandal of Panama', fed the fears and the resentment felt by retail investors – not to speak of the press. Thus, in 1901, in order to warn investors about the link between debt securities (including foreign government bonds) issued by Crédit Lyonnais and past experiences, *L'Éclaireur National* republished articles which had appeared in 1894 under the title 'The truth regarding Crédit Lyonnais, a second Panama, a loss of two billion.' It was a fact that the surge of gold bonds in the 1890s had resulted in renewed speculation on the Paris stock exchange and the emergence of bullying money-makers setting up new banks to lure speculative investors.

Doubts and apprehensions regarding the fate of the funds collected by banks resurfaced during the *Belle Époque*: 'Were banks gambling with savings by placing them in dubious projects abroad?' It was at this time that the first part – in anticipation of the part constituted after the Bolshevik Revolution – of the charge sheet against the 'Russian loans' was formulated. A section of the financial press suspected these bankers of making a handsome profit by charging a commission on investor applications without giving a thought to their future, in short, of turning these investors into so many more *gogos*. And it was Crédit Lyonnais which bore the full brunt of these attacks.[53] Sure, the successive crashes and losses endured by investors could have blurred the perception of bankers, swallowed by a crisis of confidence because they had often been intermediaries between savings and the financial market – all the more after big banks had developed wealth management through their networks. And banks could have fallen victim to the global unpopularity of the Stock Exchange, accused of being a temple of speculation[54] and deceit,[55] as well as to its crisis; its bad image being extended to investors, as stakeholders involved in the process of luring savings towards the financial market.

Anti-patriotic bankers?

The apparent dichotomy between the banking establishment and national interests was a topic of hot debate when the nationalists gathered momentum in the years leading up to the First World War. What until then had been the bankers' greatest strength and sturdiest mainstay – their international networks, their strong links with the Diaspora and the unabashed use of competent personnel of all nationalities – were the very things which now raised patriotic eyebrows. Bankers were accused of putting the interests of their international community before those of the national stock exchange. Everyone knows of the disputes regarding 'the Russian loans' and the investments, via bank partnerships, made in the Rhine and Danube region, which, though profitable, did not seem to take into account the proximity of the national border.[56] The Lysis–Testis controversy typified these journalistic debates: 'The financial oligarchy is nothing more than a vast agency for the export of French capital.'[57] A major issue revolved around the strengthening of the national economy in the face of British and German competition:

> While our money is being spent building railroads in Russia and ports in Brazil, nothing is being done to relieve the miserable condition of the equipment and communications infrastructure in our own country. Many believe that this has continued for far too long. They feel it absurd that while on one hand we set up a protectionist policy to help develop domestic industry, on the other, we continue with a financial policy which drives all our capital abroad.[58]
>
> A hundred and fifty thousand French workers would not be out of work if the billions in misplaced investments had been used by Crédit Lyonnais to help our commerce and industry. Even the organizations which have been marked for liquidation have done less harm than this scandalous corporation, this state within a state.[59]

Such words rang especially true as its president, Germain, was ensconced at the heart of the centre-left of the Republican majority of these times as a member of Parliament from the 1870s till his death in 1905. The final stone against Crédit Lyonnais was cast by Sayous in his telling little booklet: 'Its policies have paralyzed the nation's commerce and industry – the living sources of the entire country's wealth.'[60]

Gradually, these articles in the financial press began to influence the mainstream Parisian media where they found themselves in no way short of 'publicists'. The press clippings stored in the archives of Banque de France has made it easy for us to undertake a systematic study of these 'anti-finance company' publications – especially the writings of Jules Domergue, director of *la réforme économique* between 1909 and 1910, which appeared in *La Liberté du Commerce et les Établissements de Crédit* and the record of the big debate which took place in the Chamber of Commerce on 20 November 1909. In short, it came down to 'preventing French capital from being used exclusively for the betterment of other countries is good – to bring it back home would be better'.[61] 'Cosmopolitan' became the stiffest accusation against bankers, whom publicists reproached for orienting French savings towards investment in Tsarist Russia or abroad to sustain the deployment of big business instead of favouring small and medium-sized enterprises in French provincial regions. Investment banks thus became targets of such harsh pamphlets.[62] The result was a resurgence of ideas and laws in favour of closer and friendlier local banks and regional banking, with increasing calls for a cooperative or a people's credit system. Finally, the whole thing culminated in the law of 1917 regarding Banques populaires.[63] And, as a first step, some circles of populist parties or segments of opinion shared in the assaults and caricatures[64] against Big Capital led by the Russian Communists, which were adopted in the form of pictures published by the French Communist Party.

The image of banks in the inter-war years

The First World War brought a temporary end to the wrangling. Banks played an essential role in expediting transatlantic money flows and, more importantly, they maintained a successful public relations campaign by attaching publicity posters to their contributions to the war chest for the repayment of war debts, as well as for the reconstruction. As a result, people began to see banks in a whole new light and their image gained a sparkle that it had never had before.[65] After all, it was their large networks, which allowed the people to mobilize their liquidity and forge the indispensable financial tool for the benefit of the country – whether in times of war or peace. As is the way of fickle fortune, bankers now found themselves the toast of the nation – it was they who united the forces 'to forge a stronger France' (from a poster of Crédit Commercial de France in 1920).

The German model against the 'too-soft' French banks

The diplomatic and military tussle between France and Germany led many observers to question the capacity of French banks when pitted against their German rivals. Many felt that there was a deplorable lack of understanding between French bankers and industrialists – a wide and sterile no-man's land between finance and production. In their view, banks were making too meagre a contribution to modernizing the national economy – what was then called 'national tooling'. In fact, throughout and after the war, the French evinced a keen interest in 'the German methods of economic expansion',[66] and especially in the workings, efficiency and impact of the all-purpose banks.[67] These banks were based on the concept of credit on personal property, on the common interests between banks and industry, the financing of exports and on the setting up of foreign branches to support their entrepreneurs abroad. The years 1916–1917 saw a slew of articles on banking reforms, organizing the banking sector, the role of banks in the post-war era, etc. In 1919, there appeared the new orientation of the banking industry in France.

The *German model* captured the French imagination. The rapid rise of Germany from the mid-1920s and the 'renaissance of German credit'[68] further strengthened the suspicion that French banks lagged far behind their German counterparts. A special edition of *L'Illustration économique et financière,* which appeared in December 1926 titled *France. L'Allemagne. Leurs positions économiques* (France. Germany. Their economic situation) put the focus on all these comparisons. There is no doubt that several initiatives launched at the time aimed to imitate this model, such as Banque Nationale du Commerce Extérieur, Société Française pour favoriser l'assurance-crédit, Banque Française d'acceptations, medium-term credit Crédit National, Caisse Centrale de Crédit Agricole, etc. Nevertheless, while scholars continued to push for what they felt was an absolute must if France were to 'win the economic battle of the future',[69] the big banks themselves gave the impression that they lacked the required vigour and entrepreneurship – even though the reality may have been different.

The effects of the monetary crisis 1923–1926

Banks were the first to feel Prime Minister Édouard Herriot's ire when he felt the Leftist Cartel weakening (1924–1926), at a time when his own majority was being eroded and the financial situation was turning critical. Not only were they his first prey, but they were also the easiest. On one hand, they functioned as intermediaries for the investment of Treasury Bonds (then called National Defence Bonds, which they also stockpiled in their portfolio of short term investments), on the other hand they served as conduits for the transfer of liquidity towards other currencies than the Franc. Even though there is no doubt about the banks' role as intermediaries, the left-centre government's painful lack of manoeuvring space could very well have been the cause of the difficulties within the Treasury. Or the blind mule-headedness of the radical party in what regarded the necessity of consolidating the debt by forging a pact with the world of retail investors. Be that as it may, it is not easy for historical study[70] to suggest opposing views to the ones held by the public – especially when the perception has crystallized into such expressions as the *Mur d'argent* (wall of money).[71]

> The problems of our treasury … have put us at the mercy of French banks in general and the Banque de France in particular. All too often, in order to meet a difficult maturity deadline, we have had to depend on their benevolence, a kindness which they are at full liberty to deny. A democratic government cannot accept such servitude. It cannot continue to function at the mercy and oppression of these money cartels, these hostile forces which are taking advantage of the difficulties faced by this government – difficulties raised by others. … They feel that they have at

> last found the ideal weapon against the majority of 11 May [1924], a weapon they will relinquish only when they have felled the government and the majority itself.[72]

It was, as Herriot had already hinted at the Conference of London regarding war reparations and the Dawes loan, 'a dictatorship of money'.[73]

> The bankers exerted enormous pressure on the Conference. As Léon Blum was to say at the Chamber [of deputies], they thought themselves to be kings. Unfortunately, we needed them for obtaining a loan which was fundamental to the Dawes plan and which had become very difficult because of the crash of the German currency. Just a few months earlier, they had rescued a tottering French Franc, something which they would not let us forget.[74]

It is precisely this feeling of dependence on the banking establishment's capacity to set up networks, financial syndicates and the power to mobilize transatlantic money, which frustrated the government and led to resentment. Politicians turned towards the public to stand witness to their dependence and supposed impotence in a pitiful bid to escape and hide their inability to do the job. Though not entirely true, a section of the public came to a more or less explicit conclusion that the fate of money and that of the Treasury depended greatly on the good will, or at the least, on the activation of certain relational networks controlled by bankers such as Lazard.[75] Be that as it may, the mid-1920s saw the public's opinion of banks reach an all new low point – France had become a 'Republic of bankers':[76]

> Can you imagine a Minister of the Republic begging of the Bank for some charity in order to meet a deadline? What a painful scene! [...] It is high time that we progressed from simply condemning this hegemony of high finance on our nation and democracy to decisive action. Something must be done if the Republic is to be liberated from the clutches of this financial oligarchy.[77]

This was the scenario of 'The Financier in the City'[78] but in a negative sense, because the Republic was thought to be dominated by bankers and their networks that had a strong influence on the money flows and the issuance of national defence bonds and their consolidation by repeated loans. The 1931 publication of Raffalovitch's book regarding the bribing of newspapers by the promoters of pre-war Russian loans[79] further inflamed the common opinion against such banking practices.

Bankers and the world of the 'Two Hundred Families'

The shocks sustained by the Republic between 1931 and 1934, a new wave of scandals and affairs (Oustric,[80] Stavisky, Marthe Hanau), which swept through the economic landscape and the fall of the second Leftist Cartel (1932–1934) in February 1934 brought bankers right back into the cross hairs of public debate. This time, they found themselves hemmed in by a burgeoning middle-class that was against reform and staunchly opposed to the Left party (and therefore democracy). This increasingly powerful faction was capable of influencing the parliament through pressure groups, which favoured protectionism and the Colonial Party, while being against any reform regarding the rights of companies or regulation of the financial sector. It was at such a time that there arose the myth of the Two Hundred Families.[81] These latter included several banking dynasties which either directly controlled some of the big banking houses (such as Mirabaud, Rothschild, Mallet, etc.) or indirectly influenced the policies of Banque de France or of some of the other corporate banks – most notably Banque de l'union Parisienne[82] through the mediation of Mirabaud, Neuflize or Mallet.

One of the key players in the spread of the anti-money cartel offensive was the *Crapouillot*, a magazine which scrupulously and deftly reported all the miss-steps (real or supposed) committed by the political and economic powers. Its special editions of March 1936, titled *Les Deux Cents Familles* (The Two Hundred Families) and of November of the same year, on *Les Financiers et la Démocratie* (Financiers and Democracy),[83] turned out to be profoundly influential. They, along with Augustin Hamon's articles (an expert analyst of capitalist ramifications) were instrumental in initiating a prolonged effort (which lasted till the 1960s) at restructuring the maze of networks – be they protestant, Jew, Anglo-Saxon or a combination of all three. These networks supposedly interlinked capital, spheres of influence, collusions and the control mechanisms, which allowed money-power to exert a covert dominance on the entire nation and even the world. Giraudoux echoed in his *La Folle de Chaillot*[84] that these 'Masters of France',[85] as Hamon called these two hundred families, and the financial oligarchy covertly controlled the destiny of France and Europe. The character of the big banker Emmanuel Moise in *Bella* (1926) was based on Horace Finaly, executive director of the commercial bank Paribas,[86] who, in 1923–1924, came to symbolize all such people of influence suspected of colluding with politicians and political parties.[87] At around the same time, several booklets spread sordid insinuations (sometimes confirmed) regarding bankers and their corruption. Maurice Privat accused the banks of stifling Marthe Hanau and *La Gazette du Franc* (launched in 1925)[88] and Finaly himself of instigating the 'big interests'[89] to take over control of the Paris stock market.

> 'Who are these big bankers?' he asked, 'Simply money merchants. They buy cheap and sell or loan at high rates. Our lending institutions have no interest in developing the nation's trade or industry. Their method is as simple as it is selfish: to loan their surplus cash at usurious rates.'[90]

The socialists too held a similarly dim view of the economy in the mid-1930s, and their electoral success of 1936 showed that it was a view shared by many of their countrymen. The general feeling was that 'to save the Republic from these money powers, something more needs to be done than simply removing the Banque de France from this great financial feudalism'.[91] Other extremist groups too joined the socialist outcry:

> Everywhere we see that it is the financial and banking oligarchy which has recruited, formed and commanded fascist organizations. What gives them so much power? We know at least some of these Napoleons of capitalism. Their power lies in the major interests that they command.[92]

Even in our times, the historian Annie Lacroix-Riz has renewed these aspersions and has succeeded in putting together an impressive resume from such titbits of text.[93] Pamphlets, the leftist press and recent reconstructions all depend on the addition of ad-hoc case studies. We, on the other hand, would like to express our doubts regarding the justification for this finger pointing. We feel that the examples given are not representative. The reports and records of the vast majority of bankers show little or no tendency towards any form of extremism.

French bank or Anglo-Saxon plutocracy?

Elsewhere, the devaluation of the Pound and the Dollar and the vagaries of the Franc between 1936 and 1940 did not fail to throw more mud on the banking establishment. Banks were branded as disease carriers – infected with a trans-border virus that caused instability, promoted the flow of dubious capital, and encouraged stock market speculations – especially by the Swiss stock exchanges or their London branches. The news of the investments made in Germany (1931–1933) shocked an already resentful public: while France was falling victim to deflation and was running desperately short of money, hundreds of millions of Francs had gone down the drain. Despite the frantic attempts at excuses and explanations (such as: *Ce qu'il faut connaître de la finance internationale*[94] [What one should know about international finance] in the journal *Banque*), there was no stopping the myth of an international 'cartel' which included all manner of reviled terms such as banker, Jew, protestant, Anglo-Saxon – the same characters which constituted this famous worldwide plutocracy and were the target of basic anti-bourgeois stances.

It was also thought that behind these secret powers that controlled the nation and Europe, a growing core of anti-communist and anti-democratic elements was preparing a pact with the Nazis. Historians still[95] debate the formation of a sinister network of financiers and industrialists – nicknamed the *Synarchic network*, several of whom occupied high offices in the Vichy regime[96] during 1941–1942 – and mysteries which shroud the *réseau de la Cagoule* (network of the Hood). To the myth of a Jewish Conspiracy[97] was added the opposing myth of an anti-communist and pro-Nazi conspiracy.

The return of the speculators

Unfortunately for the vast majority of bankers, a few 'bad apple' money manipulators again managed to evoke lasting resentment against the entire profession. A slew of crises, mini-crashes (in 1923 and again in 1925–1926) and the plague of bankruptcies, which ruined some five hundred banks in the years 1931 to 1935, highlighted the reckless gambles taken by these bankers. They mingled commercial banks, financing of their personal interests and collusions with equal-minded partners to ruin themselves and their dependents. The fall of Banque Nationale de Crédit's president André Vincent,[98] the collapse of the Oustric group and several other reputed regional banks (in regional cities like Boulogne-sur-Mer, Reims, Nantes) and the ruin of numerous financial intermediaries at the Paris Stock Exchange inflamed the smouldering animosity towards these unscrupulous bankers. The whole campaign surrounding the *Marthe Hanau affair* and the arguments proffered by the banks and their cartels against those who defended the interests of the small investors launched a thousand virulent pamphlets against these 'Goliaths' and felled the reputation of the entire banking establishment.

The revolution in cinema, which helped firms to promote their activities or favoured movies insisting on the 'black face' of capitalism[99] – was turned into yet another weapon in the 'war against the banking establishment'.[100] Films such as *La Vérité* (Henry Roussel, 1922), *La Justicière* (Gleize & De Marsan, 1925) and *Le Prince Jean* (René Mevil, 1927) helped in building and establishing banker notoriety:

> In these three silent movies, bankers are portrayed as rapacious ogres, completely unsuited for a job whose first requirements are virtue and integrity.... They are vengeful, they fail in their stock market ventures, seek to ruin their competition (often a love rival) and finally, having ruined themselves, have no other option left except suicide.[101]

In 1928, Marcel L'Herbier transposed Zola's famous character, the banker-financier-speculator Saccard, into the world of 1920s finance by turning *L'Argent* into one of the greatest movies of the silent era (*L'Argent*, 1928). In his play, *Ces Messieurs de la Santé* (with Raimu, 1933), Pierre Colombier had a crooked banker escape from jail, only to finally atone for his sins with a life of hard labour. In René Clair's *Le Dernier Milliardaire* (1935), a banker, after having made his fortune, returns to his country, takes over the finances and becomes a quasi-dictator before ruining himself and ending his last days in prison. In short, the big screen used the image of the banker to spread the lore of the corrupting power of money – although there is no way to know the actual impact such films had on the people. Even a musical, *Arsène Lupin banquier*, written by the cousin of novelist Marcel Leblanc – the author of the *Arsène Lupin* series – and staged in May 1930, showed a rogue banker simultaneously speculating on love, diamond trading, and banking.

Though these assertions lack the force of reasonable argumentation or any clear-cut evidence, there is no doubt that as far as public opinion was concerned, such feelings were clearly gaining momentum and ground. No wonder that political repercussions were not far behind: Let us not forget that it was the public outcry for 'not doing enough to safeguard savings' which had felled the André Tardieu government and brought to fruition the *Poincaré era* on 14 November 1930 – The *Poincaré era* had begun in July 1926 and was backed by a coalition of the Right and the Centre under Prime Minister Raymond Poincaré[102] in 1926–1929. Then, when the economy crashed, a parliamentary enquiry was commissioned in March 1930 – the third within a span of eighteen years: the first was in 1913 and the second in 1924 – to look into these 'affairs' (especially Oustric). As a result, Émile Moreau, the governor of Banque de France, was forced to step down on 23 March 1931. In a way it was inevitable that the man at the centre of the private banking sector be made a scapegoat while the other key players, who belonged to both the banking and political hierarchies, escaped being censored by the Audit Department as well as the High Court. The press too, though mollified by judicious sweeteners, did not fully accept the accusations hurled by *L'Humanité* against *le Panama de 1930* and *Les Oustricards* (12 March 1931 – with the sulphurous name of banker Oustric) or those by *L'Action française* or by some financial newsletters such as *Aux écoutes de la finance.*

War capitulation and subsequent resurgence of banking domination (from the 1940s to the 1980s)

The accumulated weight of the charges against banks resulted in serious efforts made at regulation and control. Nevertheless, the banking establishment remained, more or less openly, both fascinating as well as worrisome.

Bankers and the Vichy regime

When the first stage of the Second World War led to the defeat and occupation of France by the Nazis, as well as the relative influence of a few financiers, bankers and businessmen within the dictatorial Vichy regime, some segments of the 'informed' elite and middle classes perceived a kind of hidden influence of bankers on political life and on the decision-process of the State. First, a very elite group of bankers from small houses were part of a network, *la Synarchie,* which plotted against the Republic and pleaded for an authoritative regime, before being involved in the Vichy regime and even in the economic collaboration with Nazis – thus raising resentment against *le Complot de la Synarchie.* Beyond arguments about the reality of such a conspiracy,[103] more generally, a large majority of well-thinking bankers indeed became part of the regime of financial and economic collaboration with Nazi Europe,[104] socialized in German circles and organized a top-down reshaping of the French economy.[105] This fuelled resentment among *Résistants,* who thus prepared sanctions. Finally, these bankers succeeded in convincing the new authorities of the new regime in 1944–1946 that they had struggled to preserve a large part of French interests against Germans. They escaped thus a thorough business purge or the nationalization of investment banks[106] – before a few of them were recycled as heads of a few family banks (Worms) or at Banque de l'Indochine.

Reigning in the power of bankers

Such controversies among State, business and the *Résistants* elite, with presumed genuine effects on public opinion (through mass newspapers), explained the growing popularity of divesting banks of their supposed over-power. Even during the pre-war years, the Left had begun a campaign for the 'nationalization of credit'[107] in order to break 'the power of the banks' and their 'concentration of capital'. They argued that:

> These credit establishments had governments by the short hair, as evidenced by the billions which have been invested in treasury bonds. They could, at any given time, threaten entire governments with a demand for massive redemptions. … Profits, losses and even entire account statements are more or less entirely cooked.

Too many individuals held too many posts on the boards of various banks, showing that:

> The French banking establishment controls and regulates the nation's entire production. All businesses, industries, trade, etc. are no longer managed by technicians or specialists, but by the bankers. We now begin to understand the power of this 'Wall of Money'. All these bankers would naturally resist any attempt at a nationalization of credit. They know full well that such a nationalization [would] open the doors to a rapid collectivization of all the other means of production and trade.[108]

Other, anti-Semitic currents (whether from the Left or the Right) also targeted bankers in the early 1940s. They accused them of being defeatists and held them responsible for the country's weakness and for its eventual defeat in the war. The first days of the Vichy regime saw a resurgence in anti-banker sentiments and cries of a 'conspiracy of the Synarchy', with bankers accused of weakening the Republic and of having instigated the war for the benefit of the Anglo-Saxons: 'It is the Jews and bankers who have initiated this Anglo-American war'.[109] It was no coincidence that Jean Dréville filmed *Les Affaires sont les Affaires* (*Business is Business*) in 1942. Whatever might have been the ideological grounds for this anti-capitalism – whether mediated by the extreme Left or Right – we know[110] that the end result was that the Finance Ministry and some political circles came together in an effort to regulate the economy. Though the liberals had prevented 'the passing of any law regarding the regulation and control of banks' which had been proposed by the socialists in 1925, banking laws were finally passed in 1941 and 1945. After the war, the widespread suspicions regarding the attitude of bankers under the Occupation[111] ensured a heavy hand was kept on the banking establishment. The nationalization of the big clearing banks and of three dozen insurance companies helped to reduce their power and supposed hold on the City and other enterprises.

A return of the fearsome spectre?

Nevertheless, the fact that a large number of directors had been retained on the board of both the nationalized and private banks, and the rapid reinstatement of several compromised directors opened the doors to renewed fears and speculation regarding such a 'restored France'.[112] Even though two thirds of credit was controlled by the public and semi-public sectors,[113] the growing power of the market-based economy and business initiatives was beginning to re-knit those feared and influential banking networks, especially those of the business banks like Banque de l'union Parisienne[114] and Paribas which had, for some time, been augmented by Banque de l'Indochine – the new power on the Paris market.

Subsequently, an upswing in the economy and the significant improvement in the general standard of living led to a major redistribution of wealth and consequently, to a reduction in anti-capitalist sentiments. Still, the Far Right, led by Henri Coston,[115] continued to wage a pamphlet war against French banks and the supposed collusion between French bankers and 'Anglo-Saxon finance'. Maurice Druon, a Right-leaning novelist, re-evoked the myth of the all-powerful banks in his *Les grandes familles.* Though situated during the inter-war period, its widespread popularity and the fact that its first volume – *La fin des hommes* – received the *Prix Goncourt* in 1948 and that it was made into a movie[116] in 1958, show the mood of the 1950s. People were fascinated by tales in which the action took place in between the 'big shots' of the banking and stock market world, in between 'those whose power determines people's destiny'.[117]

Notwithstanding a resurgence of such fantasies and the fear of the power of banks, the banking establishment still retained an impressive facade all through the 1950s. Though the offices of Crédit Agricole, Crédit Mutuel, Banques Populaires were built modestly and the regional offices of even the big banking houses were relatively plain and simple, the majority of them still sought to impress the City, to convince their urban clients of their safety and solidity. It was, and had been for decades, 'a closed world, with majestic facades and imposing grills … an opaque universe' often with 'a magnificent décor'. 'The hall was monumental and radiated an undeniable aura of power'.[118] Many of the agencies too were literally 'money palaces'.[119] Even with the coming of the 'third banking revolution' and the introduction of the 'bank for the masses' and the 'outlets bank', the established banking houses retained their strong brand image as air-tight coffers which guaranteed the safety of all deposits, savings and investments against any contingency. Much of the artwork and symbolism that embellished the imposing facades of their corporate headquarters evoked this sentiment.

Conclusion

We have seen how the media have often negatively portrayed bankers and the banking establishment as ogres let loose in the land of the small (retail) investors; how popular novels and magazine articles have blamed the financial industry for the country's economic woes and of completely ignoring the good usage of money (investing in the nation's infrastructure, agricultural development, or even savings which could be passed on to one's children). It is true that, lacking any systematic method for determining the public's perception of banks, we cannot draw clear conclusions regarding the impact of the novels, scurrilous reports, pamphlets, film and magazine caricatures on the population at large. Still, our study has unearthed a strong current of distrust, if not a downright negative perception of the banking establishment. Much of it can be explained by the widespread disappointment and disillusionment experienced by investors and borrowers who felt let down by meagre returns or the high interest rates. The press was simply the mouthpiece for a section of the professional, financial and investment sectors that were constantly demanding other types of banks and other ways of banking. At the same time, we should note the widespread belief in a sort of conspiracy between money power, political power and the media – a collusion which gave bankers the power to block all initiatives to augment market transparency or the implementation of reforms which could lead to better control over the money market. It all comes down to the field of political morals.[120]

In France, banks had never been in fact considered as normal or usual intermediaries of the market economy, contrary to the British situation where the banking and insurance sectors were key parts of the London (and Scottish) economy and a means to leverage Britain's worldwide power, and later of its services renaissance from the 1960s. On the other hand it should be noted that some novels and social critics – like often satirical novelist Anthony Trollope[121] whose fiction mirrored the Victorian Establishment, especially *The Way We Live Now*, which featured immoral people greedy for money – also targeted financiers and bankers when they describe their practices. Our hypothesis is that in France the legacy of the French Revolution created the myth of an economic and social democracy that transcended the conquest of political democracy, whereas in Great Britain 'gentleman-like capitalism' based on the preserved social balance between the gentry, the bourgeoisie and 'self-made' elites was the presuming ideology. In the USA, the 'self-made man' myth obviously prevailed – even if the country had sustained a long tradition of populism against bankers – the debate going back to the very founding of the First Bank of the United States indeed and to its opponent, *bankophobian*

Andrew Jackson. This opposition later continued against 'robber barons',[122] the 'moneyed aristocracy' or 'big capital', which also inspired pamphlets at the time of 'the age of the moguls'[123] like John Pierpont Morgan or Jay Cooke, or more recently pamphlets about 'tycoons'. Novels and sociological comedies of manners[124] carried stiff portraits of financiers and investment bankers,[125] and big business stirred resentment among public opinion[126] and arguments among business historians of the 1940s–1970s.

Such apparent and widespread discrepancy between public opinions in the USA, Great Britain and France could be explained by a few key points. France benefitted from a revolution – *la Révolution* – that led to the fall of leftist *Montagnards* in 1794 and even of democratic structures in 1800. Disappointment prevailed among large segments of opinion – even fuelling anti-Napoleonic positions – which started imagining some 'conspiracy' in business circles to re-establish the power of money and of bankers – suspected to have financed the *coup d'État du 18 Brumaire* (1799), which was somewhat true. And later on, the *Monarchie de Juillet* regime was perceived as controlled by businessmen and bourgeois, before a repetition of events ripped the Second Republic from its democratic aspirations in favour of the *Parti de l'ordre* (rightists) and then of the Napoleonic dictatorship till 1870. Even after the stabilization of a democratic Republic since 1877, broad segments of opinion grumbled about compromises set up between the State and 'big business' for the sake of growth, the equipment of the country, and economic colonization. In a nutshell, such positions could more largely be explained by the commonplace admission that French people had been durably more concerned about the sharing of wealth than the production of it, about the distribution of the fruits of capitalism more than taking the forces behind a developing market economy into account. Another type of explanation is to be found in the mind-set delivered by a long-term rural and agrarian society. Whether landowners, easy peasants (400,000) or small peasants (more than 5 million), many people were reluctant to see a *grande bourgeoisie* gathering momentum from big business and money-makers – with then a few layers of bankers and financiers belonging to minorities and Diasporas.[127] French opinion balked repeatedly at the British model – perceived as a cause of cyclical crisis, proletariat, and rapid urbanization and uniformization – at the City and its cosmopolitan money makers. Then from 1900 into the 1920s public opinion indicated further distrust for the 'Anglo-Saxon model' and its City and Wall Street financiers. Such opinion held much more sway than ideas of 'progress' or 'modernity', which meant that both types of models seemed to be imported, and that they contradicted French 'values' and social or cultural order, with many remnants of such attitudes still pervasive in the 21st century.[128] This continued to raise the issue of the legitimacy of big business, of the *grande bourgeoisie, of big banks*… The trend was emphasized by the fact that generally French companies lacked the regional or community embeddedness that German firms (both the *Mittelstand* or *Konzerne*) enjoyed in their *Länder* through an intense practice of welfare capitalism and of social (or cultural) foundations (*Stiftungen*).

Conversely, the French model was for long resolutely middle class, *la France des petits*,[129] with an aspiration to egalitarianism, i.e. a reduced scale of richness. Furthermore, wealthy people were suspected of gaining their fortune either by corrupting political powers or by swindling their enterprise and their customers. This explains the ever-assumed strong values of local or regional banks when compared to the big Paris banks, or the promotion of Caisses d'épargne, Banques Populaires, and Crédit Agricole throughout the nineteenth and twentieth centuries. And each banking crisis and stock exchange crash reignited discontent and suspicion – up to the very recent 2007/2009 crisis, which struck Société Générale heavily after proprietary trading on its own permanent funds in January 2008, and which swept the banking sector after the sub-prime mortgage crisis, caused by attempts to achieve ever higher-returns on capital. But one could also add that the taste for secretive operations, numerous examples of collusion between the State – itself often condemned by public opinion[130] for its profligacy – and big banks, and deplorable (or even for long non-existent) public relations policies contributed to tarnishing the corporate image of banks on the Paris market and amongst public opinion. Bankers seemed not to have understood that serving the State, the economy or firms and fostering profits and employment ought not to have prevented them from developing convincing arguments in support of their own practices – notwithstanding the fact that for decades they had commissioned articles, albeit in subdued newspapers.

Notes

1 de Balzac, H. 1835. *La fille aux yeux d'or*. Paris: Furne.
2 And that was already the case in previous periods, as analysed by Jacques Le Goff for the Middle Ages for example.
3 See Garcia, S. 2007. L'Europe du savoir contre l'Europe des banques? La construction de l'espace européen de l'enseignement supérieur. *Actes de la recherche en sciences sociales*, no. 266–67, pp. 80–93.
4 See Bonin, H. 1989. *L'argent en France depuis 1880. Banquiers, financiers et épargnants dans la vie économique et politique*. Paris: Masson.
5 See Osborne, E. 2007. *The Rise of the Anti-Corporate Movement. Corporations and the People who Hate Them*. Oxford, Greenwood, 2007.
6 See Michie, R. 2007. *Guilty Money: The City of London in Victorian and Edwardian Culture, 1815–1914*. London: Pickering & Chatto.
7 See Bonin, H. 2007. De la littérature populiste au film populaire: l'angoisse de la conspiration et du sur-pouvoir capitalistes avant Fleming (1830–1930), in F. Hache-Bissette, F. Boully and V. Chenille, *James Bond (2)007. Anatomie d'un mythe populaire*. Paris: Belin, pp. 38–48.
8 Bonin, H. 2007. Des banquiers cosmopolites? Le monde de la banque et les diasporas (des années 1730 aux années 1930). *Diasporas. Histoire et sociétés*, no. 9, *Chercher fortune*, March 2007, pp. 11–31.
9 Or *Beautiful Era*: a golden age in European history, which began in the late 19th century and lasted until the First World War.
10 Also referred to in the case study of Lagneau-Ymonet, P. 2007. *Ferragus*, une 'sociologie-fiction' de la confiance. *Actes de la recherche en sciences sociales*, September 2007, no. 169, pp. 94–104 (Ferragus being a novel by Balzac).

11 Schama, S. 2009. Gilt complex. America's long love–hate relationship with money and banks. *The Financial Times*, 16 May 2009, Life & Arts supplement, pp. 1–2. See Phillips, K. 2008. *Bad Money. Reckless Finance, Failed Politics, and the Global Crisis of American Capitalism*. New York: Viking-Penguin Grou.

12 de Blic, D. 2009. Chaque crise financière rouvre le débat sur la moralisation de l'argent. *Le Monde*, 10 March 2009. See de Blic, D. and Lazarus, J. 2007. *Sociologie de l'argent*. Paris: La Découverte.

13 See Gueslin, A. 2007. *Mythologies de l'argent. Essai sur l'histoire des représentations de la richesse et de la pauvreté dans la France contemporaine (XIX*[e]*–XX*[e] *siècles)*. Paris: Économica.

14 A topic often raised by Professor Gerry Feldman, whom we met first during a conference in his research department at Berkeley University in 1998.

15 See Birnbaum, P. 1979. *Le peuple et les gros. Histoire d'un mythe*. Paris: Grasset.

16 See Barbier, F. 1991. *Finance et politique. La dynastie des Fould, XVIII*[e]*–XIX*[e] *siècles*. Paris: Armand Colin.

17 See Bergeron, L. 1991. *Les Rothschild et les autres… La gloire des banquiers*. Paris: Perrin; Gille, B. 1965/67. *Histoire de la maison Rothschild (1817–1870)*. Geneva: Droz.

18 d'Almeida, F. 1992. La pieuvre, essai d'interprétation. *Image fixe* Journal, no. 1, 1992.

19 These *Grievance Books* had been written by local communities against the Old Regime and the privileges of the First and Second Estates as part of the election to the Estates-General in the spring of 1789.

20 Mollier, J.-Y. 1991. *Le scandale de Panama*. Paris: Fayard; Bouvier, J. 1964. *Les deux scandales de Panama*. Paris: Julliard.

21 Romains, J. 1933. *Les hommes de bonne volonté*, Vol. 5. Paris: Flammarion.

22 See Bellet, R. 1983. La Bourse et la littérature dans la seconde moitié du xixe siècle, in *L'Argent, Romantisme*, 1983, no. 40, pp. 53–64.

23 See Éveno, P. 2003. *L'argent de la presse française de 1820 à nos jours*. Paris: Éditions du CTHS.

24 Daudet, A. 1878. *Le Nabab. Moeurs parisiennes*. 29 ed. Paris.

25 Claretie, J. 1882. *Le Million. Roman parisien*. Paris: E. Dentu.

26 Claretie, J. 1882. *Le Million. Roman parisien*. Paris: E. Dentu.

27 Duchêne, G. 1867. *Études sur la féodalité financière*. Paris: Librairie Centrale; Delaisi, F. 1910. *La démocratie et les financiers*. Paris: La guerre sociale.

28 *Le Journal de Rouen, passim*, 5 April 1909, 4 November 1910 and 29 May 1913.

29 Lysis, 1911. *Contre l'oligarchie financière en France*, new ed. Paris: Albin Michel.

30 Lysis, 1911. La domination générale de l'Oligarchie financière, sa mainmise sur la presse et le government, p. 157.

31 Lysis, 1911, p. 164. On the theme of the power of influence of businessmen, see Garrigues, J. 1997. *La République des hommes d'affaires (1870–1900)*. Paris: Aubier [even though I do not share some of the analyses about the submission of political apparels to the power of money business].

32 France, A. 1908. *L'Île aux pingouins*. Paris: Calmann-Lévy.

33 de Balzac, H. c.1823. *Les paysans*. Paris: Honoré de Eldarion 1er. See Barbéris, P. 1971. Balzac, *Une Mythologie réaliste*. Paris: Larousse.

34 de Vallée, O. 1858. *Les manieurs d'argent: Études historiques et morales, 1720–1857*. Paris: Michel Lévy frères.

35 See the tales by Guilleminault, G. 1976. *La France des gogos: trois siècles de scandales financiers*. Paris: Fayard.

36 Claretie, J. 1882. *Le million*. Paris: E. Dentu, p. 90, pp. 94–95.

37 Claretie (1882), pp. 94–95.

38 Dumas fils, A. 1857. *La question d'argent: comédie en cinq actes*. Paris: Calmann-Lévy; Dumas, A. and Henning, G.N. 1898. *La question d'argent; comédie en cinq*

actes. Boston, D.C.: Heath & Co., 1898; Dumas, A. and Wells, B.W. 1896. *La question d'argent: comédie en cinq actes:* Boston: Allyn & Bacon; Dumas, A. 1915. *The Money-Question, Comedy in Five Acts.* Boston: R.G. Badger.

39 Ponsard, F. 1854. *L'honneur et l'argent: comédie en cinq actes et en vers.* Paris: Michel Lévy frères. Ponsard, F. 1856. *La Bourse, comédie en cinq actes, en vers.* Paris: Michel Lévy frères; Maret-Leriche, J. 1856. *Examen critique de la Bourse: Comédie en cinq actes en vers de François Ponsard.* Paris: Taride; Poitevin, P. 1856. *Êpitre à M. François Ponsard à l'occasion de L'examen critique de la Bourse [Jules Maret-Leriche].* Paris: [Dr.] Thunot; Guedalla, H. 1883. *Memorandums Relating to the Egyptian Debt… To Which Are Added Various Other Topics, Including Some Extracts from Ponsard's 'La Bourse' and Jenkin's 'A Paladin of Finance'.* London; Guedalla, H. and Ponsard, F. 1873. *Syndicates and Their Baneful Influence on Foreign Loans and Public Companies … To Which Is Added Some Extracts from Ponsard's Comedy of 'La Bourse'*, London; Laya, L. 1864. *Le duc Job: comédie en quatre actes et en prose*, Paris: Michel Lévy.

40 Mirbeau, O. 1904. *Les affaires sont les affaires.* Paris: Libraire Charpentier et Fasquelle. This play from 1904 describes a rogue financier, Isidore Lechat.

41 Soubeyran had invested large amounts of capital in Egypt in risky business ventures, using the cash from French bank Crédit foncier without informing its board.

42 See Gille, B. 1968. Un épisode de l'histoire des métaux: le krach des cuivres. *Revue d'histoire de la sidérurgie*, volume 9, no. 1.

43 Feydeau, E. 1868. *Un coup de Bourse; étude dramatique en cinq actes.* Paris: Michel Lévy frères.

44 Toussenel, A. 1847. *Les juifs, rois de l'épargne. Histoire de la féodalité financière.* Paris: Gabirel de Gonet. See Crossley, C. 2004. Anglophobia and Anti-semitism: The Case of Alphonse Toussenel (1803–1885). *Modern & Contemporary France*, 2004, 12–14, pp. 459–472.

45 See Birnbaum, P. 1988. *Un mythe politique: la ' République juive'.* Paris: Fayard.

46 See de Navery, R. 1883. *Les drames de l'argent.* Paris: Blériot & Gautier, pp. 196, 241.

47 Navery (1883), p. 164.

48 Navery (1883), p. 164.

49 Navery (1883), p. 195.

50 See Bouvier, J. 1960. *Le krach de l'Union générale (1878–1885).* Paris: Presses universitaires de France.

51 Navery (1883), p. 241.

52 Daudet, A. 1878. *Le Nabab. Moeurs parisiennes.* 29 ed. Paris: G. Charpentier; A little later, in 1885, was published Drumont, E. 1885. *La France juive.* Paris: Flammarion. For a broader perception see Sternhell, Z. 1978. *La droite révolutionnaire, 1855–1914. Les origines françaises du fascism.* Paris: Seuil.

53 See Éveno, P. 2002. L'image du Crédit Lyonnais à travers la presse française, in B. Desjardins, M. Lescure, R. Nougaret, A. Plessis and A. Straus. 2002. *Le Crédit Lyonnais, 1863–1986. Études historiques.* Geneva: Droz, pp. 833–850.

54 See Stanziani, A. 2007. Spéculation, in A. Stanziani, ed. *Dictionnaire historique de l'économie-droit, XVIIIe–XXe siècles.* Paris: LGDJ.

55 See Reffait, C. 2007. *La Bourse dans le roman du second XIXe siècle. Discours romanesque et imaginaire social de la spéculation.* Paris: Honoré Champion.

56 See the analysis about Crédit Lyonnais in Éveno (2002).

57 Lysis (1911).

58 Lysis (1911), p. 311.

59 Éveno (2002), p. 835. The figures of 150,000 unemployed was perhaps linked to the slight downturn caused by a little European recession in 1901.

60 Sayous, A.-E. 1901. *Les banques de dépôt, les banques de crédit et les sociétés financières.* Paris: Sirey.

61 Domergue, J. 1909. Pour faire revivre en France la banque d'affaires. *La Réforme économique*, 28 May 1909, p. 644.
62 See Favre, J.-E. 1917. *Le capital français au service de l'Étranger. Un cas: La Banque de Paris et des Pays-Bas et son œuvre anti-nationale.* Paris: Bibliothèque financière; Favre, J.-E. 1918. *Les Métèques à la Bourse de Paris: À l'assaut de la France. À propos du naturalisé austro-boche Oskar Lustgarten, nommé, en pleine guerre, directeur de la Banque de l'union parisienne.* Paris: Bibliothèque financière.
63 See Albert, E. 1997. *Les Banques populaires en France (1917–1973)*. Paris: Économica.
64 For example the caricatures by Russian Victor Deni (1893–1941), like *Kapital* (1924), where three French, US and British capitalists are prospering on a heap of starving people, with the legend: 'World Unite, 1914–1920'.
65 Bonin, H. 2000. *Les banques françaises de l'entre-deux-guerres.* Paris: Plage, volume 1, chapter 1.
66 Hauser, H. 1916. *Les méthodes allemandes d'expansion économique.* 3rd ed. Paris: Armand Colin.
67 Hauser (1916), pp. 61–105.
68 Dernis, G. 1927. *La renaissance du crédit allemand.* Paris: Presses universitaires de France.
69 Boret, V. 1916. *La nouvelle revue*, Paris, p. 211. Concerning issues of economic war, see Soutou, G.-H. 1989. *L'or et le sang. Les buts économiques de la Première Guerre mondiale.* Paris: Fayard.
70 Blancheton, N.B. 2001. *Le Pape et l'Empereur. La Banque de France, la direction du Trésor et la politique monétaire de la France (1914–1928)*. Paris: Albin Michel; Jeanneney, J.-N. 1981. *La faillite du Cartel, 1924–1926*. Paris: Seuil-Points.
71 See Néré, J. 1985. *Le problème du Mur d'argent. Les crises du franc, 1924–1926.* Paris: La pensée universelle.
72 Letter from Léon Blum to Édouard Herriot, 25 March 1925, in É. Herriot 1952. *Jadis*, volume 2. *D'une guerre à l'autre, 1914–1936*. Paris: Flammarion, p. 216.
73 'Politique intérieure. La dictature de l'argent', in Herriot (1952), p. 199.
74 Herriot (1952), p. 155.
75 See Philippe, R. 1931. *Le drame financier de 1924–1928*. Paris: Gallimard-NRF; Sabouret, A. 1987. *MM. Lazard frères et Cie. Une saga de la fortune.* Paris: Olivier Orban.
76 Chastanet, J.-L. [a socialist Parliament deputy from Isère]. 1925. *La République des banquiers.* Paris: Éditions Georges-Anquetil.
77 Chastanet (1925), pp. 11–12.
78 Homberg, O. 1926. *Le financier dans la cité:* Paris: Grasset.
79 Raffalovitch, A. 1931. *L'abominable vénalité de la presse.* Paris: Librairie du travail, 1931.
80 See Privat, M. 1932. *Oustric & Cie.* Paris: series *Documents secrets*; Hubert Bonin, B. 1996. Oustric, un financier prédateur? (1914–1930). *Revue historique*, October 1996, 295/2, pp. 429–448.
81 Sédillot, R. 1988. *Les Deux Cents Familles.* Paris: Perrin, 1988.
82 See Bonin, H. 2011. *La Banque de l'union parisienne (1874/1904–1974). De l'Europe aux outre-mers.* Paris: Publications de la SFHOM.
83 It is in fact the re-edition of Delaisi (1910).
84 See Bussière, E. 1996. *Horace Finaly, banquier, 1871–1945*. Paris: Fayard.
85 Hamon, A. 1936. *Les Maîtres de la France. La féodalité financière dans les banques.* Paris: Éditions sociales internationale.
86 See Bussière, E. 1992. *Paribas, l'Europe et le monde, 1872–1992*. Anvers: Fonds Mercator.
87 See several chapters in Jeanneney, J.-N. 1984. *L'Argent caché. Milieux d'affaires et pouvoirs politiques dans la France du xx*^{e} *siècle*, 2nd ed. Paris: Seuil.

88 Desanti, D. 1968. *La banquière des Années folles: Marthe Hanau*. Paris: Fayard.
89 Privat, M. 1929. *Le scandale de la Gazette*. Paris: March; Maurice Privat, M. 1930. *Haute finance et basse justice*. Paris: Alexis Redier.
90 Privat (1930), p. 101.
91 Paul Faure, general secretary of socialist party SFIO, *Le Populaire*, 2 July 1935, quoted by Pierre Birnbaum (1988), p. 47.
92 Léon Blum, *Le Populaire,* 4 August 1935; Birnbaum (1988), p. 47.
93 Lacroix-Riz, A. 2006. *Le choix de la défaite. Les élites françaises dans les années 1930*. Paris: Armand Colin. – and this book used an impressive amount of archives from French police and from German series.
94 Compeyrot, J. 1929. *Ce qu'il faut connaître de la finance internationale*. Paris: Boivin.
95 See Lacroix-Riz (2006). The book broadened the spectrum of an antidemocratic conspiracy theory by a 'synarchic' clan to almost the whole business community and therefore became an opposition statement to the studies of the entire French community of historians.
96 See Lacroix-Riz, A. 1999. *Industriels et banquiers sous l'Occupation. La Collaboration économique avec le Reich et Vichy*, 2nd ed. Paris: Armand Colin. Several analyses of this work are questionable despite their tonic approach and the mobilisation of archives' funds.
97 Coston, H. 1942. *La finance juive et les trusts*. Paris: Éditions Jean-Renard.
98 Bonin, H. 2002. *La Banque nationale de crédit. Histoire de la quatrième banque de dépôts française en 1913–1932*. Paris: Plage.
99 Pessis, G. 1997. *Entreprise et cinéma. Cent ans d'images*. Paris: Ministère de l'Emploi & de la Solidarité, La Documentation française.
100 Pessis (1997).
101 Dou, M. 1986. Sur l'écran: la banque, in D. Nibourel, ed. *Banque et société humaine*. Paris: APB, pp. 62–67.
102 Beforehand Poincaré had been many times a minister since the 1890s, a Prime Minister in 1912–1913 and 1922–1924 and even the President of the Republic in 1913–1920. He was a kind of 'father of the nation' who inspired 'trust', although he managed a parliamentary majority of the centre-right.
103 See Dard, O. 1998. *La Synarchie ou le mythe du complot permanent*. Paris: Perrin. He is seriously contesting A. Lacroix-Riz's analysis.
104 Lacroix-Riz (1999). Lacroix-Riz, A. 1986. Les grandes banques françaises de la Collaboration à l'épuration, 1940–1950. I. La collaboration bancaire, *Revue d'histoire de la Seconde Guerre mondiale*, no. 141, pp. 3–44.
105 de Rochebrune, R. and Hazéra, J.-C. 1995. Quand les banquiers font la loi. Henri Ardant, le père du corporatisme bancaire, in *Les patrons sous l'Occupation*. Paris: Odile Jacob, pp. 693–722; Andrieu, C. 1990. *La banque sous l'Occupation. Paradoxes de l'histoire d'une profession, 1936–1946*. Paris: Presses de la Fondation nationale des sciences politiques.
106 Bonin, H. 2014. French investment banks' renewal after WWII (1945–1960): Differenciation and pathbreaking, in H. Bonin and C. Brambilla, eds. *Investment Banking History. National and Comparative Issues (19th-21st Centuries)*, series Euroclio. Studies and Documents. Brussels: Peter Lang, pp. 201–266.
107 Philip, A. and Monceau, A. 1935. *La toute-puissance bancaire et la nationalisation du crédit*. Paris: Librairie populaire.
108 Philip and Monceau (1935).
109 Title of an article in *La France au travail*, 18 May 1941.
110 Notably thanks to Andrieu (1990).
111 de Menthon, P.-H. 1994. Les banquiers français sous l'Occupation. *Le Nouvel Économiste*, no. 937, 18 March 1994, pp. 44–48; Annie Lacroix-Riz, A. 1986. Les grandes banques françaises, de la Collaboration à l'épuration, 1940–1950.

La Collaboration bancaire. *Revue d'histoire de la deuxième guerre mondiale*, no. 141, January 1986, pp. 3–44.

112 Bouvier, J. and Bloch-Lainé, F. 1986. *La France restaurée, 1944–1954*. Paris: Fayard.

113 Quennouëlle-Corre, L. 2000. *La direction du Trésor, 1947–1967. L'État-banquier et la croissance.* Paris: Publications du Comité pour l'histoire économique et financière de la France.

114 Bonin (2011).

115 For example: Coston, H. 1955. *Les financiers qui mènent le monde.* Paris: La librairie française.

116 de la Patellière, D. 1958. *Les grandes familles* (with the actors Jean Gabin and Jean Dessailly).

117 From the blurb which appeared on the cover of the 1989 pocket edition.

118 Fischer, G.-N. 1986. L'espace en jeu: une nouvelle lecture de la banque, in Danièle Nibourel, ed. *Banque et société humaine.* Paris: Association française des banques, pp. 3–23.

119 See Bonin, H. 1993. La révolution des banques françaises (1850–1930). In: J.-F. Pinchon, ed. *Les palais d'argent. L'architecture bancaire en France de 1850 à 1930.* Paris: Éditions de la Réunion des musées nationaux, pp. 3–41.

120 See Bonin, H. 1991. Morale et entreprise dans l'histoire. *Le Débat*, no. 67, November–December 1991, Gallimard, pp. 167–185.

121 See Mullen, R. 1992. *Anthony Trollope: A Victorian in His World.* Savannah: FC Bell. And especially Trollope, A. 1875. *The Way We Live Now.* London: Chapman and Hall.

122 Debouzy, M. 1972. *Le capitalisme 'sauvage' aux États-Unis, 1860–1900*. Paris: Seuil. She synthetized and discussed the harsh arguments among American historians, for instance: Hacker, L. 1954. The anti-capitalist bias of Americans historians, in F.A. Hayek, ed. *Capitalism and its Historians.* London: Routledge & Kegan Paul; Bridges, H. 1958. The Robber Baron concept in American history. *Business History Review*, 30, Spring 1958, pp. 1–13; Cole, A.H. 1959. *Business Enterprise in its Social Setting.* Harvard: Cambridge University Press; Solganick, A. 1965. The Robber Baron concept and its revisionists. *Science and Society*, 29, Summer 1965, pp. 257–269; Jones, Peter d', A. 1968. ed. *The Robber Barons Revisited.* Boston: Heath.

123 Holbrook, S. 1954. *The Age of the Moguls.* London: Gollancz; Moody, J. 1919. *The Masters of Capital.* New Haven: Yale.

124 Like the recently successful books: Phillips, K.P. 2008. *Bad Money: Reckless Finance, Failed Politics, and the Global Crisis of American Capitalism.* New York: Viking; Phillips, K.P. 2004. *American Dynasty: Aristocracy, Fortune, and the Politics of Deceit in the House of Bush.* New York: Viki; Phillips, K.P. 2002. *Wealth and Democracy: A Political History of the American Rich.* New York: Broadway Books; Phillips, K.P. 1994. *Arrogant Capital: Washington, Wall Street, and the Frustration of American Politics.* Boston: Little, Brown & Co.

125 See Augar, P. 2005. *The Greed Merchants. How the Investment Banks Played the Free Market Game.* New York: Portfolio; Augar, P. 2000. *The Death of Gentlemanly Capitalism: The Rise and Fall of London's Investment Banks.* London: Penguin. Canada is also involved: Langlois, R. 1998. *Requins: l'insoutenable voracité des banquiers,* series *Partis pris actuels.* Montréal: VLB.

126 Galambos, L. and Barrows Spence, B. 1975. *The Public Image of Big Business in America, 1880–1940. A Quantitative Study in Social Change.* Baltimore: John Hopkins University; Geisst, C.R. 2000. *Monopolies in America: Empire Builders and Their Enemies, from Jay Gould to Bill Gates.* Oxford: Oxford University Press.

127 Bonin, H. 2007. Des banquiers cosmopolites? Le monde de la banque et les diasporas (des années 1730 aux années 1930). *Diasporas. Histoire et sociétés*, no. 9, *Chercher fortune*, March 2007, pp. 11–31.

128 Bonin, H. 2006. L'histoire comme outil de légitimation politique de l'entreprise durant la Grande Crise de la fin du xxe siècle (1974–1993), in M. Crivello, P. Garcia & N. Offenstadt, eds. *Concurrence des passés. Usages politiques du passé dans la France contemporaine*, Aix-en-Provence: Publications de l'Université de Provence, pp. 157–168.

129 Berstein, S. and Rudelle, O. eds. 1992. *Le modèle républicain.* Paris: Presses universitaires de France.

130 See Delporte, C. 1999. Du bon et du mauvais usage de l'argent des Français. Réflexions sur le ministre des Finances, le fisc et la politique financière dans la caricature de l'entre-deux-guerres. *Cahiers d'histoire,* 75, 1999, pp. 93–110.

6 'Many a slip between cup and lip'

Initiating Austrian stabilisation, 1922–1923[1]

P. L. Cottrell

One aspect of the *Great Disorder* in central and eastern Europe – Austrian inflation and hyperinflation – finally began to be addressed in September 1922. The wrangles between members of the Entente and their associates over how Austrian reconstruction that had begun in January 1921 should be undertaken, were brought almost to an end with the Geneva Protocols. These were signed at the League of Nation's Assembly on 4 October.

The protocols had been formulated by the League's Austrian sub-committee. The first addressed the question of Austrian sovereignty and independence. It restated the Treaty of St Germain's article 88 – the ban on the *Anschluss* – and required states assisting Austrian reconstruction not to seek any particular economic and financial advantage. The second specified aspects of the 650 million gold crowns stabilisation loan, including its guarantee, the composition of the committee of guarantors, and established the post of Commissioner General. Appointed by the League, he was to be responsible for executing the stabilisation plan negotiated by the League's Financial Committee. He was to accomplish his role through being resident in Vienna to oversee stabilisation and regulate the disbursement of the loan's proceeds. His powers were augmented by Protocol Three. This laid down the Austrian government's tasks, namely, to take all necessary powers to ensure that stabilisation would be accomplished within two years. To prevent stabilisation becoming a political football in the Austrian parliament, it was to be undertaken through ordinances and, furthermore, the Austrian government was to pass a constitutional law setting aside parliament's fiscal powers.[2]

The protocols were the necessary political compact for allowing Austrian stabilisation to proceed and provided an outline of the mechanism for bringing it about, but no more. It was to take a further 15 months before the Austrian government was able to draw upon the stabilisation loan's proceeds. Such a long delay, which threatened stabilisation, was due to a wide range of problems and issues that arose from within days of the League plan being put into effect. This essay reviews and analyses the various 'slips' on the path to Austrian stabilisation that continued to occur until 31 December 1923.

As the protocols' framers had anticipated, there was continuing, strong opposition from two Austrian political parties – the Social Democrats and the

Pan-Germans – to the protocols' stipulations and the stabilisation programme. Their hostility went with disputes between League delegates and the Austrian government over the latter's conception of the necessary domestic economic and financial measures for achieving stabilisation. The threats to stabilisation caused by Austrian politics were compounded by continuing Italian designs to bring the Federal Republic within Rome's sphere of influence. Flash points of dispute were also sparked by differences over who should fill the key posts: The Commissioner General, the president of the Austrian National Bank and the foreign adviser to the National Bank. It was to take until the close of 1922 for an agreed stabilisation plan, and its executive personnel, to be in place.

The slow pace of the negotiations in Vienna over how stabilisation should be accomplished, and who should steer it, increased Western bankers' already great reluctance to provide the Austrian government with the external short- and long-term finance required to bring about reconstruction. Austria's prostrate state since the Armistice of 1918 made it an extremely poor risk in the view of nearly every potential investor. Furthermore, this negative attitude was increased day by day as the Ruhr crisis developed. The disinclination to invest in Austrian securities was also made greater by problems arising from how the League stabilisation loan's security – the Geneva bond – had been drafted. Consequently, an outline basis for raising external finance was not to be established until 15 January, and the possibility of the critical American contribution not until three months later. Even so, the last portion of the stabilisation loan – the Spanish tranche – was not placed until December 1923.

The following sections consider chronologically, rather than thematically, how these issues arose and how attempts were made to resolve them. This approach has been taken to emphasise both how the execution of stabilisation was continually threatened for some 15 months and how the issues that endangered it were intermeshed. It also allows a view of *money doctors* at work – the various roles of treasury officials, western bankers and central bankers and, with regard to the latter, above all Montagu Norman, Governor of the Bank of England, in bringing about Austrian stabilisation.

Political agreement in Geneva over Austria had not taken into account bankers' attitudes to the stabilisation loan. It had aroused some interest amongst financiers from late August 1922 when the Federal Republic's reconstruction was put on the League's agenda once more. J.P. Morgan & Co. had been closely involved in previous abortive League initiatives for Austria and, on 23 September, responded to press reporting from Geneva by asking its London partner house – Morgan Grenfell – to clarify the situation.[3] However, Edward C. Grenfell had to point out to his New York associates that the Entente was apparently not yet prepared to guarantee an Austrian loan. Therefore he maintained that its issue had passed out of the 'sphere of loans which could be handled by bankers on their own merits'.[4] Nonetheless, the New York Morgan partners were keen on not letting a chance slip and so asked Morgan Grenfell to remain in close contact with the Anglo-Austrian

Bank and Baron Georg Frankenstein, the Austrian minster in London. The Morgans were not alone amongst finance houses expressing interest as both Kuhn, Loeb & Co. and Hallgartens contacted Sir William Goode, who relayed their approaches to the Austrian government.[5]

From the outset, the New York Morgan partners were concerned about the loan's security, and went as far as suggesting:

> An arrangement whereby the obligation could be jointly and severally guaranteed by the nations insofar as the holder of the bond was concerned, although a separate agreement would provide that the guaranty was several as between nations – a plan in effect similar to that of the Anglo-French loan.

As they recognised, this involved a heavy contingent burden for Britain, but they thought that such security would provide a basis for a £15m loan, of which 20 to 25 per cent could be placed in the United States.[6] Their assessment was also an early indication that America would not provide the lion's share of the required financial resources. However, their suggested security formula was not accepted by Grenfell in London. He felt that the Anglo-French loan arrangements had been hardly satisfactory, while hoping that the League discussions would not result in the Austrian loan having a joint and several guarantee by which Britain would in effect shoulder the whole contingent liability.[7]

Jay, of the Paris Morgan house – Morgan, Harjes – was in Geneva and obtained an outline of the loan arrangements from Jean Monnet, the League's secretary, and Basil Blackett of the British Treasury and a member of the League's Financial Committee. By 9 October, Grenfell in London was scathing of the details becoming available since they appeared to have been framed 'by people with no practical knowledge of finance'.[8] His concern was to prove well founded as the loan's security – the *Geneva bond* – subsequently created difficulties on a number of markets including London and New York. He also thought that the proposed issue of Austrian Treasury bills to provide bridging finance would not interest his New York partners and was better left to Kuhn, Loeb & Co. Grenfell summarised his views to Thomas Lamont of Morgans in New York as 'to do nothing except to advise you that we are keeping our eyes on this somewhat undesirable business'.[9]

The London financial community's views of the affair gradually coalesced. Governor Montagu Norman of the Bank of England saw Pierre Bark of the Anglo-Austrian Bank on 6 October. A week later, the Governor had a long discussion with Sir Arthur Salter, head of the League's Finance and Economic Section, which concentrated on the question of filling the post of the League Commissioner General.[10] After these soundings, Norman drew up a memorandum on 13 October which he agreed with Charles Whigham of Morgan Grenfell. It drew the gloomy conclusion that no arrangements could be made for the Austrian loan and, on 17 October, the Governor explained the situation to Arthur Balfour, who had taken the political initiative that had led to the Geneva Protocols.

What particularly concerned both Norman and Otto Niemeyer of the British Treasury was who might be the Commissioner General. The Dutch banker, ter Meulen, favoured Zimmerman, Rotterdam's Burgomaster, and Norman approached Salter to ensure that Zimmerman would be the first to be considered for the post. A Dutch appointment fitted the Governor's long-standing view that Austria required 'neutral' external control, and a complete Dutch 'neutral' executive team for overseeing Austrian stabilisation then appeared likely. Norman had learnt from ter Meulen that Vissering, Governor of the Netherlands Bank, was willing in principle to be the president of the new Austrian National Bank for a year.[11]

As anticipated, there was vehement opposition within Austria to the Geneva Protocols. The Social Democrats objected to the government having full powers to force through the stabilisation programme, whereas the small Pan-German party opposed the reiteration of the clause of the *St Germain Treaty* that blocked the *Anschluss.*[12] Denial of the *Anschluss* was a blow to the aspirations of both the Social Democrats and the Pan-Germans, yet the latter were now tied to Chancellor Seipel. All that the Social Democrats could offer as an alternative to the League plan was domestic self-help but with its fiscal incidence biased to fall upon finance and capital. Indeed, the real concern within Austrian politics was what group, or groups, would bear the costs of stabilisation. The Social Democrats recognised that they could only protect their constituency by having a role in shaping the reconstruction programme. This was finally secured through membership of the Extraordinary Cabinet Council, which became responsible for implementing the stabilisation programme.

Parliamentary wrangling became a threatening problem as, although the crown was appreciating somewhat the exchanges, the state's budget deficit was expanding remorselessly. Seipel tried to crystallise the situation through starkly presenting the alternatives – 'Foreign Aid or Catastrophe' – with the latter outcome being increasingly pointed up by the rapidly deteriorating German situation.[13] The political furore over implementing stabilisation was to continue until November and led, ultimately, to what were in practice ultimatums from League officials and delegates.

The heated political debate resulted in Akers-Douglas, the British Minister in Vienna, urging the rapid implementation of external control as well as the provision of the external financial assistance coupled to it. Indeed, the League's Austrian sub-committee had decided that members of the League's Financial Committee should go as soon as possible to Vienna, and they had arrived by 20 October. Furthermore, Niemeyer, one of the League's delegates who went to Vienna, and Avenol, his French counterpart, agreed with Akers-Douglas. With it being planned that the League's mission would leave the Austrian capital by 4 November, its British and French members sought the rapid installation of the Commissioner General in order to place pressure on the Austrian government. Niemeyer and Avenol also prioritised one element of the stabilisation programme – cutting government expenditure – while looking to the Austrian government quickly pledging the customs revenues and the tobacco monopoly as the security for interim externally provided credit.[14] These would finance the state until the proceeds of the long-term loan were available.

As required by the Geneva Protocols, the Seipel government presented its financial reform plan to the League delegates. It was self-help, a continuation of Seipel's policy since the spring, to bring about a prospective budget deficit of 322 million gold crowns for 1923 but a balanced budget in 1924. This was to be accomplished through applying a range of measures, including the overhaul of the administrations of the tobacco and salt monopolies, and increased railway and postal tariffs. Furthermore, the payrolls of the state enterprises and the civil service were to be markedly reduced. The reduction of state expenditure along with related efficiency gains were to be coupled to raising greater revenues. These were to be obtained by putting the customs and alcohol taxes on a gold basis, and widening the tax base through new imposts on capital, turnover and land.[15] However, the plan was tentative, the subject for negotiation with the League representatives. In the meantime, the Austrian government paid the proceeds of the customs duties and the tobacco monopoly into special accounts, operated in conjunction with the League's delegates – a holding operation until the Commissioner General arrived.

Slater's visit to Vienna in early November was an attempt to head off an impasse developing in the League plan for Austria. He was disgruntled by the continuing lack of progress in achieving internal reform, caused by continuing political opposition, while being aware of the London market's negative attitude towards the stabilisation loan. His visit resulted in the League's Financial Committee making forceful representations to the Austrian government that required state expenditure to be reduced to 350 million gold crowns over the series of projected stabilisation budgets. The committee had regarded the initial Austrian proposal of a budget totalling 500 million gold crowns in January 1925 as both too high and too delayed. Their severe criticism also arose from the view that Austrian estimates for the projected rise in state revenues were either over optimistic, or, if realisable, involved too great a 'tax take'. Niemeyer was particularly anxious about this. He considered that the Financial Committee's proposals could lead to Austrians being the lowest taxed Europeans, which 'ought to make [Austria] a very attractive area for the investment of foreign capital'. He also thought, in turn, that this might constitute a reason for Britain not being 'unduly ready to make concessions … as regards the settlement of pre-war debts'.

Niemeyer's overall verdict was that the Seipel plan was not a viable basis for taxation policy, while unduly favouring agriculture – one of the supporting planks of the Chancellor's Christian Social party. Furthermore, he detected a lost opportunity, considering that it would be possible to develop a fund to finance unemployment relief. The plan proposed to reduce the civil service and other sections of the state's payroll by 100,000, taking the 'Austrian Administration from the Imperial to the Provincial Scale'. However,

Niemeyer thought this was its Achilles heel since 'Government employees … are the first and most obvious sufferers'.[16] Nonetheless, League pressure brought about cooperation between the Social Democrats and the Seipel cabinet over economic and financial reform.

Mounting concerns over Austrian progress towards stabilisation and, consequently, over issuing the required long-term loan may have been further heightened by the difficulties encountered in passing the reconstruction legislation through parliament.[17] This should not have been a surprise as the Social Democrats had indicated from when the Seipel plan had been formulated that they would oppose the required ordinary legislation, although not the constitutional law. Yet failure to ratify the Geneva Protocols and the reconstruction legislation in the *Nationalrat* on 30 November was unexpected by the British Legation in Vienna.[18] However, this proved to be but a temporary hiccough as the laws were then passed within a matter of days, after being referred back.

Equally disconcerting was the long delay in appointing the Commissioner General. His absence was felt in all the discussions between League representatives and the Austrian government over the state budget, the establishment of a central bank, and the state's interim financing. A year later, Salter described this dialogue during the closing months of 1922 as 'the great game of bluff'.[19] Niemeyer shared Salter's view, privately indicating to London during mid-November '"about a hundred to one chance" that Austria would pull through'.[20] Zimmerman only arrived in Vienna on 15 December, shortly after the passage of the Austrian stabilisation legislation.

Tariff, fiscal and administrative reforms were linked to establishing a central bank. Despite the *Notenbank* initiative of the spring, little progress had been made by late October with this important component of stabilisation beyond the projected institution acquiring the Austro-Hungarian Bank's building and having a proposed capital of 25 million gold crowns. It was to be largely autonomous. The government only had the right to nominate its president, while the state commissioners' powers were restricted to ensuring that its directors did not transgress its statutes. The bank was to have a fiduciary note issue of 155 million gold crowns, with any greater note circulation having an initial cover of 20 per cent. Cover, comprising foreign exchange and gold, was thereafter to rise to 24 per cent within five years and 28 per cent in ten, ultimately reaching its pre-war level of 33 per cent. A portion of the bank's capital – 10 million gold crowns – was earmarked for subscription by the owners of requisitioned foreign securities, which would allow the government to realise these assets. The balance of 15 million gold crowns was for public subscription, albeit with preference given to those who took up Austrian Treasury bills. However, it was evident that the Viennese banks were more than anxious to become shareholders and, therefore, would not require any special privileges or inducements.

The League representatives privately suggested to Seipel that the central bank's first president should not be an Austrian. This was also the view of the two Austrian banks that had recently become foreign companies.[21] Behind the scenes pressure had been exerted by the management of the 'Anglicised' Anglo-Austrian Bank and, even more opaquely, by their counterparts at the French Länderbank, to secure the appointment of a neutral president. Niemeyer thought, rightly, that the Austrian government would object, while 'a governor who is likely to be *ab initio* unacceptable to his board provides no real security'.[22]

Increasing politicking developed over the central bank's presidency. Seipel favoured an Austrian but Rome made it officially known that, if an Austrian were not appointed, Mussolini would insist on an Italian under the threat of non-ratification of the Geneva Protocols.[23] This was countered in Vienna by a French protest against an Italian appointment. League officials decided that they would not press for a foreign appointment, indeed they 'deposited [a] motion against foreigner'. However, Salter personally acknowledged the 'bad effect which would be produced in the City [of London] by [the] appointment of an Austrian or an Italian', and asked the British Minister to approach Seipel. Yet, the Austrian Chancellor was committed to an Austrian candidate and appointed Reisch, a former Finance Minister. Seipel met French and Italian pressure through creating the temporary post of foreign adviser to the bank, although leaving the task of making the appointment to Janssen, Chairman of the League's Financial Committee, while hoping that he would fill it.[24] This was an attempt to respond to British pressure as, after the earlier failure to secure Vissering as the bank's president, the City of London had turned to Janssen. However, Janssen first hesitated over making any response and then refused on the grounds that the post would require his continuous residence in Vienna.

Seipel's decision over the bank's presidency disappointed London. The City had hoped during late December that no appointment would be made until Avenol of the League was once more in Vienna, which it was expected would lead to the post being filled by the 'man most likely to inspire confidence in foreign lenders'.[25] However, there was one countervailing positive factor within the Austrian situation – the passage on 15 December of the British legislation guaranteeing the League loan. London used this opportunity to inquire of the other committed guarantors – Belgium, Czechoslovakia, France, Italy, Spain and Switzerland – when their comparable statutes would be passed.[26]

It had been evident from when the Geneva Protocols were signed that the Austrian government would require interim financing until the stabilisation loan's proceeds became available. Plans for Treasury bill issues had been aired from early October, with the League delegation estimating that they might amount to at least 130 million gold crowns. Nearly all Austrian banks' managements were prepared to supply 30 million in gold currencies immediately by taking up seven per cent three-month Treasury bills. These were initially secured on the customs and tobacco monopoly and ultimately to be funded by the stabilisation loan. The banks were also ready to underwrite a public issue of 20 million six-month bills which carried the right to subscribe to the central bank's capital.

However, the Anglo-Austrian Bank's management took a negative attitude to the proposed Treasury bills. They were wary of the Austrian situation and, consequently, made it clear that they were only prepared to subscribe under special conditions. These comprised an assurance that the stabilisation loan would definitely be placed, and that no subscription on the bills that it took up would be required to be paid over before the Commissioner General was resident in Vienna. Fulfilling the first condition was beyond the authority of the League's delegates in Vienna, while the second could not be met since the Austrian government required funds to pay civil servants' salaries during November. The Länderbank's management took the same cautious attitude but left it to their opposite numbers at the 'Anglo' to make the running.

Niemeyer opposed special conditions for foreign banks. Furthermore, the Anglo's requirements ran the risk of being regarded in Vienna as being those of the Bank of England and the British government. There was a real danger that the Anglo's stipulations could be seen as Britain attempting 'to get out of its Geneva promises more cleverly than Italians'. Moreover, Niemeyer, with Henry Strakosch of the Financial Committee, thought that the 'impracticable propositions from Anglo Bank will make our mission futile', of which the key aspect was 'pressing Austrian government hard to agree to economies'.[27] Nonetheless, there was greater sympathy in the City of London for the Anglo-Austrian Bank's stance, which stemmed from the fear that the stabilisation loan would not be fully issued on the terms that had been specified at Geneva. The bank's management foresaw only the British and the French tranches being floated. These would provide funds sufficient for financing the Austrian budget deficit but not the Treasury bills' repayment. Their gloomy forecast had arisen from reviews of the situation that had included discussions with Norman.[28] At the beginning of November, Norman tried to break the deadlock by seeing Strakosch together with Lawrence and Bark of the Anglo-Austrian Bank to review the Anglo's continued reluctance to subscribe to Treasury bills before the Commissioner General had been nominated.

The Anglo's management was not alone in pressing for the earliest arrival of the Commissioner General in Vienna. Blackett pointed out this had been looked for in Geneva when the Protocols had been formulated. And he was supported by his fellow members of the League Financial Committee, Niemeyer and Avenol, although they regarded the attitude of the Anglo's management as unhelpful. Further discussions with Monnet reviewed suitable persons for the post of Commissioner General. The candidature of Boyden, the American representative on the Reparation Commission, had been blocked by Washington, which left Zimmerman. Niemeyer was anxious that his appointment should be quickly announced so that he could be in Vienna by mid-December.[29] In the meantime, the only way to meet the Anglo's stipulations proved to be a letter from the League giving an assurance that all possible steps would be taken to ensure the stabilisation loan's issue during spring 1923.

Niemeyer had expected that Austrian sources of funds would finance the government until December. However, they only proved to be sufficient until November, when Morgan Grenfell's attitude to the League's Austrian financial schemes crystallised. The house had been approached to place the balance of 30 million gold crowns of an issue of 130 million gold crowns in six-month Austrian Treasury bills. While its partners were not prepared to undertake the transaction, they wondered whether American bankers would consider it.[30] However, their negative attitude was shared by the New York Morgan house which consequently felt unable 'to ask our banking friends to tie up money'.[31]

During the continuing negotiations between League delegates and the Austrian government the most pressing matter became the issue of about £3m worth of Treasury bills, in either sterling or dollars, pledged against securities under League control. The bills would be renewed, when they would be guaranteed by signatory governments to the Geneva Protocols, and be funded by the first instalment of the planned guaranteed £26m long-term loan.[32] However, Charles Whigham of Morgan Grenfell thought that the London market would only take these bills if their repayment in gold was fully secured as opposed to being solely dependent upon the long-term loan's proceeds. It also seemed that, as the stabilisation loan's issue so largely hung in practice upon the British government's support, especially its guarantee of a considerable portion, the Bank of England rather than private houses would undertake any London issuing operation.[33] Morgan Grenfell therefore expected to be underwriters to, rather than issuers of, the British tranche.

Norman approached the Morgan group during November over the question of the Austrian long-term loan, especially the placing of an American tranche. J.P. Morgan thought that this was out of the question, sharing the Governor's own pessimism arising from the difficulty of determining the loan's value in terms of its security. Nonetheless, he wanted his New York partners' opinions before giving a definite verdict which could affect legislation being drafted by the League.[34] Their collective view continued to be that the loan would have to be jointly and severally guaranteed by the countries involved rather than simply jointly as was being planned. There were precedents: the 1898 Greek loan and the 1855 Turkish loan. An alternative was splitting the loan into local issues, with the British guaranteed portion sold on the New York market. Yet this could lead to various unfortunate comparisons between issuing markets regarding the loan's price/yield. Another approach was a loan much smaller in amount but with the attraction that the pledged revenues would amply cover its service. More generally, the New York market for all foreign securities was unsettled in late 1922 due to the growing storm clouds over the reparations question, a condition which did not favour an immediate issue of the Austrian loan.[35] Such considerations confirmed the more general view in London.

Norman's talk with J.P. Morgan on 16 November had been a thorough review, as had been his previous discussions with Niemeyer and ter Meulen. Consequently, the Governor on 4 December carefully explained to Frankenstein that, as far as he was aware, nothing could be immediately undertaken on Western markets with respect to either placing Treasury bills or issuing the long-term loan. Austrian assets alone were not regarded by Western bankers as sufficient security for a long-term loan, whereas the ratification of the Geneva guarantees required legislation in the parliaments of the various signatory states.[36] Nonetheless, British and French diplomacy was trying in tandem to ensure through representations to Denmark, the Netherlands, Norway, and Sweden that the stabilisation loan would be issued on the largest number of European financial markets and that, thereby, subscriptions would have a sizeable neutral participation.[37]

The Austrian government's finances became precarious in mid-December. There were sufficient funds possibly only until the close of the year. Thereafter, the government's finance depended on either the conclusion of negotiations for a Czechoslovak credit, albeit complicated by the Czech crown's recent depreciation, or resort to using its gold reserves. The Devisenzentrale had £3m but it was planned that these resources would go to the central bank. Furthermore, League officials were concerned about the impact on confidence, if Austria physically exported gold.[38]

The pressing need for interim financing led the Austrian government and League officials to consider every possible source. In late December, the issue of bills secured on francs, lire and gold was explored. As earlier, London bankers were doubtful of the collateral's status, which appeared to conflict with that pledged earlier. What worried Whigham of Morgan Grenfell was whether 'we [were] back in the vicious circle whereby innumerable would-be friends of the Austrian government possibly without full knowledge or authority are promulgating innumerable different plans for dealing with the situation'. His anxiety had been caused by a proposal relayed to London by a broker related to the Viennese Rothschilds. The London Rothschilds had then approached Morgan Grenfell but both houses felt unsure, especially with regard to any possible conflict arising with the League stabilisation plan. Therefore it was decided to ask Young, a British government official in Vienna, to talk to the Viennese Rothschilds.[39]

Young found that the Austrian government required £3.25m and was offering gold and the unexpended portions of French and Italian credits as security. However, with the depreciation of the franc and the lire, there was the difficulty of establishing an acceptable arrangement for guaranteeing the exchange values of their respective portions of the collateral. The only sound security was the gold, and the question was whether the London market would advance £2m immediately. There were also technical difficulties arising from both the availability of the unexpended franc and lire credits and the relationship of the advance's repayment to the future League loan. Consequently, Young advised discussions with Niemeyer, while offering to come to London with Baron Louis de Rothschild.[40] Even this did not clarify the situation, as Morgan Grenfell wanted it established that the gold, francs and lire were not only readily available but could be deposited with their agents.[41]

Furthermore, as Young had recognised, the London market was only prepared in practice to advance against gold. The provision of £1.25m against francs and lire could not be considered because 'the whole position of the grand loan is at present so intangible that the prospects of repayment from this source offers no adequate security'.[42] Yet another complication arose from Schroders trying to integrate the Boden-Credit-Anstalt into the Viennese group of the placing syndicate. Morgans and Schroders had recently acquired shareholdings in this Austrian major bank, and Baron Bruno Schröder was anxious to maintain its prestige.[43]

The Geneva Protocols may have cut through the Gordian knot of European politics that had enmeshed the Austrian problem but they had failed to give an immediate basis for Western capital markets to provide the required resources for the Alpine republic's reconstruction. By late 1922 disquiet over the Austrian situation was spreading through the personal networks of European men of affairs. Melchior passed to Keynes the contents of a letter received from 'a friend of mine, a high state official in Austria,' from which the German banker concluded that '[T]he beginning of 1923 smells extremely badly'.[44]

The questions of how, and when, the stabilisation loan would be issued were brought to a head by League meetings in late January 1923 to consider the Austrian situation. Part of the necessary preparations for this review had been accomplished by Anglo-French diplomacy that had brought Belgium, Spain and Switzerland within the guarantors for the loan. In order to ensure that it was fully guaranteed, joint representations were also being made to Denmark, the Netherlands, Norway, and Sweden, which, if successful, would also give a significant neutral participation on which London laid great store.[45] Furthermore, an attempt to interest bankers in issuing the stabilisation loan was made on 15 January at a meeting convened by the Deputy Governor of the Bank of England.

The 15 January meeting was attended by representatives of Barings, Rothschilds, Schroders and Morgan Grenfell along with Bark of the Anglo-Austrian Bank, Niemeyer of the Treasury and Strakosch of the League's Financial Committee. The starting point of their discussions was that Austria required a long-term loan of £28m, of which £5.6m would fund advances. It was recognised that its first tranche could not be issued before April, or even May, and that, in the meantime, further bridging finance of £2m to £3.5m was needed.

Strakosch tried to gain the London market's involvement by pointing out that the Austrian government had instituted the reforms required. He outlined the progress to stabilisation. Inflation had ceased on 18 November 1922, while the central bank's constitution precluded it from financing the government. Deposits with banks and savings institutions had increased by 107 billion paper crowns between 1 September and 30 November 1922, and private capital had returned to the country – £3.5m during the last quarter of 1922. Since 1 December 1922, 47 million gold crowns had been raised internally through the issue of Treasury bills, and 22 million gold crowns had been subscribed to the central bank's capital. Having accomplished these various forms of self-help, Vienna now looked to the League to make good its implicit promise of mobilising the required external financial resources. Continuing delay had caused disappointment with the result that there was a possibility of declining confidence undermining the progress that had been achieved. Niemeyer emphasised Strakosch's appraisal through maintaining that the whole Austrian question had reached the stage where the stabilisation plan either went forward or broke down with all the consequences that that would involve.

Like all the other bankers present at the meeting, Vivian H. Smith and Whigham of Morgan Grenfell were impressed by Strakosch's account of the steps forward made in Austria. However, they reminded those in the room of their earlier adverse opinions regarding the stabilisation loan's security provisions. These had the effect of each signatory government guaranteeing its own loan portion and no more. However, the security now seemed to be 'more substantial than had been previously realized'. Yet, this faint optimism was tempered by the London Morgan partners remaining undecided about the security's value, and all present having the rapidly deteriorating German situation at the forefront of their minds.[46] Nonetheless, a positive consensus developed as a result of the lead given by Revelstoke and Gaspard of Barings.

It seemed that, once the necessary formalities had been completed, a long-term loan of £5m could be immediately raised on European markets, with London supplying the bulk. However, it was recognised that this would only be accomplished if a like amount was issued in the United States. The matter could possibly be resolved by the Bank of England undertaking the London issue and inducing other European central banks to follow its lead. If outline agreements for the long-term loan could be reached, the London bankers present were prepared to consider taking, and holding firm, £1m worth of Austrian Treasury bills but only so long as American bankers acted in concert. The bills would finance the Austrian government until 1 April, by which time it was hoped that the long-term loan's first tranche would have been issued. As these arrangements were aired and discussed, Smith and Whigham felt increasingly trapped because they recognised that it would be practically impossible for Morgan Grenfell to stand apart if the meeting's emerging conclusions were accepted.

Informally and with great care, Morgans in New York discussed the London formulae of 15 January, particularly those for the Treasury bills, with National City Bank, First National Bank, Guaranty Trust and Bankers Trust. As in London, the German situation clouded the picture. American bankers were so discouraged by the central European situation that they felt it both futile to contact distributing houses about the long-term loan 'and almost, if not quite equally useless to discuss' with heads of banking departments the possibility of temporary advances. However, Morgans regarded the Austrian situation as crucial since the League plan's successful execution could possibly pave the way for a similar operation for Germany. Nonetheless, the New York house's partners felt unable to take on alone any considerable obligation or risk. Moreover, they had reached the conclusion that American markets would not take up any substantial proportion of a long-term Austrian loan issued during the coming April, even if the German situation was resolved, because of the varying standings of its guarantors. Consequently, Morgans were only prepared to review the situation again if the reserve expressed by their London associates 'be cleared up so as to give a very different aspect to [the] affair'.[47] J.P. Morgan expressed his personal regret at this discouragement, but offered the possibility of assistance to Morgan Grenfell if its partners felt it necessary to become involved in any London scheme with a commitment greater than was convenient for their house.[48]

Norman was in the United States when London bankers discussed financing Austria on 15 January, and Morgan Grenfell wanted him fully briefed about what had been considered. Furthermore, with New York's subsequent negative response, all those involved had decided that no further step could be taken, maintaining that it was probably better to let things drift until Norman had returned.[49] Edward C. Grenfell, who was in Cannes, agreed with his partners' decisions, including Morgan Grenfell not standing back from financing Austria should the other three London merchant banks decide to proceed. His basic grumble with the proposed London formulae of 15 January was that they constituted moral blackmail. He maintained that, if an Austrian breakdown was regarded as being so bad for the world, the governments involved in Austrian stabilisation should stand behind the City of London 'privately, if not openly'. Furthermore, he was concerned, like his fellow partners in London and New York, that, should the Ruhr crisis deteriorate further, divisions between Britain, France and Italy would open up to such an extent that they would prevent any issue of an Austrian long-term loan.[50] The result of these London discussions and their trans-Atlantic airing was that Strakosch and Niemeyer were left to get along 'as best as they could' at the League discussions of Austrian reconstruction during late January.[51]

Although Niemeyer could not bring agreed loan subscriptions to the meeting of the Austrian Committee of Control, he presented a plan for raising £3.5m through the issue of 12 month Treasury bills in various countries. This was approved with the expectation that the first tranche would be floated in London. Consequently, the Austrian delegation wrote to the Bank of England, and Reisch, President of the Austrian National Bank, held himself ready to visit London. Similarly, Balfour at the session of the League Council's Austrian Committee tried to dispel any pessimism over the question of credits, and over Austrian progress in carrying through the reforms.[52]

It was left to Niemeyer to try and prepare the ground for discussions between the City of London and the Austrian government for the Treasury bill issue. British diplomats laid great stress on the need for success: 'The raising of even a small sum of money abroad at once will do a great deal to strengthen the hands of the High Commissioner [Zimmerman] and the Austrian Government in carrying through the reforms.'[53]

The Bank of England took the lead, applying the outline formulae discussed in mid-January. In early February, the Bank issued the Austrian Treasury bills on the London market with the hope that bankers in Paris and Amsterdam would take a share. Morgan Grenfell decided to subscribe for the same proportion of the London issue as that of each of the other houses represented at the 15 January meeting. Norman realised that this was but a first step on a long, difficult road and, consequently, sought the earliest indication of any change in either conditions on the New York market or the interest of the Secretary of State in the Austrian question following the arrangement of the British Debt Settlement.[54]

J.P. Morgan & Co. refused to be a named participant in the Treasury bill issue but agreed, as its partners had indicated earlier, to relieve its London associates of any amount in excess of that taken individually by the other three London merchant banks.[55] The New York Morgan house's general adverse attitude was shared by both Max Warburg, American correspondent for the Credit-Anstalt, and Kuhn, Loeb & Co. However, Paribas tried to induce Kuhn, Loeb & Co., its American correspondents, to change its mind to the extent of making a public issue denominated in dollars, but to no avail.[56] Norman wanted no further trans-Atlantic haggling, however well intended, informing the Anglo-Austrian Bank that it seemed likely that the bills could be placed fully within Europe.[57] By 1 March, the British tranche – £1.8m – had been fully subscribed as a result of pressure from Norman and, although most of the issue was subscribed in London, the Governor's influence had led to other European centres taking small amounts.[58]

Niemeyer took advantage of the presence of the British delegation in Washington for the talks over funding the British War Debt to try and obtain the United States' involvement in the guarantees for the Austrian long-term loan. He pointed out that Belgium, Denmark, the Netherlands, Spain, Sweden and Switzerland had now joined the signatories to the Geneva Protocols, commenting that: 'This represents a work of international co-operation for reconstruction of Europe without parallel', and crisply adding 'Want of interest in America is surprising'.[59] The ratification of the Anglo-American debt agreement only went through Congress a few days before it was adjourned on 4 March. This prevented any immediate discussion of the United States joining the guarantors for Austria, an outcome not unexpected by Thomas Lamont of Morgans. However, the New York Morgans regretted that the United States had been unable to take up what they regarded an excellent opportunity 'to participate helpfully in European matters without compelling the American people to undertake any burden whatsoever in the way of additional taxes'.[60] The British Embassy in Washington issued a press release on Austrian reconstruction 'but few papers appeared to publish it'. America was proving to be stony ground, and all that Morgans could offer as a gesture of good will was to take up a small portion of the planned long-term loan on their own account, should it be issued in May.[61]

Niemeyer was surprised at the Treasury bill issue's success, for which he gave full credit to Norman, but this British Treasury official had been equally fully engaged in all the negotiations with Belgium, France, the Netherlands, Switzerland and Sweden. He stated candidly to Zimmerman that:

> I did not myself think that we should be able to raise more than something like $1^1/2$ million, and the achievement of placing $3^1/2$ million in six different countries on a security hitherto unknown to the market is I think a very satisfactory one.[62]

Yet, his understandable elation was tinged with pessimism because he was concerned that the Austrians involved, especially Victor Kienböck, the new Minister of Finance, should not get the impression that they were now in 'calm waters'. This worry was coupled with others. Niemeyer did not want the Austrian National Bank to allow 'a too lavish inflation of commercial credit', which he thought would undo 'all our work in Austria'. Closely related was the prevention of the crown appreciating as a result of the inflow of remittances. Niemeyer looked to Reisch to control the situation, while wanting the most rapid instalment of Schynder von Wartensee to the still vacant and controversial post of foreign adviser to the Austrian National Bank. Lastly, Niemeyer regarded the Austrians who had been involved in the negotiations for the Treasury bill issue as 'gifted amateurs', and so now wanted a properly constituted delegation to conduct the talks for floating the League loan.

Niemeyer had discussed the loan with Norman and felt that its negotiation should be handled by a small commission which would tour Europe from early March and, if propitious, visit America. He had put this to Kienböck and Salter. He saw his proposed commission as ideally led by an Austrian who was fluent in French and English, and preferably not a Jew; 'what is wanted is a man with some knowledge of the world, some dignity and some personality, e.g. an ex-diplomat, if they could get one'. As to the other members, Niemeyer suggested Bark of the Anglo-Austrian Bank, 'who would be acceptable in financial quarters generally', and Salter of the League. In his plan, the commission should have full powers and immediately begin the loan negotiations. When arrangements had reached an outline stage, they could be presented to the League's Commission of Control, possibly early in May. Niemeyer also recognised the importance of American participation and hoped that this would be encouraged through Boyden handing a statement to American journalists in Paris, paralleled by the Austrian Ambassador distributing it in Washington. It was a repeat of his earlier attempt to raise American interest in Austria through the British Financial Delegation in Washington.[63]

Niemeyer's commission was ready by 12 March and comprised Frankenstein, the Austrian Minister in London, Bark and Salter. Although it was 'in no sense a British mission', 'His Majesty's Government are anxious that the negotiations on which the future stability of Austria depends should be successful'.[64] In London, the matter was handled by the Bank of England, together with Bark, Binder, the accountant who had been involved in the Anglo-Austrian

Bank's *Anglicisation*, and Frankenstein. Morgan Grenfell regarded Bark as 'a first class fellow', bearing out Niemeyer's assessment, but it was known that the French disliked him. This was not regarded as a major impediment because of the generally strained relations between London and Paris caused by the Ruhr occupation.

By mid-March the loan mission had been approached by some American houses – Hallgartens and Speyers – but they did not carry weight in the City of London where it was felt that their proposed participations could give Austria false hopes. Norman wanted the mission to cross the Atlantic and see J.P. Morgan & Co. first, so much so that the Governor sought an early intimation of the New York Morgan house's attitude.[65] The partners of J.P. Morgan & Co. were particularly anxious to have discussions with Salter, but warned that the Ruhr occupation along with the general situation in Europe could preclude American co-operation on any considerable scale. However, they indicated that when the issue was arranged, they were prepared at the very least to give a certain amount of banking support to indicate their interest in, and sympathy with, the Austrian situation.[66] The New York Morgan partners also remained concerned about the loan's security and continued to ask for the joint and several guarantee of the principal guarantors – Czechoslovakia, France, Great Britain and Italy. It was appreciated that it would be difficult to change the guarantees, but Morgans' motive was to be enabled 'to place a round amount with the American investors rather than the comparatively trifling amount' that would come forward as a result of sentiment.[67] Their search for changes was out of the question since they would involve a re-negotiation of the Geneva Protocols, while the security had proved to be acceptable on European markets for the February/March issue of Treasury bills. Furthermore, it was felt in London that nothing would induce the British government to accept a joint and several guarantee for the loan's whole amount.[68]

Anglo-American discussions, conducted by cable, were cut across by an Italian protest to the nomination of Schnyder of the Schweizer Nationalbank as foreign adviser to the Austrian National Bank. 'Expressed … very violently', it was made by Pantaleoni, which further muddied the waters as he chaired the Committee of Control for Austria. The Committee had not been consulted over Schnyder's selection but the City of London had made it a condition for the Treasury bill issue. Furthermore, the Foreign Office regarded the appointment 'of a subject of one of the major guarantors' [i.e., an Italian] as being inconsistent with the spirit of the Geneva Protocols. London left the resolution of the matter to the Austrian Government and its foreign creditors.[69]

No direct approach was made to Seipel, then in Italy. During this visit the Austrian Chancellor found that some major Italian banks were prepared to subscribe to the Austrian loan 'if the Italian Government gave the word'.[70] Seipel was aware of Pantaleoni's protest and thought that it might be raised at League meetings in April. He did not expect formal representations from the

Italian government and looked to the required amendments to the Austrian National Bank's statutes for creating the advisory post to be accepted at its forthcoming general meeting. This would leave the Commissioner General to make the formal nomination of the candidate to fill it. Seipel was not prepared to recognise overtly the existence of a problem and, if it had substance, he considered it to be for either the League or the loan guarantors to resolve.[71] Such a disinterested approach was actually misleading because one of the reasons why Seipel did not intend to be at the League's Finance and Austrian committees was to ensure that the Austrian National Bank's statutes were amended to allow the appointment of a foreign adviser.[72] The Austrian National Bank's Italian director opposed the required amendment at the bank's general meeting, while the Social Democrats voiced a protest in parliament because the appointment widened the extent of foreign control over Austria.[73]

The threatened Italian protest was not made at the meeting of the Austrian Control Committee, which, therefore, was able to work into the early hours to establish the long-term loan's technical details. Only the guaranteed portion could be issued but merely two per cent of the amount remained to be guaranteed. The major signatories' guarantees, accounting for 80 per cent of the loan, were altered to allow the Italian portion to rise to 18.6 per cent through reducing those of Britain, Czechoslovakia and France to 21.8 per cent each.[74] A further 18 per cent was guaranteed by Belgium, Denmark, the Netherlands, Spain, Sweden and Switzerland. The loan was to have a term of 20 years and be further secured by the Austrian state tobacco monopoly and the customs revenues. Issuing conditions were established as an average yield of 7.75 per cent, with issuing commissions not to exceed an average of 4.5 per cent of the nominal value of the amount to be floated.

Strakosch had expected difficulties at the League's Austrian sub-committee, and they came in the form of Italian pressure for some control body over Austria to replace the Commissioner General when his task was completed. The Italian plan for this new organ involved it having powers exceeding the supervision of assets assigned to service the loan. It was plain, as with earlier similar initiatives from Rome, that an Italian presidency for this future body was being sought. Britain made no commitment, leaving the matter to be settled when the Commissioner General's term came to an end.[75]

Shortly after the League meetings, the Italian government indicated to Vienna that a prior condition for the discussions over issuing the stabilisation loan in Rome would be the settling 'of the question of foreign adviser to the Austrian National Bank… to Italian satisfaction'. Niemeyer arranged a rebuff from the British Foreign Office.[76] Nonetheless, Italian opposition continued even after Zimmerman had formally offered the post to Schynder. A growing concern in early May was that Rome might bring pressure to bear upon the Swiss government in order to abort Schynder's appointment.[77] Schynder accepted the post on 18 May but Italian representatives then raised questions about the whole nature of the League loan. Despite the matter having been resolved at Geneva in autumn 1922, Rome raised again the problem of Austrian Relief bonds held by the Italian government, and demanded that the Austrian loan should be placed upon a gold basis, rather than being denominated in the respective currencies of the countries where it was proposed to issue tranches. In order to discuss these points, the Italians asked for the Committee of Control to reconvene in late May, an initiative opposed by Salter and the British and French governments.[78]

Continuing Italian prevarication could have had serious consequences as, by mid-May, it seemed likely that J.P. Morgan & Co. were prepared to issue the loan in New York. The Foreign Office in London thought that the ultimate source of the problems created by Italian representations was probably 'departmental jealousies in Rome' and, consequently, instructed the British Ambassador to approach Mussolini directly.[79] Inter-ministerial communication in Rome did indeed prove to be one difficulty, but the problem was a more fundamental one as Graham, the British Ambassador, discovered. The Italian Treasury's real concern was the possibility of incurring a loss should the lira appreciate, hence the desire to put the loan onto a gold basis. Graham made daily representations and, on 2 June, Italian banks were authorized to subscribe for 200 million lire.[80]

By the time of the League spring meetings, Frank Nixon, a former director of the League's Economic section, had joined the loan mission, acting as an alternate to Salter. The mission's continuing prime concern was how to attract American subscriptions and, consequently, its members were considering taking up Ivy Lee's offer of co-operation.[81] Lee was a publicity man and, although Morgans thought highly of his character and capacity, the New York partners considered it inadvisable for any such person to accompany the mission to the United States. They wanted the principal loan negotiations to take place in London, with the mission crossing the Atlantic solely to explain the Austrian situation in general terms, following the pattern of its visits to European centres.

Without further prompting from London, the New York Morgan house constructed a tentative financial group of sufficient composition and strength to undertake the loan, if the operation proved feasible.[82] To assist its presentation in America, Dwight Morrow of J.P. Morgan & Co., with Salter, was trying to arrange for Zimmerman to come independently to New York and address the meeting of the United States Chamber of Commerce, arranged for 7 to 11 May. American bankers had clear ideas of how the loan was to be launched publicly in the United States, but the loan mission had become accustomed in European centres to a pattern of business involving discussions with a range of banks. London agreed with J.P. Morgan & Co. that it would be inadvisable to give the impression in New York of hawking the business around which might be created by negotiations with a number of houses. Consequently it was impressed upon the mission that its members in New York should not only see J.P. Morgan & Co. first but also abide with its partners' advice with regard to the American market.[83]

The American approach was clarified during late April, when partners of Morgan Grenfell met Norman and the loan mission. It was planned to issue the loan around 1 June and the mission regarded it as essential that London and New York took together not less than half of the £21m to be issued publicly. It had been already agreed that tranches were to be confined to their respective issuing markets so as not to internationalise the loan. J.P. Morgan & Co. approved because, if the American market proved less receptive than other issuing centres, this would not be an obstacle to floating a tranche in New York. London now needed to know from Morgans in New York whether the mission should cross the Atlantic, or continue the principal discussions in London.[84] An urgent reply was required as the mission was proceeding to Paris, and was not planning to return to London.

Morgans continued to prefer to centre the discussions in London but there was a chance of direct contact as Lamont was sailing for Cherbourg on 28 April, arriving in Paris on 5 May. However, it was still considered in New York that it would be advantageous for Salter and Zimmerman to cross the Atlantic, so they could meet Morgan's proposed associates.[85] The overall aim envisaged for the two European officials was that they should convince first Morgans and then their associates that the Austrian loan was secure without any state guarantees. This was required because, with the Ruhr crisis, French loans, along with those of other guarantors of the Austrian loan, were being traded on the American market at such low prices that any Austrian loan would have to be issued on very attractive terms. In this situation, even with a high yield, Morgans thought that the American public would take very little of it. Consequently, the house would have to look to other bankers to hold the loan until Austrian recovery justified a wider sale. This pointed to the terms for an American issue to be bonds bearing at least eight per cent with the issuing syndicate taking a discount of four points on the public flotation price.

In all these trans-Atlantic discussions by cable and as had been evident since October 1922, Morgans were only considering a small issue in New York, in the range of $10m to $25m (£2m to £5m). This would mean that London would have to absorb £5.5m to £8.5m if the Anglo-American markets were to take in an aggregate half of the loan. One way of overcoming this problem involved splitting the Anglo-American block in two. The second part's flotation might benefit from any greater than planned reduction of the Austrian budget deficit through being consequently smaller in amount and cheaper in issue price. This option was rejected; it being decided that the best way forward was to issue all the stock that the American market could take. However, the American tranche's success depended upon there being no further deterioration in the Ruhr situation. Morgans once more stressed to London that most American bankers were sceptical about the soundness of central European conditions in general and the Austrian situation in particular.[86]

In seeking to enable the largest possible American issue, London tried to respond to American requirements. It was made clear to J.P. Morgan & Co. that the detailed terms for the flotation of the European tranches had not yet been agreed, with the exception of the Swiss. Nonetheless, a general basis had emerged, involving substantial parity of issuing conditions on those financial centres where the local currency approximated to a gold basis, but concessions for markets with heavily depreciated currencies as, for instance, those of Belgium, France and Italy. All in all, this could allow some small differentiation in the American issuing terms, if warranted by circumstances.[87]

Technical problems also arose. London sent J.P. Morgan & Co. a copy of the loan's general bond. The New York house promptly pointed out that certain features were not in accord with American practice, as had been anticipated in October 1922, and these would further complicate making a public issue.[88] Lamont later laid the blame for the bond's flaws on the Bank of England's solicitors having had apparently little regard for any market usage other than London. Actually this was not the case; the League, through Strakosch, had arranged for the legal drafting of the bond in London, and Norman would have preferred certain alterations. This was now practically impossible as the bond had been approved at Geneva and so had to be considered finalised. Alterations could only be made by the Control Commission and there would be great difficulties in bringing this body together and securing unanimous approval. Furthermore, it would give Rome an opportunity to air its own required revisions, so creating further diplomatic problems.

Despite this problem, Morgans called a meeting of its associates on 28 April, subsequently assuring London that they were all like-minded in agreeing 'to leave no stone unturned in assisting in this situation'. Morgans' discussions in New York with the 'technical bondmen' of both Guaranty Trust and Bankers Trust established a market composed of banks and corporations but not private investors. Yet whatever hopes this generated in London needed to be tempered, and Morgans reiterated that they had no undue confidence in the issue's American reception.[89] At the Investment Bankers Association meeting, George Whitney had sounded out a number of the 'more intelligent and co-operative dealers', gaining the impression that 'while they theoretically acknowledged the value of [the] operation, they did not express the slightest hope of any substantial purchasing by investors'.[90]

Although transatlantic cables, augmented by personal letters, carried information and views, perhaps their stress and emphasis were not always clear, with the result that the two parties to the ethereal conversation did not fully appreciate diverging opinions and conclusions. This became apparent when Lamont met the loan mission, including Salter and Frankenstein, in Paris. The American banker had to hammer home that there was no discernible American interest in Austrian bonds, especially as the United States had no important commercial connections with the country. He felt that the mission's members were either not facing up to this situation or did not want to digest fully its unpalatable consequences. It was evident to him that they hoped for not only a larger proportion of the loan to be issued in New York but also for it to be issued at a lower rate of interest.

Lamont had to restate that the American tranche would have to yield eight per cent. The loan mission indicated their preparedness to accept any terms ensuring the American issue's success, but feared that a high yield on the New York issue would have an untoward effect upon European markets.[91] Bark, who Lamont acknowledged was experienced, amplified the point, and tried to find a compromise in an American tranche nominally bearing seven or 7.5 per cent but issued at a discount to raise the initial yield. This was not quite the compromise which Norman had suggested; the Governor's device had been the issue in New York of eight-per-cent bonds at par, coupled with six-per-cent bonds in London floated at 80, which would give an average yield of 7.75 per cent, so meeting the requirement agreed with the Committee of Control.[92]

The loan mission was able to convince Lamont that the loan was sound. Its members argued that it was amply secured in various ways. The governments of the Alpine Republic's neighbouring states were assuring Austria's continuing political integrity and economic viability. Therefore, the successor states, and in particular Czechoslovakia, had every reason to assist Austria. With the political and financial guarantees that they had given, it was equally in the guarantors' interest not to be called upon to fulfil them. Lastly, the guarantors would deposit collateral with the Swiss National Bank as trustee that would permit, should Austria default, 'immediate realisation of the loan'.[93]

In Western Europe preparations for the loan had progressed, with Lamont learning that preliminary arrangements had been made to issue £8.25m in London, of which £2.5m would be taken by the Treasury as a funding of earlier short-term advances to Austria. In Paris the Ministry of Finance had imposed a limit of £2m, but Italy was prepared to take £2.5m, as was Czechoslovakia, although in Prague it would be primarily a funding operation. Similarly, the Spanish authorities were ready for Madrid to issue £1m, Belgium would participate to the extent of £0.3m, whereas Dutch banks regarded £0.5m as the ceiling for a local issue, while preferring to participate in a dollar-denominated tranche.

In these talks, which more than cleared the air, some decisions were taken. It was evident to all that the situation in Vienna would not permit Zimmerman to travel to New York. League considerations of the Austrian problem, with all its complications, meant that Salter similarly felt that it was more important for him to remain in Geneva. Looking to the immediate future, the mission feared, following Lamont's pessimism, that any American visit would be useless and disappointing, a depressing conclusion with which Salter concurred. Furthermore, time was becoming increasingly short if the loan was to be issued around the desired date of 1 June. This implied that the mission would have to conclude its European arrangements by 18 May in order to give the guarantors time to deposit their collateral with the Swiss National Bank. This timetable was pressing and, moreover, did not provide an opportunity to make any progress in American negotiations. Consequently, the only way forward was to place the American operation entirely in the hands of J.P. Morgan & Co. Lamont reassured the mission that his house would try to assemble a syndicate that would attempt to carry out their wishes.

Draft letters to New York requested an American tranche of $25m (£5m), carrying a coupon of either 7.5 or eight per cent but with a strong preference for the lower rate. The mission sought to maximise the issue's proceeds as well as reducing its flotation costs. However, Lamont knew privately that his New York partners favoured an eight-per-cent coupon precisely because it would net Austria more valuable dollars. The mission offered the issuing houses a turn of three to five points which was to cover all expenses, except the preparation of the temporary and then the definitive bonds, expected to be printed in Austria. The mission stressed that the saving of even half a point 'would be of great advantage to the Austrian government'. Once issued, as with the London tranche, the dollar proceeds were to remain on deposit until the loan had been floated on all the various markets involved.

Lamont entered three reservations in his draft letters of acceptance. One was a technical point, which had been much discussed, stemming from the trustees' powers determined by the 'Geneva' bond. This was without precedent in American practice and was considered by the New York banker to be an effective bar to a dollar issue. Subsequently, it was found that some of the consequent difficulties could be side stepped through separate issuing contracts, signed by each banking group. The bond also raised difficulties for the British tranche, which led to Sir William Leese, a partner at the Bank of England's solicitors, Freshfields, to make enquiries in Vienna. Morgans were offered the results of his investigation that enabled the General Bond's troublesome clause 22 to be eliminated by agreement amongst the major parties, leaving only assent from two minor centres being required. The domestic securities that Austria was pledging were being freed through the Reparation Commission, with the loan mission subsequently providing an official letter stating that all liens on them had been lifted in favour of the proposed loan.[94]

Second, Lamont asked for permission to proceed even if the New York market only proved capable of raising $20m. Third, there was a saving clause by which the operation could be suspended as a result of either a marked change in market conditions or force majeure and, with the situation in the Ruhr, this latter standard condition had considerable significance.

Privately, Lamont commented to his fellow partners that he had assured the mission that Morgans would act 'invariably for their best interests' but, in asking for a spread in fixing the coupon rate, he was following the precedent of previous large operations for the British and other governments. He hoped that his New York house would be able to raise $25m since any shortfall would gravely affect the Austrian government, emphasising that 'we have always shown that when we put our backs into it we can better the best estimates'. Lamont also looked to Morgans being able to induce their associates not to require an initiating commission, thereby cutting costs and maximising the proceeds. Despite what he had trenchantly put to the loan mission, Lamont favoured a 7.5 per cent coupon, with operation for the loan's American tranche being moved rapidly forward by a small group taking blocks of $5m at 91 as an underwriting operation and, then, selling on to the public issuing syndicate.[95]

Lamont had not told the loan mission that a commitment from Morgans to form an issuing syndicate, either verbal or written, was 'almost equivalent to saying we shall accomplish it barring force majeure'. He was also well aware that a letter of intent from Morgans to the mission would be of great value in their continuing discussions, especially at one or two European financial centres. Yet the banker diplomat remained concerned about stimulating a response within the United States to the Austrian loan and so his last suggestion to his New York partners was to inquire whether Herbert Hoover would make a supporting statement. Lamont was aware of the niceties of the Secretary of Commerce's political position but felt that it might prove valuable if Hoover gave some public interviews in which he explained 'the great and favourable change in Austrian conditions'. With Hoover's past links to Austria, he could make a friendly unofficial gesture whereas Secretary of State Hughes would only be able to offer an official pronouncement. Another personage who could fulfil such a role was Julius Barnes who, with Hoover, had overseen American post-war relief of Austria; he had recently returned from Austria and it was known that his personal assessment had greatly impressed Hoover.

The Morgan partners were committed to an American participation in the loan as they, and other New York houses, considered it to be of great importance that the United States assisted in the resolution of the Austrian situation. But their appreciation of the mood in American financial markets pointed to substantial issuing difficulties, while they were concerned about the possible impression created by the dollar tranche bearing eight per cent since it would add further fuel to 'Shylock' propaganda.[96] Consequently, Morgans in New York wanted to know whether Norman and the City of London would prefer J.P. Morgan & Co. underwriting and subscribing for an enlarged sterling tranche as an alternative to a dollar flotation at eight per cent or more. Lamont, with Norman, rejected this alternative since they regarded the crux of the situation as being a direct and public American participation to encourage continental European subscriptions. Lamont argued that European bankers would understand that the New York pricing of the dollar tranche arose from American market conditions.

A further impediment to a New York public issue was American bankers' criticisms of the loan for being 'unproductive' since its proceeds were to finance Austrian budget deficits for the ensuing two years and fund earlier advances. In order to counter this negative point, Morgans wondered whether there had been sufficient improvement in Austrian conditions for the budget to be balanced during the loan expenditure period 'thus freeing some of [it] for constructive purposes'.[97] The mission considered that there were substantial grounds for maintaining that some loan proceeds would finance productive investment. The currently planned Austrian stabilisation budget contained expenditure on construction, outlays which Zimmerman had approved, while, overall, the budget appeared to be moving faster towards balance than anticipated by League experts. Morgans were initially sceptical of this interpretation because they presumed that budget items for the railways, post office and telegraphs and the tobacco monopoly were to meet operating deficits rather than financing constructive investment.[98] The mission countered by pointing out that 278 billion crowns had been invested in state enterprises during 1922, with a like sum planned for 1923. Furthermore, it increasingly appeared that a considerable amount of the proposed loan would be available for investment purposes, especially railway electrification.[99]

Despite Morgans' continuing pessimistic view of the American market's receptiveness to the Austrian loan, other American houses competed for undertaking at least part of the proposed dollar tranche. Hallgartens made an offer, as did Speyers in conjunction with Chase National, but in their case through London.[100] Whigham informed Frankenstein that Morgan Grenfell considered it unusual for London representatives of New York houses and banks to make applications 'at this end' for inclusion in an American syndicate. It was suggested to the Austrian Minister that he ask the European agents' principals to apply direct to J.P. Morgan & Co. for inclusion.[101]

On 18 May 1923 J.P. Morgan & Co. announced to the loan mission that it was ready to proceed with the attempt to form a syndicate for underwriting $25m (£5m) of seven-per-cent bonds to be issued to the public at 90.[102] Morgan Grenfell informed its New York associates that their European partners in the venture were those shown in Table 6.1.

Within a day, the New York Morgan house felt able to state that the formation of the American syndicate was assured, barring totally unforeseen developments.[103] Actually J.P. Morgan & Co. had by the evening of 19 May commitments of $35m from 30 subscribers, made up of various banks, local private bankers, industrial corporations 'and a few prominent individuals such as J.D. Rockefeller Jr., Thomas F. Ryan and Payne Whitney'. Consequently, the house's partners confidently expected to increase the amount of underwriting subscriptions to $50m within three or four days. Dwight Morrow and Thomas Cochrane remarked to Lamont: 'for the past 48 hours we have all been working unremittingly … we are not done yet'. By 22 May, the underwriting syndicate had topped $40m and $50m was well within sight. The American partners attributed their considerable success to first their leadership 'to which the response has never been more impressive' and second 'to the common

Table 6.1 Morgan Grenfell's European partners

Austria	*Syndicate of all chief banks*
Brussels	Société Générale
London	Bank of England
Netherlands	Hope & Co.
Paris	Paribas
Sweden	Syndicate of all chief banks
Switzerland	Syndicate of all chief banks

feeling among all public spirited bankers that this country should do something for Europe in general and that Austria is a fine place to begin with'. It was planned to make the public issue through a nationwide selling syndicate of about 1,100 distributors.[104] However, there were still great doubts about whether the public would take the issue, but Morrow and Cochrane were now striving for 'a great triumph' – achieving the goal of relieving the underwriters of their commitments in full.[105]

The first objective was to counteract the impression of the 'average bondman and investor ... that the whole Austrian proposition is pretty hopeless'. This was to be achieved by a press campaign and, therefore, Lamont's fellow partners wanted him 'to get some good information into the hands of American correspondents' in Europe. In this publicity drive the League's role was going to be down played because of continuing intense controversy within the United States over the League of Nations. Instead, stress was to be given first to the Austrian loan being good in itself; second, that real reconstruction was beginning in Austria; and third, that the European governments' guarantees, although important financially, had more bearing upon Austria's future political security.[106] To assist this campaign, J.P. Morgan & Co. once again wanted Zimmerman to come to New York in order to give the widest publicity to his assessment of the Austrian position. It was felt that statements from the Commissioner General would both calm the underwriters' fears that they would have to take up a large portion of the issue, and draw in public subscriptions.[107] As previously, it proved impossible for Zimmerman to cross the Atlantic. He was at the crucial point of 'getting the railways and other important matters under control'.[108] Lamont therefore suggested that he meet Zimmerman in Paris, and thought that this would give him the chance to 'secure additional selling points to cable to New York'.

By 19 May, the New York house had drawn up the first page of the prospectus for the American issue while continuing to negotiate with potential underwriters and distributors.[109] However, press stories had begun to circulate and, consequently, Morgans were forced to announce publicly on 24 May that they were organising an underwriting syndicate for the Austrian League loan. This was justified within terms of the agreed strategy for the publicity campaign, namely, that Morgans believed that the bond for the loan was well secured, while the loan itself was:

> The first step towards the economic rehabilitation of Central Europe taken by all the countries working together and we believe that the American market should take its part when such a concerted effort is being made to better general business conditions of the world.[110]

The formation of an American issuing syndicate led to a rapid development of cable traffic between, variously, New York and London, London and Paris, and Paris and New York. By 24 May, some of the partners in the various banks of the Morgan group were concerned that unless there was some co-ordination, there was going to be 'a slip up on some details'.[111] Considerable tying up and tidying up was indeed required. Neither the loan mission nor Morgans had signed formal letters. There was no formal contract for the dollar tranche, and Whigham of Morgan Grenfell was also uncertain of the progress made in this direction by the Bank of England for the London sterling issue.[112]

Some preparations for completing this important paper work were undertaken through Whigham going to Paris on 26 May to report to Lamont. Additionally, Norman held a meeting at the Bank of England on 30 May at which many of the still outstanding difficulties were reviewed. These consisted of the various legal opinions required, the deposit of collateral, and the problem of issuing dollar-denominated securities in Austria that in the medium term had to be isolated from the American market. The Governor was adamant that the operation should not fail; he had already despatched a personal telegram thanking J.P. Morgan for his 'willingness to take a hand in the Austrian issue' and assuring the American banker 'that we here are not sparing ourselves to help its success'.[113] The Bank of England planned to issue the British prospectus on 9 June for publication in the Sunday press the following day. The sterling issue price was to be 80 with a six per-cent coupon, the flotation closing on 11 June.[114] New York considered that the British issue price, higher than expected, could lead to some unfortunate consequences for the American market.[115]

On hearing that Morgans had brought together in New York an underwriting syndicate for more than $50m, Lamont raised the possibility of increasing the dollar tranche to parity with the London issue, reminding his partners of the earlier hopes of both Norman and the loan mission.[116] New York would not accept his suggestion, a refusal confirmed by Morgan staff's tour of American cities during which they were asked for assurances that the American market would not be required to absorb more than $25m.

The loan mission continued its negotiations in European capitals. Before its arrival in Rome, Lamont learnt that the Banca Commerciale Italiana could proceed no further with its tranche since the Ministry of Foreign Affairs was maintaining that the Austrian loan was still in suspense.[117] This arose from continuing Italian opposition to the foreign adviser to the Austrian National Bank, questions about post-war relief advances to Austria, and concern about tranches being denominated in local currencies and not gold, with consequent fears over a loss should the lira appreciate. How these issues were resolved, proving to be but a temporary impasse in Rome, is unclear.

An increasing problem for the loan mission was to establish a common issue date, caused by the varying degrees of preparedness at each financial centre. It was finally decided to twin the American and British issues, the loan mission having to accept that the domestic flotation of state loans in both France and Italy would postpone the franc and lire tranches until July.[118]

The necessary preliminary letters for the dollar tranche were exchanged on 26 May,[119] whereupon J.P. Morgan & Co. drew up a statement giving details of the Austrian economy, the loan and reconstruction for insertion in the prospectus.[120] This was paralleled by Upson, the American relief controller in Vienna sending a memorandum to Hoover.[121] On his arrival in London to meet Lamont and after reading Morgans' draft, Zimmerman provided his own statement. This stressed that the Austrian government had given an undertaking not to alienate the independence of the Alpine Republic.[122] This was for American houses undertaking the public distribution.[123] However, Morgans found that there were parts in the text 'which, from the standpoint of the local atmosphere here, would we believe add little to the strong points of his picture and might well detract'. The partners therefore sought authorisation to quote parts of the text rather than releasing it en bloc.[124] Lamont subsequently reported to his fellow partners that Zimmerman was 'a "real fellow", strong, vigorous and intelligent and very much pleased with [the] way in which we have handled [the] American participation'.[125]

On 7 June, Morgan Grenfell received notification from the loan mission of the practical completion of the entire operation. The Italian government had, at last, formally released its liens on Austrian state assets but there were some reservations over French arrangements since the franc tranche was only partially underwritten. The London underwriting details were complete and the sterling issue was to close on 11 June, as set in the timetable of 30 May.[126] This enabled Morgans to proceed promptly with the American issue. J.P. Morgan had decided to release a personal statement to herald the issue of the dollar tranche, and his New York partners wondered whether the British Prime Minister would make a similar gesture for use in the American papers.[127] Norman had already agreed to such public involvement, accepting the suggested draft from New York practically without alteration.[128] Lamont offered his American partners a cable which would state that the British subscription books 'have been opened and [are] already closed' as the London underwriting had been 'handsomely completed'.[129] The attitude in the New York Morgan offices was that 'we are not going to quit working until the thing is over the top but we can say to-night [9 June 1923] that all the preliminary indications are that the public offering will be a success'.[130]

The British lists closed at 11.15 a.m. with the sterling tranche heavily oversubscribed.[131] Norman sent a cable to J.P. Morgan, stating:

> I am grateful for your message and feel sure that you will be able to close your list as quickly as we have done this morning. Let us remember in days to come that this sort of international co-operation of which you have now set such an example is just what the world needs.[132]

The Times had supported J.P. Morgan's personal statement in its financial editorial, while all the London press had featured it.[133]

The loan achieved the same success in New York – a substantial oversubscription – and the Morgan partners were able to close the issue books within one hour.[134] The house had received $100m in applications but what staggered the partners was that they had come from 'all sections of the country and in very small units indicating that the loan was very well sold and the great bulk of it to real investors'.[135] J.P. Morgan considered the over-subscription as 'almost bewildering', and wrote to Norman that 'we may all feel satisfied with this first experiment in international co-operation of markets'.[136] Keynes, when commenting upon the Austrian loan for *The Nation and Athenaeum*, gave praise to others, including Sir William Goode, who had 'been Austria's bravest friend through everything and saved Vienna from disaster in her darkest days'. He also felt that the League reconstruction of Austria was a pointer for its general role in 'Fields which are not the subject of acute controversy between the major powers, but where, in the absence of the League, the necessary organisation and enthusiasm for constructive work would have been lacking'.[137]

The success of the Austrian loan had a positive impact in Vienna, especially with the ever-deepening German crisis. Calculations showed that the loan in its entirety would eventually provide the Austrian government with 346 million gold crowns, although they could only be dispensed under Zimmerman's signature. However, implementing the stabilisation programme was causing difficulties, as in the increasingly protracted salary negotiations with state employees provoked by continuing rising prices. Although the crown was stable on the foreign exchanges, prices had increased by 25 per cent over the first half of 1923 and, consequently, the government was reluctant to cease wage indexing. A compromise had been developed whereby indexation was suspended but state officials and employees received enhanced special allowances.[138] While Zimmerman pressed for the abolition of indexation, the government was trying to deal with some state officials' 'passive resistance'. This situation made the final outcome of the draft 1923 budget difficult to establish. When it passed its third reading in the *Nationalrat*, the budget had a projected gross deficit of 2,664 billion crowns but 'this … may probably be exceeded owing to the rise in the cost of living'.[139] Stabilisation was creating internal stresses, and the transfer of the proceeds of the American tranche of the loan issue to the Austrian government was dependent upon the success of continental European tranches.

There were no difficulties in the Netherlands; the Dutch tranche was floated on 16 June and taken up primarily by holders of Austrian Treasury bills who had preferential subscription rights.[140] Lamont gave the news of the American and British over-subscriptions to both Swiss and Italian bankers, encouraging and urging them to complete their parts of the overall loan operation.[141] The Swiss tranche consisted, in essence, of a government advance to the Austrian state and the Swiss operation was successfully completed by the end of June 1923.[142] The Italian tranche, which had been troublesome during the early spring, was taken by a banking syndicate on 30 June and issued publicly the following month.

Initially, the Spanish trance was comparable in nature to the Swiss but progress in Madrid was a source of anxiety as there were doubts, arising from elections, over whether the Cortes would authorise the advance, following the King issuing the necessary decree.[143] Moreover, the mission was strongly advised that no issue, even if authorised, should be made during the summer since it was a financial 'dead period'. This assessment was accepted by the Austrian Finance Minister, and the issue of the Spanish tranche was consequently postponed until the autumn.[144] In any case, proceedings in the new Spanish parliament did not allow the necessary bill's consideration before the summer recess. The arising difficulties were covered, initially, by Nixon of the loan mission receiving a written assurance from the Spanish Foreign Secretary of his government's determination to push the necessary law through in October. Furthermore, Marquis de Cortina, representing Spanish bankers, maintained that there would be no market impediment to raising the necessary funds, once the tranche had been authorised.[145]

The other area of concern in early summer was the French tranche, Morgans having informed the loan mission that American investors' subscriptions would be returned if no issue had been made in Paris by 15 July. The French government was embarrassed that a Crédit National loan on 14 July and a reconstruction issue for the Department of Somme et Meuse meant that the French tranche could not be marketed before the end of July.[146] Furthermore, the tranche was still only partially underwritten. Lamont thoroughly explored these problems not only with 'Paribas' but also the Finance Minister. He received assurances that the French government intended 'to favour the issue in every way legitimate'.[147] Yet, although it seemed that the tranche could be issued on the Paris market by 25 July at the latest, one French banker:

> Dared not [to] be over optimistic as to [the] time it would take as issues here [are] not so rapidly covered as in America and in the particular case of Austria, public feeling is quite different from what it is in England and America and very little publicity will be possible.[148]

Morgans in New York put forward the solution of the French banking syndicate underwriting the entire franc tranche instead of just 25 per cent.[149]

Negotiations in Paris continued until the end of July, when the issuing syndicate indicated a preference not to make the float of the tranche free of French tax. Although the loan mission agreed with this change so long as the tranche's nominal amount was increased to secure the agreed franc proceeds, it had wider implications that created further difficulties. As issuing arrangements in Rome were based on the French, the Italians had to be informed and their agreement obtained.[150] There were other repercussions because the British government was not prepared to deposit further collateral to cover the payment of the 12 per cent French tax, necessitated by the type of security that the French syndicate proposed to issue. This developing impasse resulted in the French tranche failing to be issued by the end of July, which had other knock-on and more grave consequences. The New York Morgan partners had delayed making a decision over the return of funds to American subscribers until 31 July. By the beginning of August they were perturbed about the growing delays, not only in Madrid but also Paris.[151] They covered the situation by not exercising their right to return the proceeds of the American tranche and, thereby, accepted the responsibility of 'possibly causing the bondholders to lose a substantial amount in interest'.[152]

During early August, the Italian government continued to refuse to deposit the extra collateral required for the French tranche, being only prepared to accede if the Austrian loan's guarantors also guaranteed the Italian income tax on the lire bonds. It appeared that the only way forward was for the Austrian government to deposit with the Italian issuing banks a sum equivalent to the amount of the Italian income tax over the period to maturity of the Italian tranche of the loan – approximately 5 million gold crowns. If this arrangement was accepted, the French tranche could be issued during the second week in August.[153] Morgans felt that the only person who could take such a serious decision was Zimmerman, and the necessary authorisation was received from Vienna on 10 August.[154]

The continuing problem of the issue of the Spanish tranche was passed by New York to Whigham of Morgan Grenfell and Norman for discussion with J.P. Morgan who was in Europe. After hearing the Spanish Foreign Minister's further assurances to the loan delegation, Morgan decided that his New York house could proceed with winding-up the loan details. Nevertheless, this meant that Morgans in New York would have to find some way of surmounting any problems caused by the Spanish authorities and bankers being unable to discharge their commitment. Although the Morgan partners had not returned the subscriptions to the American tranche, they were not prepared to release funds to the Austrian loan mission until the Spanish issue had been definitely assured.[155]

Other problems arose which also endangered the success of the whole venture. The movement of the foreign exchanges, in particular of the lira and the franc, meant that the loan's net proceeds were likely to fall somewhat short of the stipulated 630 million gold crowns. Zimmerman calculated the possible deficiency in mid-August as approximately 2–3m French francs. The Morgan partners in New York became greatly concerned as they considered that the American prospectus, and the interim receipt that they had issued, had committed them technically, as well as morally, to ensure that the whole operation netted 630 million gold crowns. Failure in this regard meant that the dollar subscriptions would have to be returned. This opinion was reinforced by Gardiner, the house's counsel, who considered that it would be a variation of the plan if any tranche failed to produce its allotted percentage of the grand total in gold crowns at the time of issue.[156] Some reassurance came when the French tranche was at last floated on 21 August.[157] It was all sold within ten days, and it seemed that the proceeds, at current rates of exchange, would provide the required proportional amount.[158]

This still left the matter of the Spanish tranche. H.H. Harjes of Morgan, Harjes & Co. learnt on 15 October from the Spanish Ambassador in Paris that the necessary decree would be promulgated during early November. Frankenstein and Bark decided to go to Madrid to see if matters could be accelerated.[159] Eventually, Bark went alone but it would appear that his visit had little effect.[160] With the continuing delay in transferring the proceeds of the loan to the Austrian government, the Bank of England inquired on 5 December whether the only obstacle was the issue of the Spanish tranche. Bark returned to Madrid but was still forced to conclude that he was 'still very far away from a loan agreement'.[161] Increasingly frustrated, Bark drafted the necessary contract with the Bank of Spain, and requested the Austrian Minister in Paris to join him.[162] This galvanised matters and Morgan, Harjes & Co. learnt unofficially from the Spanish Ambassador in Paris that the agreement for the Spanish tranche would probably be signed on 15 December.[163] Completion of the contract was made subject to a declaration by the League of Nations, made on 18 December.[164] Ultimately, the Spanish authorities decided that the tranche should be an issue guaranteed by the state, rather than a government advance.[165] Banca Privada, an association of bankers, eventually took the Spanish tranche, and Morgan Grenfell considered it immaterial whether the loan's peseta portion had actually been issued publicly.[166]

On 18 December Zimmerman informed J.P. Morgan & Co. that all tranches of the Austrian loan had been negotiated successfully, with the Committee of Control recording that the net proceeds to date had reached 585–7 million gold crowns. This allowed the New York house to dissolve the American selling syndicate at the end of the year. However, with the continuing fluctuations on the European exchanges, it was going to be 'a vain task' to establish an annual annuity in gold. In this situation, the Commissioner General put forward his considered opinion that all the conditions stipulated in the American prospectus had been met. Whigham cabled Lamont:

> I cannot help feeling that there is a limit to which technicalities should be pressed … I hate to urge you unduly but if … [the categorical statements given by Zimmerman] … do not satisfy your legal advisers, we really are at a loss to suggest what further steps can be taken.[167]

They did prove to be sufficient for New York, and on 31 December 1923 Morgans credited the Austrian National Bank with $21,688,721.48.[168] This allowed the Austrian government to draw from the beginning of 1924 on all the funds that had been raised over the previous six months.[169]

Establishing when Austria was 'stabilised' is a difficult exercise. One indicator of instability – 'disorder' – with which many, if not most, Austrians would have been familiar (the dollar quotation in Vienna), began to fall from 29 August 1922 when it became apparent that the League of Nations would once more intervene to institute stabilisation. Nonetheless, as the likelihood of the success of the stabilisation began to be questioned, this indicator began to rise, albeit slowly, from mid-January 1923 and did not resume its decline until two months later. Furthermore, the quotation of the dollar in Vienna did not stabilise until early July, a fortnight after the issue of the American and British tranches of the stabilisation loan.[170] Austrians, in particular the Viennese, would have perceived the success of stabilisation more directly through the cost of what they bought in the markets and shops. There are a variety of cost of living indices available but none are ideal. The two considered the most satisfactory display rises between October 1922 and December 1923 of 7.6 per cent (Mixed Commission, excluding housing), and 13.9 per cent (*Oesterreichische Volkswirt,* excluding housing), with the difference between the two arising from the former not fully capturing movements in retail prices.[171] More telling is that both indices rose during 1923 until June and July and then fell back, which again emphasises the importance of the successful flotation of the American and British tranches of the stabilisation loan.

> Austrian stabilisation was seen by some members of the 'Morgan group' along with others, such as Norman, as the starting point for confronting central Europe's 'Great Disorder'. This, indeed, proved to be the case. The methods employed for externally financing the Austrian government from the Treasury bill issue of March 1923 shaped in many respects how the Dawes loan was to be raised. More directly, the Austrian stabilisation model was applied first to Hungary and then to other European states in disorder.[172] The 'money doctors' took pleasure in their rolling back of disorder, with Strakosch commenting in late October 1924 to Clegg, a member of Norman's circle of central bankers, "The German Reparations question [is] in a fair way of settlement and [...] Austria and Hungary [are] on the high way to financial and economic recovery: in other words, [...] the most important economic units of central are fairly equipped to resume – gradually it is true – their normal measure of production in condition of monetary stability'.[173]

Notes

1 I am grateful to the Governor and Company of the Bank of England for permission to use the Bank's archives. The underlying research could not have been accomplished without the very considerable assistance of the Bank's archivists: Henry Gillett, Sarah Millard and Roy Harris. I am equally obliged to Professor K. Burk, who enabled agreed access to specified files in the archive of Morgan Grenfell, London.

2 See League of Nations, 1926. *The Financial Reconstruction of Austria: General Survey and Documents.* Geneva: League of Nations; Freund, F. 1924. Die Genfer Protokolle, *Sozialwissenschaftliche Forschungen.* Berlin:Walter de Gruyter; Gartner, F. 1924. Die Stabiliserung der österreichischen Krone, *Schriften des Vereins fur Sozialpolitik*, 169; Kienböck, V. 1925. *Das österreichische Sanierungswerk, Finanz- und Volksitirtschaftliche Zeitfragen Heft 85.* Stuttgart: F. Enke; Pillet, M. 1928. *Le Relevement financier de l'Autriche.* Paris: A. Pedone; Reimann, V. 1968. *Zu gross für Österreich. Seipel und Bauer im Kampf um die Erste Republic.* Vienna: Moldern.

3 Morgan Grenfell papers [hereafter MG]: Cable 22/2375, J.P. Morgan & Co. New York [hereafter JPM] to Morgan Grenfell [hereafter MG], 23 Sep. 1922. On the

'Morgan group', see Carosso, V.P. 1987. *The Morgans: Private International Bankers 1854–1913*. Cambridge: Havard University Press; Burk, K. 1989. *Morgan Grenfell 1838–1988. The Biography of a Merchant Bank*. Oxford: Oxford University Press.

4 MG: Cable 22/4885, E.C. Grenfell, MG to JPM, 25 Sep. 1922.

5 See Leith Ross, F.W. 2009. Goode, Sir William Athelstane Meredith (1875–1944), rev. Brodie, M. *Oxford Dictionary of National Biography*. Available at: www.oxforddnb.com/view/article/33449 [accessed 23 Apr. 2009].

6 MG: Cable 22/2387, JPM to MG, 3 Oct.1922.

7 MG: Cable 22/4893, E.C. Grenfell, MG to JPM, 3 Oct. 1922.

8 Grenfell was not alone in holding such a view as the Dutch banker, ter Meulen, also considered that a loan 'could never be floated on League Plan'. See Bank of England, Historical Archive [hereafter BoE]: ADM 20/11, Norman's diary, 18 Oct. 1922.

9 MG: E.C. Grenfell, MG, to T. Lamont, JPM, 9 Oct. 1922.

10 BoE: ADM 20/11, Norman's diary, 6 and 12 Oct. 1922.

11 BoE: ADM 20/11, Norman's diary, 17 and 18 Oct. 1922.

12 Medlicott, W.N. and Dakin, D. eds. with Bennett, G. 1922. *Documents on British Foreign Policy 1919–1939* 1st series, 24, *Anglo-Italian Conversations June–July 1922; Central Europe and the Balkans, 1922–3; The Corfu Crisis 1923*. London: HMSO, 1983 [hereafter *DBFP*]; No. 179, Akers-Douglas (Vienna) to Curzon (FO), 6 Oct. 1922; No.188; and No. 188, Akers-Douglas (Vienna) to Curzon (FO), 20.x. 1922.

13 März, E. 1984. *Austrian Banking and Financial Policy. Creditanstalt at a Turning Point 1913–192*. Translated by C. Kessler. New York: St Martin's Press, pp. 495–6.

14 *DBFP*, 1st series, 24; No.186, Akers-Douglas (Vienna) to Curzon (FO), 24 Oct. 1922.

15 *DBFP*, 1st series, 24; No. 189, Akers-Douglas (Vienna) to Curzon (FO), 26 Oct. 1922.

16 *DBFP*, 1st series, 24; No. 197, Keeling (Vienna) to Curzon (FO), 10 Oct. 1922.

17 *DBFP*, 1st series, 24; No. 229, Curzon (FO) to Keeling (Vienna), 22.Oct. 1922.

18 *DBFP*, 1st series, 24; No. 214, Keeling (Vienna) to Curzon (FO), 30 Oct. 1922.

19 Jones, T., Middlemas, K. eds. 1969. *Whitehall Diary, I, 1916–1925*. London: Oxford University Press.

20 *DBFP*, 1st series, 24; No. 198, Keeling (Vienna) to Curzon (FO), 10 Nov. 1922 and n.10.

21 See Natmessnig, C. 1998. *Britische Finanzinteressen in Österreich. Studien zur Wirtschaftsgeschichte und Wirtschaftspolitik*, 5th ed. Vienna: Böhlau; Cottrell, P. L. 1983. Aspects of Western Equity Investment in the Banking Systems of East Central Europe, in A. Teichova and P.L. Cottrell, eds. *International Business and Central Europe, 1918–1939*. Leicester/New York: Leicester University Press/St Martins Press, pp. 316–21.

22 *DBFP*, 1st series, 24; No. 191, Akers-Douglas (Vienna) to Curzon (FO), 29 Oct. 1922.

23 *DBFP*, 1st series, 24; No. 281, Keeling (Vienna) to Curzon (FO), 8 Dec. 1922.

24 *DBFP*, 1st series, 24; No. 255, Keeling (Vienna) to Curzon (FO), 21 Dec. 1922; and No. 226, Keeling (Vienna) to Curzon (FO), 21 Dec. 1922.

25 *DBFP*, 1st series, 24; No. 228, Curzon (FO) to Keeling (Vienna), 22 Dec.1922; and see also Nos. 230, 231, 232, 233.

26 *DBFP*, 1st series, 24; No. 219, Curzon (FO) to Hardinge (Paris), 12 Dec.1922.

27 *DBFP*, 1st series, 24; No. 191, Akers-Douglas (Vienna) to Curzon (FO), 29 Oct. 1922, and n.1.

28 See BoE: ADM, 20/11, Norman's diary, 26 and 30 Oct. 1922.

29 *DBFP*, 1st series, 24; No. 205, Curzon (FO) to Keeling (Vienna), 17 Nov. 1922, and n.1; and No. 206, Keeling (Vienna) to Curzon (FO), 17 Nov. 1922.

30 MG: Cable 22/4935, MG to JPM, 16 Nov. 1922.
31 MG: Cable 22/2442, JPM to MG, 18 Nov. 1922.
32 MG: Young (Vienna) to C. Whigham, MG, 30 Nov. 1922.
33 MG: C. Whigham, MG to Young (Vienna), 6 Dec. 1922.
34 MG: Cable 22/4937, MG to JPM, 17 Nov. 1922.
35 MG: Cable 22/243, JPM to MG for J.P. Morgan, 20 Nov. 1922.
36 *DBFP*, 1st series, 24; No. 208, Curzon (FO) to Marling (The Hague), 21 Nov. 1922.
37 *DBFP*, 1st series, 24; No. 208, Curzon (FO) to Marling (The Hague), 21 Nov. 1922.
38 *DBFP*, 1st series, 24; No. 223, Keeling (Vienna) to Curzon (FO), 19 Dec. 1922.
39 MG: Whigham, MG to Young (Vienna), 22 Dec. 1922.
40 MG: Young (Vienna) to Whigham, MG, 27 Dec. 1922.
41 MG: MG to Young (Vienna), 1 Jan. 1923.
42 MG: Whigham, MG to Young (Vienna), 1 Jan. 1923.
43 MG: B. Schröder to E.C. Grenfell, MG, 10 Jan. 1923; see Cottrell, P.L. 1994. 'Mushrooms and Dinosaurs': Sieghart and the Boden-Credit-Anstalt during the 1920s, in A. Teichova, T. Gourvish and A. Pogány, eds. *Universal Banking in the Twentieth Century*. Aldershot: Edward Elgar, pp. 159–62.
44 Johnson, E. ed. 1978. *The Collected Writings of J. M. Keynes*, 18, *Activities 1922–1932: The End of Reparations*. London: Macmillan for the Royal Economic Society [henceforth *CWJMK*], Melchior to Keynes, 2 Feb. 1923.
45 *DBFP*, 1st series, 24; No. 252, Curzon (FO) to Barclay (Stockholm), 16 Jan. 1923.
46 MG: Cable 23/4512, MG to JPM, 16 Jan. 1923; and Cable 23/4513, MG to JPM, 17 Jan. 1923.
47 MG: Cable 23/2012, JPM to MG, 18 Jan. 1923.
48 MG: Cable 23/2013, J.P. Morgan (JPM) to MG, 18 Jan. 1923.
49 MG: Whigham to E.C. Grenfell (Cannes), 18 Jan. 1923.
50 MG: E.C. Grenfell (Cannes) to Whigham (MG), 18 Jan. 1923.
51 MG: Whigham, MG to E.C. Grenfell (Cannes), 22 Jan. 1923.
52 *DBFP*, 1st series, 24; No. 262, Phillpotts (Paris) to Akers-Douglas (Vienna), 31 Jan. 1923.
53 *DBFP*, 1st series, 24; No. 264, Phillpotts (Paris) to Akers-Douglas (Vienna), 2 Feb. 1923.
54 MG: Cable 23/3423, MG to JPM, 5 Feb. 1923.
55 MG: Cable 23/2023, JPM to MG, 6 Feb. 1923.
56 MG: E.C. Grenfell (MG) to Norman, 14 Feb. 1923; Cable 23/4528, MG to JPM, 14 Feb. 1923; and Cable 23/2026, JPM to MG, 16 Feb. 1923.
57 MG: Cable [copy] Norman to Geneva, 15 Feb. 1923.
58 MG: Cable 23/4533, MG to JPM, 1 Mar. 1923; and E.C. Grenfell (MG) to T. Lamont (JPM), 20 Mar. 1923.
59 *DBFP*, 1st series, 24; No. 277, Curzon (FO) to Geddes (Washington), 19 Feb. 1923.
60 MG: T. Lamont, JPM to E.C. Grenfell, MG, 9 Mar. 1923.
61 MG: T. Lamont, JPM to E.C. Grenfell, MG, 10 Mar.1923.
62 *DBFP*, 1st series, 24; No. 281, Niemeyer (Treasury) to Lampson (FO), 23 Feb. 1923.
63 *DBFP*, 1st series, 24; No. 281, Niemeyer (Treasury) to Lampson (FO), 23 Feb. 1923.
64 *DBFP*, 1st series, 24; No. 295, Curzon (FO) to Crewe (Paris), 12 Mar. 1923.
65 MG: E.C. Grenfell, MG to T. Lamont, JPM, 22 Mar. 1923; E.C. Grenfell, MG to T. Lamont, JPM, 26 Mar. 1923; and Cable 23/4549, MG to JPM, 20 Mar. 1923.

66 MG: Cable 23/2020, JPM to MG, 21 Mar. 1923.
67 MG: Cable 23/2074, JPM to MG, 13 Apr. 1923.
68 MG: Cable 23/4579, MG to JPM, 17 Apr. 1923.
69 *DBFP*, 1st series, 24; No. 314, Curzon (FO) to Keeling (Vienna), 6 Apr. 1923.
70 *DBFP*, 1st series, 24; No. 317, Keeling (Vienna) to Curzon (FO), 6 Apr. 1923.
71 *DBFP*, 1st series, 24; No. 321, Akers-Douglas (Vienna) to Curzon (FO), 10 Apr. 1923.
72 *DBFP*, 1st series, 24; No. 328, Akers-Douglas (Vienna) to Curzon (FO), 13 Apr. 1923.
73 *DBFP*, 1st series, 24; No. 342, Akers-Douglas (Vienna) to Curzon (FO), 20 Apr. 1923.
74 *DBFP*, 1st series, 24; No. 332, London (Geneva) to Curzon (FO), 17 Apr. 1923.
75 *DBFP*, 1st series, 24; No. 343, Comments by Tufton (Geneva), 24 Apr. 1923.
76 *DBFP*, 1st series, 24; No. 346, Curzon (FO) to Graham (Rome), 25 Apr. 1923 and n.10.
77 *DBFP*, 1st series, 24; No. 361, Akers-Douglas (Vienna) to Curzon (FO), 7 May 1923; and see also No. 364, Curzon (FO) to Akers-Douglas (Vienna), 9 May 1923.
78 *DBFP*, 1st series, 24; No. 370, Akers-Douglas (Vienna) to Curzon (FO), 11 May 1923; No. 371, Curzon (FO) to Graham (Rome), 12 May 1923; and No. 372, Akers-Douglas (Vienna) to Curzon (FO), 14 May 1923.
79 *DBFP*, 1st series, 24; No. 377, Curzon (FO) to Graham (Rome), 15 May 1923.
80 *DBFP*, 1st series, 24; No. 385, Graham (Rome) to Curzon (FO), 18 May 1923 and n.6.
81 MG: Cable 82276, MG to JPM, 18 Apr. 1923.
82 MG: Cable 23/2078, JPM to MG, 19 Apr. 1923.
83 MG: Cable 23/4582, MG to JPM, 19 Apr. 1923.
84 MG: Cable 23/4585, MG to JPM, 21 Apr. 1923.
85 MG: Cable 23/2082, JPM to MG, 23 Apr. 1923.
86 MG: Cable 23/2083, JPM to MG, 24 Apr. 1923.
87 MG: Cable 23/4588, MG to JPM, 26 Apr. 1923.
88 MG: Cable 23/2087, JPM to MG, 27 Apr. 1923.
89 MG: Cable 23/2089, JPM to MG, 28 Apr. 1923.
90 MG: Cable [copy] 61.800, JPM to T. Lamont, Morgan Harjes, Paris [hereafter MH], 9 May 1923.
91 MG: Cable [copy] T. Lamont, MH to JPM, 6 May 1923.
92 MG: Cable [copy] Bank of England to P. Bark, Paris, 12 May 1923.
93 MG: Cable 82.294, T. Lamont, MH to JPM, 7 May 1923.
94 MG: Cable 23/4632, MG to JPM, 18 May 1923.
95 MG: Cable 82.307, T. Lamont, MH to JPM, 10 May 1923.
96 MG: Cable 23/2117, JPM to MG, 12 May 1923.
97 MG: Cable 23/2120, JPM to MG, 17 May 1923.
98 MG: Cable 23/2139, JPM to MG, 24 May 1923.
99 MG: Cable 23/4640, MG to JPM, 22 May 1923.
100 MG: Cable 23/4629, MG to JPM, 17 May 1923.
101 MG: C. Whigham, MG to Lamont, 18 May 1923.
102 MG: Cable 23/2122, JPM to MG, 18 May 1923.
103 MG: Cable 23/2129, JPM to MG, 19 May 1923.
104 MG: Cable 61.830 [copy], JPM to T. Lamont, 19 May 1923.
105 MG: Cable 61.835 [copy], D. Morrow and T. Cochrane, JPM to T. Lamont, 22 May 1923.
106 MG: Cable 61.840 [copy], D. Morrow, T. Cochrane and G. Whitney, JPM to T. Lamont (Paris).
107 MG: Cable 23/2126, J.P. Morgan (JPM) to MG, 19 May 1923.

108 MG: Cable 82.327, T. Lamont (Paris) to JPM, 22 May 1923.
109 MG: Cable 23/2128, JPM to MG, 19 May 1923.
110 MG: Cable 23/2136, JPM to MG, 24 May 1923.
111 MG: Cable 82.331, T. Lamont (Paris) to JPM, 24 May 1923.
112 MG: C. Whigham, MG to T. Lamont (Paris), 24 May 1923.
113 MG: Cable 23/4651, M.C. Norman to J.P. Morgan, JPM, 30 May 1923.
114 MG: Cable 23/4652, MG to JPM, 30 May 1923.
115 MG: Cable 23/2148, JPM to MG, 31 May 1923.
116 MG: Cable 61.841 [copy], JPM to T. Lamont (Paris), 23 May 1923.
117 MG: Cable G. F. (Rome) to T. Lamont (Paris), 23 May 1923.
118 MG: Cable 82.345, T. Lamont (Paris) to JPM, 26 May 1923.
119 MG: Cable 82.346, T. Lamont (Paris) to JPM, 26 May 1923.
120 MG: Cable 61.864, JPM to MH, 28 May 1923.
121 MG: Cable 82.348, T. Lamont (Paris) to JPM, 28 May 1923.
122 MG: Cable 23/4667, MG to JPM, 2. Jun. 1923.
123 MG: T. Lamont (London) to Zimmerman (London), 1 Jun. 1923.
124 MG: Cable 23/2169, JPM to MG, 5 Jun. 1923.
125 MG: Cable 23/4675, MG to JPM, 5 Jun. 1923.
126 MG: Cable 23/4685, MG to JPM, 7 Jun. 1923.
127 MG: Cable 23/2187, JPM to MG, 8 Jun. 1923.
128 MG: Cable 23/4694, MG to JPM, 8 Jun. 1923; and 23/4695, MG to JPM, 8 Jun. 1923.
129 MG: Cable 23/4693, MG to JPM, 8 Jun. 1923.
130 MG: Cable 23/2192, D. Morrow and T. Cochrane, JPM to T. Lamont or E.C. Grenfell, MG, 9 Jun. 1923.
131 MG: Cable 23/4700, MG to JPM, 11 Jun. 1923.
132 MG: Cable 23/4699, M. Norman to J.P. Morgan, 11 Jun. 1923.
133 MG: Cable 23/4701, T. Lamont, MG to JPM, 11 Jun. 1923.
134 MG: Cable 23/2200, JPM to T. Lamont, MG, 11 Jun. 1923.
135 MG: Cable 23/2211, JPM to T. Lamont, MG, 13 Jun. 1923.
136 MG: Cable 23/2201, J.P. Morgan, JPM to M. C. Norman, 11 Jun. 1923.
137 *CWJMK*, 18, 'The Austrian Loan and Preparations in South-Eastern Europe', *The Nation and Athenaeum*, 16 Jun. 1923, pp. 176–7.
138 *DBFP*, 1st series, 24; No. 430, Akers-Douglas (Vienna) to Curzon (FO), 15 Jun. 1923.
139 *DBFP*, 1st series, 24; No. 458, Akers-Douglas (Vienna) to Curzon (FO), 28 Jun. 1923.
140 MG: Cable, ter Meulen (Amsterdam) to Whigham, MG, 16 Jun. 1923.
141 MG: Cable, T. Lamont (MG) to F.D.U. (Geneva), 11 Jun. 1923; and Cable, Lamont to Giofumi (Rome), 11 Jun. 1923.
142 MG: Cable 23/4763, MG to JPM, 30 Jun. 1923.
143 MG: Cable 23/4706, MG to JPM, 11 Jun. 1923.
144 MG: S.V. Baevenklaii (Vienna) to MG, 21 Jul. 1923.
145 MG: Frankenstein, Nixon and Bark (Paris) to MG, 28 Jul. 1923.
146 MG: Cable 82.373, MH to JPM, 14 Jun. 1923.
147 MG: Cable 61.899, JPM to MH, 20 Jun. 1923.
148 MG: Cable 82.382, H. H. Harjes, MH to JPM, 20 Jun. 1923.
149 MG: Cable 61.891 [copy], JPM to MH, 15 Jun. 1923.
150 MG: Cable [copy] Frankenstein, Bark and Nixon (Paris) to Norman for Niemeyer (London), 28 Jul. 1923.
151 MG: MG to Austrian Loan Commission, 11 Aug. 1923.
152 MG: Cable 82.471, A.M. Anderson (Paris) to JPM, 4 Aug. 1923.
153 MG: Cable 23/4812, MG to JPM, 8 Aug. 1923.
154 MG: Cable 23/2331, JPM to MG, 10 Aug. 1923; Frankenstein and Bark to MG, 10 Aug. 1923.

155 MG: Cable 23/4817, C. Whigham, MG to JPM, 10 Aug. 1923.
156 MG: Cable 62.004, JPM to A. M. Anderson (Paris), 18 Aug. 1923.
157 MG: Cable 1588, A. M. Anderson, MH to MG, 21 Aug. 1923.
158 MG: Cable 82.514, MH to JPM, 31 Aug. 1923; Cable 62.022 [copy], JPM to MH, 1 Nov. 1923; and Cable 82.519, MH to JPM, 3 Oct. 1923.
159 MG: Cable 82.564, MH to JPM, 15 Oct. 1923.
160 MG: Cable 23.4895, MG to JPM, 24 Oct. 1923; and Letter [diary abstract], Bark to MG, 28 Nov. 1923.
161 MG: Bark (Madrid) to Norman, 4 Dec. 1923.
162 MG: Letter [incomplete], Bark (Madrid) to Norman, 6 Dec. 1923.
163 MG: Cable 82.651, MH to JPM, 15 Dec. 1923.
164 MG: Cable 23/4960, MG to JPM, 18 Dec. 1923.
165 MG: Letter [diary abstract], Austrian Finance Ministry to MG, 30 Dec. 1923.
166 MG: Cable 23/4975, MG to JPM, 27 Dec. 1923.
167 MG: Cable 23/4976, C. Whigham, MG to T. Lamont, JPM, 27 Dec. 1923.
168 MG: Cable 23/2497, JPM to MG, 28 Dec. 1923.
169 MG: Letter [diary abstract], Zimmerman to JPM, 18 Dec. 1923.
170 van Walré de Bordes, J. 1924. *The Austrian Crown. Its Depreciation and Stabilization*. London: P.S. King & Son, pp. 132–9.
171 van Walré de Bordes (1924), pp. 97, 101.
172 See Cottrell, P.L. 1997. Norman, Strakosch and the Development of Central Banking: From Conception to Practice, 1919–1924, in P.L. Cottrell, ed. *Rebuilding the Financial System in Central and Eastern Europe, 1918–1994*. Aldershot: Scholar Press.
173 BoE: OV37/21, Strakosch to Clegg, 24 Oct. 1924.

7 Why were there no investment trusts in Germany?

An analysis of an anomaly in the German financial industry from 1870 to 1957

Martin L. Müller

One of the major financial innovations in the 19th century was the investment fund. The basic idea was that the potential returns on investments could be substantially increased and the risk reduced if many small investors combined to make a joint capital investment. This facilitated an investment system that was otherwise only available to large-scale investors.[1] Risk diversification was guaranteed by the purchase of many different securities, while a higher return was feasible because the reduced risk meant that there was no need to restrict purchases to government bonds that were regarded as safe. Higher-yield industrial bonds and especially equities could also be included in the portfolio. The investment fund obtained its investible cash by issuing shares or certificates and usually reinvested them on a broadly diversified basis in listed securities. This diversification was achieved not only by investing in shares and bonds, but also through a portfolio mix with respect to the industries and countries invested in. By watching the market closely, the investment fund could sell securities in receptive markets and buy them when prices were falling. It could buy in large quantities, subscribe new issues and hold them until they turned in a profit. It could make arbitrage profits if, for technical reasons, securities prices differed between New York and, for example, London. In all respects the fund was in a better strategic position than the simple capital investor acting alone.[2]

From the mid-19th century onwards, the first investment funds to work on the principle described above were set up in Belgium, France, Switzerland, Great Britain and the USA. In Germany, on the other hand, investment funds did not establish a permanent footing until a decade after the Second World War. Given the clear advantages of the collective investment idea, it is astonishing that the German capital market, already highly developed before the First World War, did not adopt this innovation. This paper seeks to answer the question of why investment fund companies were so late in becoming established in Germany compared with its Western European neighbours and the US.

In the search for answers, the special situation of Germany's big banks was noted early on. In 1910 an observer of the English and German capital markets explained the absence of investment funds in Germany by the fact that:

> The management of private capital investment lies solely in the hands of banks and bankers. The latter have taken on the task of supplying the public with investment securities and advising them on which ones to choose. They inform large and small capitalists about all suitable securities and enable them to make an objective capital investment following the principle of risk distribution.[3]

Since the big banks had third-party shares in their own portfolios in many cases, for a long period they could also be regarded as investment funds of a kind themselves. As a popular textbook put it, a shareholder buying shares in Deutsche Bank 'was also buying an indirect interest in the fate of a whole row of other companies'.[4]

The question as to whether the big German banks' business model was the only reason for the delayed establishment of investment funds, or whether other factors, such as the capital market regime or the legal situation, had an important influence requires detailed consideration. First of all, the development of this type of company outside Germany will be outlined in order to provide a background with which Germany's 'special path' can be contrasted.

The first precursors in Belgium, France and Switzerland

Belgium's Société Générale, founded in 1822 in Brussels and which also became the prototype of the universal bank, is regarded as the earliest precursor of today's investment fund companies. It was not only authorized to discount bills and securities, to issue banknotes and conduct collection, current account, deposits, cash advance and loan business, it also performed a treasury function and served as financier to the state with its issuing business. Above all, though, its lending to the private sector became particularly important.[5] The new feature was that its advances were secured not against goods, but against securities. After Société Générale had acquired the first shareholdings in coal mines and metal-working companies because borrowers had defaulted and the shares given as security had changed hands, the bank began to build up its industrial shareholdings systematically and develop an investment strategy. Between 1835 and 1862, Société Générale acquired shares in 62 companies, most of them new ones. As a rule, the bank took only a minority stake. It did not seek to influence the companies' business policy. Due to Société Générale's brisk business in company formation and the acquisition of substantial share packages for its own portfolio, Belgium became the country in which the financing of early industry was most strongly supported by the banks.[6]

Société Générale even went a step further by setting up subsidiaries, which already had features typical of the separate or special funds of modern fund management companies. Société de Commerce de Bruxelles, for example, developed into an investment fund company with the coal sector as its main field of activity. Another subsidiary, Société Nationale pour Entreprises

Industrielles et Commerciales, was originally conceived as a general industrial investment company, but then, to distinguish it from Société de Commerce, it operated in all sectors except mining. The third subsidiary, Société des Capitalistes réunis dans un But de Mutualité Industrielle, was expected to attract funds from new investors to support the parent company's industrial financing activities. It was hoped, for example, that savings bank customers would invest part of their savings in Mutualité shares. In the long run, though, none of these subsidiaries was able to fulfil expectations. Société de Commerce and Société Nationale were taken over by the parent company in 1849, and Mutualité was wound up in 1873.

Generally speaking, Crédit Mobilier, founded in 1852 in the France of Napoleon III, is also regarded as a precursor of later investment trusts. This bank's business model not only focused on deposit-taking and lending to railway companies and industrial firms, but also included the issuance of the bank's own bonds. The proceeds from this issuing activity were to be used to purchase public-sector bonds, as well as railway and industrial shares as investment securities. Price fluctuations were to be balanced out through broad dispersion. Securing the bonds with mobile assets – in contrast to Crédit Foncier's mortgage bond issues, which were secured by mortgages on immobile real estate – was also the reason why the bank was named Crédit Mobilier. This business model did not, however, enjoy lasting success. Having almost gone bankrupt in 1867, the bank subsequently led a mere shadow existence, serving primarily to settle previous transactions.[7] Despite this early precursor, investment trusts did not establish a permanent footing in France until the beginning of the 1930s. The basis was created by tax privileges, the scope of which was broadened after the end of the Second World War.

While Société Générale and Crédit Mobilier had only engaged in the investment fund business as one of several business lines, pure capital investment companies emerged in Switzerland in the middle of the 19th century and can be regarded as direct forerunners of today's fund management companies. In 1849 three Genevan banking firms founded a joint stock corporation named Omnium, Société Civile Génèvoise d'emploi de Fonds.[8] Its object was the purchase and sale of public-sector bonds, industrial bonds and shares traded at the principal centres in Europe and America. In 1883 the company had a diversified portfolio worth 4.2 million Swiss francs. This capital was invested in English, Turkish and Serbian government securities, in shares of Banque de Prêts et Dépots in Geneva, the Swiss Railway Bank, the North East Railway, Société Générale, the Corinth Canal, the gas companies in Marseille, Naples and Vienna as well as the Rio Tinto mines. While the traces of these first Swiss capital investment companies disappear at the end of the 19th century, other companies were founded from 1872 onwards, especially in Geneva, such as Association Financière de Génève, which subsequently became part of Union Financière de Génève. Banque des Fonds d'Etat and Société Financière Franco-Suisse were also established there. All these companies, soon to be joined by others, were stock corporations, which primarily purchased government and municipal bonds as well as railway companies' shares and bonds.

The first investment trusts in Great Britain and the USA

The above-mentioned companies in Belgium, France and Switzerland had certain features in common with modern fund management companies, but did not cause a general breakthrough for this form of company. The idea only gained broader currency with the so-called investment trusts founded from 1860 onwards in Scotland and England.[9]

The British investment trusts emerged at a time when the domestic capital market featured a general capital saturation. A clear sign of this was that first-class English government bonds, though bearing a coupon of only 3 per cent, were trading on the stock exchange at 114 per cent, a very high level. British industry, financed to a large extent with retained profits, and the colonies, which only made modest capital demands on the mother country, offered no investment alternatives. Much more attractive to the British investors were bonds of other states and the frequently issued bonds of European and American railway companies promising returns of 5, 6 or more per cent.

These investments entailed a much higher risk than domestic government bonds. Small investors could not limit the risk of loss in the way that wealthy investors could by broadly diversifying their investments. They therefore began to organize themselves on the basis of mutuality and combine their capital to spread the risk between them in a mix of investments. They chose the legal form of a trust. This special fiduciary structure was deeply rooted in the old English legal system, but unknown in countries with a Roman law tradition. In medieval England, it originally referred to the transfer of property to a trustee, who had to pass on the revenue obtained from it to the original owner or to another beneficiary. Towards the end of the 17th century, a practice arose under common law by which all assets could be transferred to a trustee without the latter becoming the owner in legal terms. The first investment trusts worked on this principle, with several people being appointed trustees. A certain amount of capital was placed at their disposal subject to the stipulations set out in the trust agreement as to how the capital should be managed. The investors received a certificate for the capital they contributed and a corresponding share of the revenue from the purchased securities.

These first British investment trusts featured all the important characteristics of the present-day companies. The founding prospectus of the Foreign and Colonial Government Trust, formed in 1868, described the company's objective as being 'to give the investor of moderate means the same advantage as large capitalists in diminishing the risk of investing in foreign and colonial Government stocks, by spreading the investment over a number of different stocks'.[10]

The first investment trust in Great Britain can be traced back to 1860 when the Scottish-American Investment Company appeared on a London price list.

It had invested its capital of £2 million in American securities. The company was based on the close ties between Scotland and the American stock market, with transactions very often taking place directly, without the intermediation of the London market.

The year 1864 saw the formation of the Mining Shares Investment Company, which apparently specialized in the many domestic and foreign mining shares traded on the London Stock Exchange. Ten more companies were set up between 1860 and 1875. The following one and a half decades saw British investment trusts multiply at an increasing pace. Ten new ones were founded in 1888 and 15 the year after.

It is interesting to note that the initiative to set up the early investment trusts came not from established lenders, but from the potential investors/savers themselves. The new company form was not conceived in the City of London, but in Scottish provincial cities. The local petty bourgeois population, including ship owners, jute traders, small manufacturers, oil traders and high sea fishermen, was the breeding ground for the first investment trust entrepreneurs.

The legal form of trust was gradually replaced by that of a limited company, i.e. a corporation. Nevertheless, most companies retained in their names the word trust, which is particularly confidence building in English. Since 1870, new investment fund companies have only been set up as limited companies. They offered not only the advantage of restricting the scope of action of the company's director, but also gave the companies the possibility of issuing debentures.

The phase of rapid growth and brisk foundation activity of British investment trusts ended abruptly with the stock exchange crisis in 1890, precipitated by the inability of London banking house Baring Brothers to meet its payment obligations. As it turned out, the investment trusts had played a part in the speculative overheating of stock market prices since 1888. When fund companies' returns fell as prices rose, many a fund company director tried to find new sources of income by buying and selling securities on a larger scale. A further point was that the investment trusts had entered the issuing business on a substantial scale and taken securities from new issues into their portfolios, which promised stronger price gains, but carried higher risk.

In this respect the Baring crisis had a cathartic effect, in that after 1890 the investment trusts reverted to their original solid principles and left the business of securities issuance and lending against securities to specialized financing companies.

The second wave of new investment trusts in Great Britain came after the First World War. Fifty-four new companies were set up between 1922 and the start of the Great Depression in 1929. These companies did not differ from their predecessors either in terms of legal form or with regard to capital sourcing or capital investment, but now the country's big insurance companies and private banks – individually or combined in syndicates – were the founders and capital providers.

The new companies set up in the twenties included a number of firms, which invested primarily in German securities owing to the German economy's extremely strong demand for capital and the resulting high interest rate level. Big German banks also had stakes in these firms, such as the Reichs-Kredit-Gesellschaft, Preussische Staatsbank (Seehandlung), Berliner Handels-Gesellschaft and Deutsche Bank,[11] which were among the co-founders of the British & German Trust in London in 1926. On the English side, a stake was held by the banking house Herbert, Wagg & Co. The Trust's equity capital was £1 million. Furthermore, 5 per cent debentures were issued for £750,000 in Great Britain. The big German banks took on this exposure for reasons connected with their home market. With the help of the British & German Trust, they were able to provide their currency loans to their small and medium-sized corporate customers, who had no access to the international capital markets. Deutsche Bank, for example, was able to obtain Sterling loans from the Trust for at least 18 small and medium-sized firms from 1926 onwards. Aktienbrauerei Schönbusch in Königsberg, for instance, received a mortgage-backed loan for £35,000 with interest at 7.5 per cent per annum and repayable until the end of 1941.[12] In 1928, the British & German Trust's shareholdings in and mortgage loans to German firms amounted to RM31 million.[13] With the onset of foreign exchange controls in Germany in the summer of 1931, the Trust's new business dried up completely. The settlement of the loans, however, was to occupy those involved for a long time to come.

Given the reasons why investment trusts came into being in Great Britain – interest in capital investment and resulting capital export – it is not surprising that investment fund companies did not emerge on a broad front in the USA until the country changed from debtor into the most important creditor of the world economy during the First World War.

The first precursors date back, however, to the beginning of the 19th century when it was above all insurance companies that engaged in mutual fund business as a sideline. The development of the mutual fund concept was hampered not only by the lack of capital that was typical of the American market, but also the absence of selling methods and investors' preference for mortgage bonds. The era of the American companies began parallel to the second wave of new British investment trusts in the twenties. Besides American capital exports, a statutory measure, the so-called Edge Act of 1919, was a major factor behind their success. With this Federal act, the USA opened the door for American banks to engage in national interstate banking and international business. Since it was now also expressly permitted to buy foreign bonds for institutional investment purposes, the Edge Act can be described as the statutory acknowledgement of the idea of investment fund saving and the fund management company.

That this new situation did not lead directly to the foundation of investment trusts had cyclical reasons above all. In 1920, the USA, which had emerged from the First World War as the world's leading economic nation, experienced an economic crisis that lasted until July 1921. With the subsequent economic recovery, which led into a growth phase spanning almost a decade, there was a genuine boom in the formation of new fund management companies in the US. In 1926, there were already 160 investment trusts, and a further 141 were set up in 1927 alone. These figures were exceeded again in 1928 and 1929. At the end of 1929, about USD 7 billion were invested in roughly 500 American companies.

But the more the companies profited from the stock market boom in the years from 1927 to 1929, the harder they were hit by the great crash in October 1929. The American trusts now experienced their Baring crisis. The prices of investment trust shares fell far more strongly than the average of the shares traded in New York.[14] Several smaller trusts collapsed, and larger ones also suffered losses to such an extent that no dividends could be paid. A further point was that as prices rose, the propensity to speculate had steadily increased, and companies with a questionable reputation had arisen and sold their shares using advertising methods, as Alfred Lansburgh, editor of the financial magazine *Die Bank*, criticized in May 1930, similar 'to those that were used to sell cameras or soap powder'.[15]

A direct consequence of the great crash was the establishment of the Securities and Exchange Commission (SEC) in 1934. One of the important results of SEC's analysis of the crisis was the Investment Company Act of 1940, which created the formal and material foundations for investment fund saving from that date onwards in the United States of America. This Act also had a strong influence on German legislation concerning investment fund companies that finally came about in 1957 after a long period of gestation.

The beginnings of investment fund saving in Germany

Just at the time when the investment fund idea was being discussed in Germany in financial circles and was slowly gaining popularity, it was affected by the collapse of the New York Stock Exchange and the subsequent crisis at many American investment trusts. With the stock market and economic crisis that spread from the USA to Germany; in 1930 all chances were lost of setting up investment fund companies in Germany in the foreseeable future. In times of collapsing stock exchange prices, troubled big banks and industrial companies that no longer found any buyers for their products, the creation of companies devoted to securities investment for a broad retail public was out of the question.

An additional problem impeding the development of special investment fund companies in Germany was the dominant position of the big universal banks, which had developed since the middle of the 19th century. Together with the leading private banks, these big banks not only controlled the issuance of bonds and equities, they also had wealthy investors among their customers to whom many of the securities launched on the capital market by the banks themselves could be sold. 'Whoever wishes to buy or sell securities approaches a bank or a private banker', is the simple statement made in

Georg Obst's handbook on money, banking and the stock market, which appeared in several editions before the First World War.[16]

A letter from Max Steinthal, member of Deutsche Bank's management board, to Wilhelm Bode, Director of the Kaiser Friedrich Museum in 1905 shows what securities advice from a banker looked like:

> In accordance with your instructions, I have sold your M. 15,000 4 per cent Russian Bond of 1902 at today's price of 88.10 per cent [...]. To quote to you an investment where with some certainty you could recoup your loss of M. 1,500 is not so easy. You could perhaps buy some Elektrische Licht- und Kraft shares, whose price is today at 130 per cent, and which is in the process of realizing older stocks at a large profit.[17]

This form of intensive securities advisory by banks, which profited from their know-how as issuing institutions and financiers to industry, left investment fund companies no room to develop their activities.

The banks also offered a custody service for the purchased securities in a securities account where they were not only safely stored, but also managed at the same time. That means that the banks took care of the redemption of interest and dividend coupons and credited the proceeds to the securities account customer's account. To protect securities clients, a separate Securities Account Act had come into force in 1896, defining the duties of banks in connection with the custody of third-party securities.

Over and above this closed circle from production to sales to the custody of securities by the universal bank, the big banks, following the model of Belgium's Société Générale and Crédit Mobilier, had created their own investment companies devoted to the foundation of and holding of equity interests in industrial companies, and which can be regarded as precursors of present-day investment fund companies. Critics talked of 'new companies to set up new companies'.[18] In 1871, A. Schaaffhausen'scher Bankverein in Cologne, Prussia's oldest joint stock bank, had set up the Deutsche Aktiengesellschaft für Rheinisch-Westfälische Industrie together with a small group of investors. It was partly a financing company, partly an investment company. It focused on mining and the cement industry on the Rhine and Ruhr. The company owned, for example, all shares in the Aktiengesellschaft für Rheinisch-Westfälische Cementindustrie and the Blankenburg coal mine on the Ruhr. Besides this clearly entrepreneurial commitment, the company also transacted purely financial investments in a number of joint stock companies.[19] The firms and corporate shares purchased were always held by the company for a longer period. At favourable moments, however, it often sold its equity shareholdings in order to purchase others later on. Owing to this business strategy, its revenues fluctuated substantially. Years with no dividend were followed by years with 19 per cent, and a dividend of no less than 40 per cent was paid in 1906. Although the company's shares were traded at various German stock exchanges, it did not develop into a retail company, but remained largely in the hands of a number of Rheinisch banks.[20] In 1921, these banks decided to liquidate the company, which had been affected by war and the incipient inflation.

A second and similarly structured company, the Bergisch-Märkische Industrie-Gesellschaft, was also set up in 1871 by a leading regional bank, Barmer Bankverein. The object of the company was to 'promote industry and building activity, establish industrial companies and acquire equity shareholdings in such companies as limited partner or silent partner, and to purchase and develop building land'.[21] For the most part, the company's capital was invested in industrial companies. This principal objective, however, was in the foreground only in the early days of Bergisch-Märkische Industrie-Gesellschaft. In 1897, Deutsche Bank and Bergisch Märkische Bank, closely linked with Deutsche Bank in a community of interests, took equity stakes in the company. Henceforth, the company was used primarily to subscribe securities of the companies set up by the two banks. In the decades before the First World War, the dividends obtained lay between 3.5 and 7.5 per cent. In 1911, Bergisch-Märkische Industrie-Gesellschaft suffered a substantial setback due to the spectacular collapse of Berliner Terrain- und Bau-A.G., precipitated by the strong fall in prices on the Berlin property market. Owing to the necessary depreciation, the company was for the first time unable to pay a dividend.[22] After recovering again in the meantime, the company led a shadow existence after hyperinflation, and was dissolved in 1939 due to the lack of assets.[23]

Aktiengesellschaft für Rheinisch-Westfälische Industrie and Bergisch-Märkische Industrie-Gesellschaft remained the only companies of this kind in Germany until the mid-1890s. It was only with the strong upswing in the years before the turn of the century that similar companies came into being, developing, however, into financing companies and specialized banks, such as Aktiengesellschaft für Montanindustrie and Bank für Bergbau und Industrie, as well as Bank für Orientalische Eisenbahnen and Bank für elektrische Unternehmungen at European level. These two big financing companies, domiciled in Zurich, were owned by multinational bank syndicates, in each of which Deutsche Bank had a leading position. After the First World War, specialized institutions such as Kinobank and Automobilbank were founded.

Another such specialized institution was Bank für Industriewerte, set up in 1919 by leading big banks and private banks.[24] Its original object was to purchase industrial shares to support the market after the collapse of the German Empire. After this direct mandate had been completed, the bank could have constituted the solid core of an investment company, but it was assigned to other tasks by its principal shareholders. It purchased from a number of industrial companies preferred shares with a simple and in some cases multiple voting right, with a commitment to keep these equities in its possession for an agreed period. The idea was to prevent the sell-out of German shares to foreign buyers during the period of inflation.[25] The bank ultimately developed into a pure holding company for the big banks' industrial shares.

In no case, however, did the aforementioned investment companies develop into firms with a broadly dispersed capital base. They remained owned and controlled by separately formed syndicates that bundled special risks in these companies. They could therefore take investment risks in securities of specific industries or regions showing excessive volatility of the parent companies' balance sheets and were still able to participate in the partially above-average revenues. This business model ended with the First World War and the subsequent collapse of the German currency. Private initiatives by investors, which in Great Britain had led to the emergence of the first investment trusts, were not apparent in the German Empire. It would appear that investors had sufficient alternatives to the low-yield Prussian and Imperial bonds, including equities, industrial bonds and a large number of foreign bonds of public sector and private issuers.[26]

It was only under completely new capital market conditions that the first genuine investment company was set up in 1923 in Königs Wusterhausen in Brandenburg. Zickert'scher Kapitalverein (Zickert's Capital Association), renamed Deutscher Kapitalverein (German Capital Association) in 1928, and re-domiciled to Berlin, had certain features in common with the early British investment trusts.[27] Like them, it was set up far from the financial centre and with no participation by the leading banks. The founder was Hermann Zickert, a business journalist, who gave his name to the company. As editor of the *Berliner Tageblatt* and later as publisher of the financial magazine *Wirtschaftlicher Ratgeber* (Economic Advisor), he was very familiar with stock market and financial events and developments. His book *Die acht Gebote der Finanzkunst* (The Eight Commandments of the Art of Finance), published in 1924, went through several editions and was a practical guide to investment in securities.[28] In setting up the Capital Association, Zickert switched from theory to practice. The sole object of the Association was 'the joint fiduciary investment and administration of assets provided by the members of the Association'.[29] These assets could consist of cash or securities marketable on a stock exchange. Every member had a share in the joint assets in accordance with his contributed share. In the financial years 1927 and 1928, the Association paid a dividend of more than 8 per cent on its invested capital. At the end of 1928, it had 1,532 members and managed assets of RM 2.95 million.[30] In accordance with its articles of association, the Association was obliged to invest the joint assets primarily in securities listed on a stock exchange. In practice, Capital Association invested solely in equities, most of them traded on the Berlin Stock Exchange. Towards the end of the 1920s, however, it tried to reduce risk not only by investing in various industries, but also through geographical diversification. To an increasing extent, foreign shares were purchased at the trading centres in London, New York and Amsterdam.

Since Hermann Zickert had chosen the form of association without legal capacity for his Capital Association, the latter was exempted from corporation tax. Later on, the Association was also granted exemption from wealth tax. The disadvantage of this legal form, however, was that the Association was not a legal person. The issued shares were therefore almost untradeable, both legally and in practice. There were also no control possibilities, for example of the kind open to the supervisory board of a stock corporation. The Association worked solely on the basis of personal confidence in the founding chairman. This confidence was severely shaken by the collapse of the Berlin banking house Siegfried Brann, to which the Capital Association had a substantial exposure. In addition, there were the strong price falls due to the great crash in autumn 1929. The change to Deutscher Investment-Verein GmbH was therefore resolved at the general meeting of the Capital Association in March 1930. This cooperative had a three-man management board and a supervisory board and joined the Audit Association (Revisionsverband).[31] With the world economic crisis intensifying and prices continuing to fall, however, this transformation could not protect the company from collapse. It went into liquidation in 1931.

In contrast to Zickert's Capital Association, which at times generated substantial publicity, Bayerische Investment AG, founded in Munich in 1926, attracted little public attention. The conditions surrounding its start-up were relatively favourable, with the company receiving 25 per cent paid-up equity capital of RM 1 million.[32] Its founders were primarily lawyers and economic advisors from Munich. Although the company had adopted the object of capital investment along the lines of the English and American investment trusts, it devoted itself initially to loan brokerage in order to postpone its investment activity until its tax situation could be clarified. In fact, the Reichsfinanzhof (German Tax Court) determined in March 1930 that the certificate holders in total did not constitute an association of persons, but a material association with gainful objectives, from which it followed that it was exempted from company and securities tax, and that tax was deductible from capital income.[33] Bayerische Investment AG saw in these tax privileges an opportunity to promote investment fund saving, as a result of which it deleted the request for liquidation from the agenda of its general meeting on 25 April 1930.[34] Nevertheless, it went into liquidation two years later. After this sobering experience, it was noted at that time that 'the economic conditions in Germany in connection with the world crisis' showed 'that at the present time it was not possible, despite all the indisputable advantages, to introduce the investment fund concept in practice in Germany'.[35] With that, the second attempt to establish an investment fund company in the years of the Weimar Republic had also failed.

There is no doubt that the effects of the Great Depression were the main impediment to the emergence and establishment of investment fund companies in Germany at the beginning of the 1930s. Besides these cyclical obstacles, there were also structural hurdles, as already noted in connection with the two new companies described above. Tax law and company law in the period between the wars was extremely unfavourable for investment fund companies. In the form of corporation, the only feasible solution was that of a joint stock corporation, where profits were taxed at up to 50 per cent through the income and wealth tax of the German Reich, the regional states and the local councils. This was intolerable for an investment fund company, especially as its investors were subject to three-fold taxation: first at the company whose shares were owned by the investment company, second at the investment company itself, and third as the latter's shareholder.[36]

The world economic crisis induced parliament in the middle of 1930 to take a first step towards reducing the tax burden on investment fund companies. By law, the German parliament authorized the German government to ease the tax burden in order to facilitate and cheapen the supply of credit to the German economy. As a concrete measure, the text of the Act expressly referred to a tax reduction for domestic joint stock corporations which had 'the object of managing, purchasing and selling shares, mining shares, equity interests or participatory certificates of other investing companies, or of bonds in small quantities'.[37]

The political situation, however, impeded a rapid implementation of these regulations. On 18 July 1930, Paul von Hindenburg, President of the German Reich, dissolved the German parliament. But the hope of German Chancellor Brüning that he would broaden his parliamentary base in the forthcoming new elections was not fulfilled. The German parliament was almost incapable of acting. Many draft acts had been put on ice.

It was only with the Second Emergency Ordinance of the President of the German Reich to protect the economy and finances, dated 5 June 1931,[38] that the previously announced tax privilege for capital management companies was introduced. The taxation of these companies' revenues and assets with only one-tenth of the tax that would have been payable according to general taxation principles was undoubtedly an important step forward, especially as a similar reduction of trade tax was to be introduced. The aim of encouraging the foundation of investment fund companies was considered unrealistic, however, by observers at the time.[39]

Another factor also impeding the establishment of a successful investment fund company in the period between the wars was the high level of German capital market interest rates. With a real interest rate of no less than 8 per cent on domestic bonds and no less than 7 per cent on fixed-income paper placed abroad, organized capital management focusing on domestic equities was unattractive. Even with the low prices at the beginning of 1930, good German shares did not manage a dividend yield of more than 6 to 7 per cent.[40] Under conditions of chronic capital scarcity, the idea of saving in equities could not make any headway. It was not by chance that investment trusts had emerged in England when the interest rate level on English Treasury bonds had fallen to 3 per cent and investors were looking for higher-yielding, but still safe alternatives. This lack of investible capital remained basically predominant during the rest of the 1930s. It was one reason why, despite lively interest and the growing conviction in expert circles that investment fund companies had good prospects, especially in Germany,[41] there were no more serious attempts to set up investment fund companies until the early years after the Second World War.

After the National Socialists came to power, the unfavourable economic conditions were compounded by political reservations hampering the emergence of investment fund companies. The intense discussion among financial experts in the years between 1928 and 1932 about the introduction of investment fund companies in Germany came to a sudden end. An important factor here was that banks, stock exchanges and large corporations in general did not enjoy great popularity among those in power. Many of them dreamed of pre-modern times and had popular anti-Capitalist slogans such as 'breaking interest bondage' and the distinction between productive and hoarding capital in their standard repertoire. At a time when leading NSDAP[42] ideologists saw big banks as parasitical or at least dispensable, the formation of new institutions with capital investment as their sole object was out of the question. For the Nazi regime, the Great Depression had proved that the private market economy had failed and that the state must in future exercise greater control over economic activity and organize it to suit its needs. This led to interest rate control as well as restrictions on large loans and securities issues. An indirect consequence of this was that the capital market lost volume. It was no longer determined by supply and demand: the crucial factor was state demand for finance. During the war, this led to the almost complete displacement of private issuers' securities by Treasury notes of the German Reich. The full extent of the consequences of this capital market policy did not become apparent until after the war. A capital market no longer existed, and the currency was almost worthless. A new start depended on one thing: confidence in economic activity had to be restored by a currency reform.

Foundation of the first German fund management company

Though the basis for the resumption of regulated financial transactions was created with the currency reform of 1948, the formation of new investment companies modelled on English and American firms still looked a long way off. The material and psychological conditions in West Germany in 1948/49 differed clearly from those at the time when the British and American trusts came into being. These trusts had been set up in times of prosperity, not in times of shortage. The need among broad investor groups for investment opportunities offering higher returns and security had been the deciding factor. The discussion in West Germany, on the other hand, recommended the formation of investment fund companies to encourage saving and help preserve asset values in recent conditions of inflationary policy. There was no lack of suggestions. A kind of investment fund institution for shipping securities was proposed for the financing of shipbuilding, and the mining industry was interested in encouraging the propensity to save by issuing certificates intended to represent a mixed ownership of good equities.[43] None of these proposals came anywhere close to realization.

Largely unnoticed, however, a group of mainly Bavarian banks had joined forces to set up Germany's first post-war investment fund company at the end of 1949. This pioneering company received the name Allgemeine Deutsche Investment-Gesellschaft mbH (ADIG); its domicile was Munich. The legal structure chosen for ADIG was based on a Swiss model and, taking account of tax aspects, joint ownership. This means that the company's funds were jointly owned assets. Their certificates conferred co-ownership rights on bearers. The participating banks were Bayerische Staatsbank, Bayerische Hypotheken- und Wechsel-Bank, Bayerische Vereinsbank, the Munich banking house Seiler & Co. and Jüdische Industrie- und Handelsbank in Frankfurt am Main. Each of the founding companies subscribed a GmbH share of DM 100,000. While Jüdische Industrie- und Handelsbank withdrew from the consortium in 1950, other banks joined one by one.[44] Of the three big banks, however, only the successor institutions of Commerzbank participated in ADIG.

The fund management companies act

When the Fund Management Companies Act was enacted and subsequently came into force on 17 April 1957, the business of investment fund companies in Germany was finally regulated in law.[45] The legislator had tried repeatedly since 1930 to promote this type of company with tax privileges, but without success in conditions of world economic crisis. A further point was the political discrimination against the share in the years from 1933 onwards. In the following one and a half decades, the investment fund concept was practically defunct. The idea was revived with the foundation of ADIG and the legislator was induced to place investment fund saving on an orderly basis. The declared intention of the initiators of the act was 'to put broader sections of the population than hitherto – specifically from the working population – in a position to participate in raising the investment capital needed by the business community'.[46]

On 15 April 1953, the first draft act was put before the Federal German Parliament.[47] Many provisions of the *American Investment Company Act* of 1940 had found their way into it. However, it was not possible to pass the act before the end of the legislative period. Two years passed before Parliament resumed work on the project.

The driving force was August Neuburger, Member of Parliament for the CDU.[48] The lawyer and senior civil servant in the post-war government of Württemberg-Baden was a member of the Federal German Parliament from 1949 to 1961. As a well-known lawyer specializing in tax law, Neuburger was considered to be one of his party's financial experts. He was thought to have played a decisive part in the major tax reform of 1954. From 1949 to 1957, he was a member of the committees for fiscal and tax questions and for money and credit, and subsequently he was Chairman of the Fiscal Committee until he left the Federal Parliament.[49]

The original draft of the act was tabled once again in the Federal Parliament by Neuburger and the CDU/CSU[50] fraction with minor changes on 9 July 1955.[51] This was followed by intensive deliberations in the committees for money and credit, fiscal and tax questions, and for economic policy. At the beginning of 1957, the act passed through the Federal Parliament, and finally came into force after four years of consultation.

The success of the fund management companies was due primarily to the tax stipulations in the act. The exemption of first purchases and repurchases of the certificates from taxation under the Capital Transaction Tax Act placed investment fund saving on an equal footing with the direct purchase of securities. The tax discrimination of saving and securities, which for decades had impeded the establishment of fund management companies in Germany, was now removed. With the foundation in 1956 of their own fund management companies, the central institutions of the credit cooperatives (Union Investment[52]) as well as the successor institutions of Dresdner Bank (Deutscher Investment Trust[53]) and Deutsche Bank (Deutsche Gesellschaft für Wertpapiersparen[54]) had already anticipated the legal regulations. Together with ADIG, in existence since 1949, these four fund companies dominated the rapidly growing West German investment fund business. Roughly one decade after the Second World War, this finally ended an anomaly, which had existed for several decades in the German financial services system. In this respect as well, the Federal Republic had arrived in the West.

Conclusion

Unlike its Western European neighbour countries and the USA, investment fund companies were unable to get established in Germany until the years of the *economic miracle* came after the Second World War. In view of the high efficiency of the German capital market and the institutional differentiation of the financial sector in the German Empire, this is an astonishing fact, which needs explaining.

Crucial for the absence of fund management companies in the decades before the First World War was the dominant role of Germany's big banks in their specific form of universal bank. Their broadly diversified business model gave fund management companies no room to develop. The universal banks acted not only as the most important issuing houses for bonds and equities of public and private issuers, they also had the customers and the advisory competence to be able to sell large portions of their own securities issues and finally held and administered large parts of the securities held by customers in securities accounts set up specifically for this purpose.

It should also be kept in mind that the big banks not only became fund management companies of a kind themselves with large portfolios of shareholdings by acquiring interests in a large number of other companies through the purchase of their shares; they also set up companies whose sole object was to hold shares in other companies. These already had elements of today's fund management companies, but the broad diversification of these companies' capital was not the intention. They remained under the control of a small number of investors, for whom they fulfilled the function of bundling and risk transfer for their own industrial shareholding business, in which they were not dissimilar to today's hedge funds.

With no interest on the part of the big banks and apparently sufficient coverage for prospective investors, a development such as the United Kingdom had experienced did not materialize in the second half of the 19th century. There, the first investment trusts had emerged from the interest in investment among an affluent social class that was not prepared to accept the low returns on British Treasury bonds and was looking for alternatives. In the German Empire, there were a considerable number of investors who were dissatisfied with the meagre interest on Prussian and Imperial German bonds. But this did not induce them to set up their own investment institutions. The big banks were apparently able to refer them to sufficient investment alternatives in German and foreign securities.

The basis for the formation in Germany of a form of joint securities buying in the years between the two wars was much more favourable than before 1914, as the big banks had emerged seriously weakened from war and hyperinflation. At the same time, after the stabilization of the German currency there was strong demand for capital in all areas, which led to new forms of financing by specialized banks, savings and loan associations and building societies. This situation also offered new possibilities for the investment trust idea. Zickert'scher Kapitalverein, founded by Hermann Zickert, can be regarded as the first genuine German fund management company. Like its British forerunners, it had been set up in the provinces without the participation of a bank. The fact that it was not successful in the longer term can be explained primarily by the losses suffered in the Great Depression. A fund management company founded in Munich as a joint stock corporation, and not as an association with legal capacity like Zickert'scher Kapitalverein, suffered a similar fate. Having this legal form meant that its shares were tradable, but its profits also attracted a total tax burden of up to 50 per cent. For the investor saving in investment funds, such tax rates were particularly painful because he was already subject to threefold taxation: tax was paid by the company in which the fund management company invested, by the fund management company itself and finally by the shareholder in the fund management company.

A tax privilege for fund management companies came into force in 1931, but at the peak of the Great Depression, this incentive was still far from sufficient to stimulate the foundation of new companies. The high level of interest rates on the German capital market was unfavourable for fund management companies as it was even more difficult to obtain higher returns with the best mix of equities than with fixed-income securities and Pfandbriefe. The increasing political control of the capital market, which was ultimately placed wholly in the service of armaments and war financing, eliminated, from 1933 onwards, all scope for setting up fund management companies; particularly as the economic and structural obstacles were compounded by socio-political impediments, as financial institutions such as stock exchanges, banks and financing companies ran counter to National Socialist ideology.

After the 1948 currency reform, the normalization of the capital markets, the start of strong economic growth and a pronounced increase in disposable incomes, the underlying conditions were better than ever. The favourable climate for setting up new companies was supported by the deliberations in progress since 1953 for a Fund Management Companies Act, which was passed in 1957. Against this background a series of new fund management companies was set up by the banking sector from the middle of the fifties onwards. These companies became established in the market and have maintained their positions until today. In contrast to the German Empire, the banks did not regard investment fund business as competing with their own securities advisory activities, but as a genuine step forward for broad segments of the population.

Notes

1 Cottrell, P.L. 1995. Investment Trusts, in Michael North, ed. *Von Aktie bis Zoll. Ein historisches Lexikon des Geldes.* Munich: Beck, pp.175–6.
2 Anon. 1927/28. Der Investment Trust. *Bankwissenschaft*, pp.576–7.
3 Mauer, H. 1910/11. Kapitalanlage-Gesellschaften. *Bank-Archiv*, pp.378–80.
4 Weber, A. 1938. *Depositenbanken und Spekulationsbanken. Ein Vergleich deutschen und englischen Bankwesens*, 4th ed. Munich/Leipzig: Duncker & Humblot, p.277.
5 On Société Générale and its selective investments in industrial shareholdings, see van der Wee, H. and Verbreyt, M. 1997. *The Generale Bank 1822–1997. A Continuing Challenge.* Tielt: Lannoo, pp.43–50; Liefmann, R. 1921. *Beteiligungs- und Finanzierungsgesellschaften*, 3rd ed. Jena: Fischer, pp.111–30.
6 Born, K.E. 1977. *Geld und Banken im 19. Jahrhundert,* 2nd ed. Stuttgart: Kroner, pp.102–3.
7 See Born (1977), pp.135–42; Plenge, J. 1903. *Gründung und Geschichte des Crédit Mobilier. Zwei Kapitel aus Anlagebanken, eine Anleitung in die Theorie des Anlagebankgeschäftes.* Tübingen: H. Laupp'sche Buchhandlung, pp.103–7.
8 Liefmann (1921), pp.162–3.
9 On British investment trusts see Kilgus, E. 1929. *Kapitalanlage-Gesellschaften – Investment Trusts.* Berlin: Christians, pp.20–50; Linhardt, H. 1935. *Die Britischen Investment Trusts.* Berlin/Wien: Spaeth & Linde.
10 Liefmann (1921), p.132.
11 Deutsche Bank, 1926. *Annual Report for 1926.* Frankfurt am Main: Deutsche Bank.
12 *Loan Agreement of 19 November 1926.* Frankfurt am Main: Historical Archives of Deutsche Bank (HADB), P7495, pp.9–11.
13 Kilgus (1929), p.31.
14 Marten, T. 1929/30. Lehren der amerikanischen Investmenttrust-Entwicklung. *Bank-Archiv 1929/30*, pp.174–6.
15 Lansburgh, A. 1930. Investment Trusts. *Die Bank*, 10 May 1930, pp.717–21.
16 Obst, G. 1910. *Geld- Bank- und Börsenwesen*, 6th ed. Leipzig: Poeschel, p.188.
17 Max Steinthal to Wihelm von Bode, 29 May 1905, in Müller, M. and Frost, R. 2007. *Deutsche Bank. Eine Geschichte in Bildern – An Illustrated History.* Munich: Piper, p.271.
18 Glagau, O. 1877. *Der Börsen- und Gründungs-Schwindel in Deutschland.* Leipzig: Frohberg, p.417.
19 Anon. 1899/1900. *Handbuch der deutschen Aktiengesellschaften 1899/1900*, vol. 1. pp.328–9.
20 Liefmann (1921), p.171.

21 Anon. (1899/1900), p.327.
22 Liefmann (1921), pp.171–2.
23 Anon. 1939. *Handbuch der deutschen Aktiengesellschaften 1939*, vol. 6, p.8470.
24 The founders were Bank für Handel und Industrie, Deutsche Bank, Disconto-Gesellschaft, Dresdner Bank, Berliner Handels-Gesellschaft, Commerz- und Privatbank, Nationalbank für Deutschland, S. Bleichröder, Mendelssohn & Co. Delbrück Schickler & Co. and Hardy & Co. The bank was located at the headquarters of Deutsche Bank in Berlin.
25 Anon. 1920–21. *Handbuch der deutschen Aktiengesellschaften 1920–21*, vol.2, p.2. Anon. 1932. Ein deutscher Investment Trust für Industrie-Werte. *Die Bank*, 20 July 1932, pp.926–7.
26 Although German investors preferred German state and municipal bonds, 10 per cent of the total annual issue volume was invested in foreign securities in 1909. See Obst (1910).
27 Zickert'scher Kapitalverein, 1927. *Annual Report for 1927*. Frankfurt am Main: HADB, K5/295; Kilgus (1929), p.158.
28 Heeb, K., Zickert, H. 2009. *Der deutsche Börsenpionier*. Munich: Finanz Buch Verlag.
29 Deutscher Kapitalverein. *Articles of Association 1928*. Frankfurt am Main: HADB, K5/295.
30 Zickert'scher Kapitalverein, 1928. *Annual Report for 1928*. Frankfurt am Main: HADB, K5/295.
31 Anon. 1930. Differenzen im Zickert'schen Kapitalverein. *Frankfurter Zeitung*, No. 297, 22 April 1930, p.4; Anon. 1930. Umbildung des Zickertschen Kapitalvereins. *Frankfurter Zeitung*, No. 310, 27 April 1930, p.4.
32 Goldschmidt, E. 1929/30. Ueber die Voraussetzungen zur Errichtung von Investment Trusts (Kapitalverwertungsgesellschaften) in Deutschland. *Bank-Archiv* 1929/30, pp.38–40; Weber (1938), p.277.
33 Judgement of the Reichsfinanzhof, 11 March 1930. *Reichssteuerblatt* 1930, pp.205–07.
34 Anon. 1931. *Handbuch der deutschen Aktiengesellschaften* 1931, vol. 1, pp.150–1.
35 Anon. 1932. *Handbuch der deutschen Aktiengesellschaften*, 1932, vol. 3, p.3535.
36 Gentes, J. 1929/30. Anteilsscheine an gemischten Effektendepots (fixed income trust certificates). *Bank-Archiv*, 1929/30, pp.285–8.
37 *Gesetz über die Ermächtigung zu steuerlichen Maßnahmen zwecks Erleichterung und Verbilligung der Kreditversorgung der deutschen Wirtschaft*, 9 June 1930. RGBl. I, 1930, p.187.
38 RGBl. I. 1931, p.279, part 7, chapter IV.
39 Haußmann, F. 1930/31. Zur finanz- und steuerpolitischen Würdigung der zweiten Notverordnung vom 5. Juni. *Bank-Archiv*, 1930/31, p.428.
40 Lansbergh, A. 1930. Investment Trusts. *Die Bank*, 10 May 1930, pp.720–1.
41 Raumer, K. 1931. Investment Trust-Dämmerung? *Die Bank*, 30 May 1931, pp.724–5.
42 Nationalsozialistische Deutsche Arbeiter Partei: commonly referred to in English as the Nazi Party was a political party in Germany active between 1920 and 1945 that practiced Nazism. (Wikipedia: https://en.wikipedia.org/wiki/Nazi_Party, accessed 23 May 2016)
43 *Circular of Bundesverband des privaten Bankgewerbes (Association of German Private Banks)* to the members of its committees for capital market and for legal and tax questions, 27 November 1951, Frankfurt: HADB, ZA40/90.
44 Voges, B. 1953. *Investmentgesellschaften in Deutschland*, Hamburg 1953 [typed manuscript], Frankfurt: HADB, F2/226.
45 BGBl. I, 1957, 378.
46 Anon. 1967. Das Investmentsparen in der Bundesrepublik. Die letzten 10 Jahre. *Deutsche Bank AG. Mitteilungen für die Angehörigen der Bank*, No. 20, 1967, p.21.

47 Anon. 1949. Deutscher Bundestag. 1. Wahlperiode 1949, *Drucksache Nr. 4199/1.*
48 Christlich Demokraitsche Union Deutschlands (Christian Democratic Union of Germany) is a liberal, conservative, centre right party in German politics.
49 Vierhaus, R. Herbst, L. and Jahn, B. eds. 2002. *Biographisches Handbuch der Mitglieder des Deutschen Bundestages 1949–2002*, vol. 2, Munich: Saur, p.597.
50 Christlich Soziale Union (Christian Social Union) the smaller, yet more conservative sister party of CDU in Bavaria (a federal state in Germany).
51 Anon. 1953. Deutscher Bundestag. 2. Wahlperiode 1953. *Drucksache Nr. 1585/2.*
52 Baehring, B. 1981. *Investment in Deutschland. Union-Investment-Gesellschaft mbH Frankfurt am Main. Schrift zum 25jährigen Jubiläum 1981*. Frankfurt am Main: Thiele.
53 Bähr, J. 2006. *50 Jahre DIT. Aufbruch Wachstum Zukunft 1955–2005*. Frankfurt am Main: Knapp.
54 Müller, M.L. 2006. *DWS – Eine Erfolgsgeschichte 1956–2006*. Munich: Piper.

8 Comradery, the joys of work, and the struggle to improve performance

Creditanstalt–Bankverein's corporate newspaper, *Gemeinschaft*, 1939–1943

Ulrike Zimmerl

Corporate self-portrayal and information forum

Employee newspapers, magazines, and newsletters are generally edited, financed, and produced by a firm's management and, in most instances, are distributed without charge to the readership. They constitute a means of communicating with employees and furthering specific company aims. As a journalistic form, employee newspapers or magazines (*Werkzeitschriften*) are distinguished by regular but relatively infrequent publication intervals (weekly or quarterly), by being targeted at regular employees working within a single firm and affiliated with that firm's professional specialty, by recent but not up-to-the-minute coverage, and by a multifaceted but limited scope (encompassing not only the diversity of a particular company but also its procedures and practices). A rather contrary view holds that publications for employees are neither journals nor newspapers, but constitute a unique journalistic form of their own.[1] As a medium of information, employee magazines act (as does informal communication between employees) to shape attitudes and influence socio-economic outlooks. The magazines replicate, round out, and intensify information and promote certain interpretations of it.

Employees surveyed in the 1980s rated a number of topics covered by their internal company newsletter as important. These included commentaries by management, inflation, stagnation, and the economy generally, planned rationalizations, wages and how they were determined, hiring, layoffs, personal stories, and employee suggestions. Sports, business, nature, politics, and entertainment were mentioned by those surveyed as non-professional areas of interest of other print media such as employee letters, bulletins, flyers, employee handbooks, etc. as well as internal communication methods such as display windows, posters, bulletin boards, letters by pneumatic tube and public address systems, the employee magazine or newspaper rates as the most important and heavily used internal information medium.[2]

Employee newspapers in Austria first became widespread in the mid-1920s – the less industrially developed and multilingual Austrian-Hungarian monarchy was a bit behind other European countries[3] – and were patterned after the periodicals of the German Institute for Practical Skills Training

(DINTA, *Deutsches Institut für technische Arbeitsschulung*).[4] Their format (layout, type of paper, pagination) mimicked that of contemporary daily newspapers.

Under National Socialism in Germany and Austria, employee newspapers were (together with occupational training) the most visible overlap between earlier DINTA conceptions and the labour politics of the German Labour Front (DAF, *Deutsche Arbeitsfront*). Employee newspapers illuminated connections between the individual employees and the overall production process, and drew readers' attention to 'setting output targets' and 'work in its wider context' and to how the individual work station was situated within the larger operation. As a mouthpiece for corporate management, the in-house newspaper served to bridge the 'gap between the worker/employee and the entrepreneur', to help in the 'pacification' of the work force, and to develop links between work and leisure time.

> The employee newspaper is one of the best and most effective instruments for creating and further developing the sense of companionship and cooperation between all employed in the enterprise, especially the large enterprise. In it the workplace leader [*Betriebsführer*] and his retinue [*Gefolgschaft*] find not only a well-suited communication channel but also a corporate-wide umbrella spanning the occupations, attitudes, and the concerns – mundane and weighty – of all employment there.[5]

By December 1934, in the context of the National Socialist educational mission, the DAF press office had already mandated the integration of all employee magazines into the DAF press system. In August 1935 the DAF-Press was reorganized and the *DINTA* periodicals were absorbed into it. DAF, founded in 1925 by a group of German industrialists and run by Carl Arnhold, had already been integrated into the DAF in 1933, although it retained relative autonomy. In 1935, however, it was transferred to the Office of Vocational Training and Industrial Organization (*Amt für Berufserziehung und Betriebsführung*). Arnhold became director of a new DAF Office for Vocational Training and Performance Improvement (*Berufserziehung und Leistungssteigerung*); a position he held until 1942.[6]

The pre-eminent goal of the DAF was to extend the network of employee newspapers across as many large enterprises as possible, while continuing to absorb independent company periodicals not yet under its control. The companies remained responsible for the financing and free distribution of their in-house newspapers, but the ideology of the periodicals was oriented towards the principles of the DAF and the National Socialist Party (NSDAP, *Nationalsozialistische Deutsche Arbeiterpartei*).

Employee newspapers typically contained two sections. The first section offered general overviews of business and politics (although day-to-day political issues were avoided), essays on labour aesthetics, articles related to operational or technical matters, and more specific sections covering job training, local events, announcements, and entertaining news items or activities taking place within the organization. Critical letters from readers and articles contributed by employees (written in a 'candid and objective style') were welcomed, although their main purpose was to provide employees an outlet for letting off steam. Often there were special pages for women, teenagers, or children, designed to establish a link to life outside of the workplace.

Over time, increasing emphasis was placed on the second section of the in-house newspaper, which focused on internal organizational matters while also prominently covering DAF initiatives, social welfare measures and the provision of workers' housing. DAF did not manage to get full control over the newspapers' contents (not least because of a conflict between it and the Reich Group Industry), but its influence grew over time. Employers appointed editors in consultation with the DAF press office, the work of DAF was extensively covered in many articles, and the formats and titles of many employee newspapers harked back to the DAF.

After 1936, new employee newspapers could be started only with the consent of the DAF and the Reich Press Chamber (*Reichspressekammer*). Employee newspaper editors tended, however, to avoid mentioning DAF when reporting on social improvements within their enterprises, even when those improvements were a result of DAF policies or actions. Nevertheless, NSDAP ideas were prominent in all these newspapers' portrayals of the workplace community (*Betriebsgemeinschaft*) and the performance community (*Leistungsgesellschaft*) as well as the ideological education of the workforce.[7]

Gemeinschaft (community): the slogan of the new management

The newspaper of the workplace community of the Austrian Creditanstalt–Wiener Bankverein[8] first appeared in January 1939. According to Rudolf Pfeiffer, a board of management member and the bank's Workplace Leader, *Gemeinschaft* (community) was chosen as the newspaper's motto[9] in reference to both the intended audience and the newspaper's ultimate goal. This was, by the combined efforts of executives and retinue, to 'strengthen the unity of our organization, promote its further development, raise its productive efficiency, and bind the individual branches of the enterprise more tightly to one another'.[10]

Thus the very name of the employee newsletter was chosen in full accordance with the official conceptions of National Socialism. In place of the previous class struggle, a 'new harmony of the great people's community of classes' (*völkische Klassengemeinschaft*) was to be placed front and centre, and competition between individuals would be replaced by a 'common struggle' based on the guiding principle of a people's community (*Volksgemeinschaftsprinzip*).

At that time the bank had roughly 2,200 people working in 50 operating locations. About 1,800 of these employees were situated in Vienna, and the rest were distributed amongst the Austrian provinces or assigned to foreign branches. Regardless of job classification or status, all employees were called upon to participate in the employee newspaper.[11] The newspaper was under the responsibility of Rudolf Pfeiffer, the Workplace Leader, and the articles in it were intended for an audience consisting exclusively of the bank's employees. Through the newspaper, he expected

> a powerful invigoration of the sense of belonging and an enhancement [of employee] happiness in their work and lives... The striving for a deeply felt sense of community amongst all members of the organization will produce a true, honest, and lasting comradery that will become a pillar of unbreakable unity and cohesion amongst the people's community (*Volksgemeinschaft*).

The National Socialist worldview was also reflected in the final statement of Pfeiffer's preface to the first edition of the newspaper:

> So we will also express our thanks and gratitude to our liberator and leader Adolf Hitler by developing and perfecting our journal in his spirit and by his guiding principles, for the well-being of our organization and its membership and thereby for the benefit of all our people.[12]

Rudolf Pfeiffer was born on 21 November 1895 in Andrychau bei Bielitz, Galicia, and already had a 19-year career with the bank behind him when *Gemeinschaft* was founded in 1939. He joined the Wiener Bankverein on 15 December 1920, after finishing his studies in jurisprudence at the University of Vienna. After the merger of Wiener Bankverein with the Österreichische Creditanstalt, he worked for Österreichische Creditanstalt–Wiener Bankverein.[13] He joined the National Socialist Party in 1933, paying membership dues until 1937 under the name of Dr Rudolf Bankmann and holding simultaneous membership in the Fatherland Front (VF, *Vaterländische Front*).[14] From 1937 to 1938 the membership ran under his own name, and he carried the membership number 20.962/18.[15] From 1 May 1938 on he had the membership number 6.310.916.[16] Beginning in 1933, he assumed functions within the Economics Division of the NSDAP (handling financial and banking matters) and was a co-founder of the industrial group at that time under the leadership of Engineer Kern. From July 1934, Pfeiffer worked for the National Socialist News Service Berlin becoming head of a special assignment team in 1937. From 1935 to 1938, he was entrusted with leadership of a National Socialist cell within the Comrades Association (*Kameradschaftsverein*) of the Austrian telegraph corps. These activities earned him a special citation in May 1942 from the Vienna Gau leadership for his 'manly' exertions on behalf of the NSDAP during the 'time when the Party was banned' (*Verbotszeit*).[17]

A few days before the *Anschluss* (Annexation) of Austria into the German Reich, on 7 March 1938, Pfeiffer gave his first National Socialist speech at the Comrades Association to the 'delegates of all ranks of the active office corps', a speech he had to justify a few days later to the Army Group Inspector

(*Heeresgruppeninspektor*). He also had to prepare a report for newly named chancellor, Arthur Seyss-Inquart. On the day when the German Wehrmacht marched into Austria, he gathered together 200 members of the German Club, which he had been a member of since 1933, led their march to the Federal Chancellor's Office, where they broke through a police barricade to sing for the new Chancellor Seyss-Inquart. Pfeiffer was also a member of the German Association of Front Soldiers (*Verein Deutscher Helm*), was made a member of the Association for Legal Science (*Verein für Rechtswissenschaft*) in 1934 under the direction of Seyss-Inquart and Ernst Schönbauer, and had been a member of the Association for Racial Hygiene (*Verein für Rassenhygiene*) since 1935. Following the *Anschluss*, he joined the National Socialist Public Welfare Organization (NSV, *Nationalsozialistische Volkswohlfahrt*), DAF, the Reich Air Defence League (RLB, *Reichsluftschutzbund*), the German Red Cross (DRK, *Deutsches Rotes Kreuz*) and the National Socialist Lawyer's League (NSRB, *Nationalsozialistischer Rechtwahrerbund*), and became an SS Hauptsturmführer [officer rank in of SS; *Schutzstaffel* (Protection Squadron)].[18]

His character was said to be 'strong, steady, friendly, and accommodating', and his attitude towards the NSDAP was considered 'exemplary'. The Party also rated favourably the membership of his wife in the National Socialist Women's League (*Nationalsozialistische Frauenschaft, NS Frauenschaft*) and that of his only daughter in the League of German Girls (BDM, *Bund Deutscher Mädel*).[19] After the *Anschluss* he had positions of responsibility with a range of organizations, serving, for example, as honorary comptroller of the Austrian branch of the German League Abroad (VDA, *Volksbund für das Deutschtum im Ausland*), and, by appointment of the Mayor of Vienna, Hermann Neubacher, as financial advisor to the Vienna Racing Club. He was also a trusted advisor to the Vienna Police Chief in the commission responsible for judiciary or jury selections and he served as a member of the Economic Policy committee of the German-Hungarian Chamber of Commerce in Budapest, and on the advisory council of the Cooperative Association for Reich Accident Insurance.

In his 'supplemental report on my national activities after the Upheaval',[20] Pfeiffer gives a detailed description of the events of 12 and 13 March 1938 and the days immediately following. This account makes clear his changed position and future role relative to the new political situation. In his own words, as early as 12 March he was directing staffing changes not only at important positions within the Creditanstalt, but also at numerous bank-dependent firms, in order to 'install National Socialist personnel so that asset smuggling or sabotage can be avoided'. On the following morning, 13 March, Pfeiffer and organization cell leader (*Betriebszellenleiter*) Josef Dienst had a conversation with the 'still' General Director of the Creditanstalt–Wiener Bankverein, Josef Joham. Pfeiffer told Joham that no economic decisions would be allowed without his approval as Economic Consultant of NSDAP and ordered the recognition of Dienst as the 'official representative of the employees'.[21]

One hour after the conversation with Joham, at ten o'clock, an announcement was circulated to all departments and branches of the bank and to all the NDSAP representatives newly installed by Pfeiffer, prohibiting any executive decisions or funds transfers not previously agreed to by him. The employees of the bank were informed by circular of their new 'special supervisors assigned by the NDSAP to be responsible for economic questions at the Creditanstalt–Wiener Bankverein'. In this function, Pfeiffer was charged with the duty of 'ensuring the smooth transfer from the economic policy of liberal-capitalism to that of National Socialism'. The employees were instructed to keep Pfeiffer informed about the important business matters and developments, and, in urgent cases, to get into immediate direct contact with him personally. Pfeiffer expected from all employees, especially from the comrades of the DAF, their 'workmanlike support' and asked them, 'with increased diligence to cheerfully work for reputation and prosperity of our institute within the framework of the German People's community'.[22]

On the same morning, a conversation similar to that with Joham took place between Pfeiffer and the General Director of the Länderbank, Henry Reuter. Reuter was also instructed to grant decision-making or vetoing authority to representatives of the NSDAP in all important matters. On that morning Pfeiffer also mentioned his obligation to immediately dismiss 'some Jewish bank directors'. At the Creditanstalt–Wiener Bankverein that meant Franz Rottenberg and Oscar Pollak; both board directors were expelled from the board immediately following the Anschluss.[23]

On the afternoon of 13 March, Pfeiffer chaired a meeting of the illegal banking association at the Creditanstalt, in which the official banking association was 'effectively taken over'. On that same day, Pfeiffer was appointed to be the special representative of NSDAP for economic matters at the Creditanstalt–Bankverein. The appointment was ordered by the regional leadership (*Landesleitung*) of NSDAP with the approval of Odilo Globocnik,[24] the then *Gauleiter* (National Socialist regional district administrator) of Vienna, and was later verbally confirmed by Hubert Klausner.[25]

On 15 March, the SA (*Sturmabteilung*) senior command (*Obergruppe*) gave Pfeiffer full decision-making authority over personnel matters at the Creditanstalt–Bankverein group. Two days later, upon the recommendation of Robert Hammer,[26] General Director of the Central Bank of German Savings Banks, he was appointed the designated delegate for Banking and Credit. The same day, 17 March, also marked his appointment by National Socialist Leadership for the Province of Austria in Vienna as their trustee at Creditanstalt–Bankverein overseeing banking and credit services.[27] These powers gave Pfeiffer considerable oversight authority over both incoming and outgoing mail, and throughout the business of the bank as a whole. If needed, he could file reports to Robert Hammer.

In his notes, Pfeiffer mentions the decree from Göring to carry out *Arianization* in the banking sector as fast as possible. This mission is said to have been communicated to him in the presence of *SS Oberführer* (senior leader)

Franz Langoth.[28] Once it was established, the Office of State Commissioner for the Private Economy confirmed Pfeiffer in his position as a trustee of NSDAP at Creditanstalt–Bankverein, in which he was to carry out all personnel changes in the sector in consultation with the State Commissioner. Based on the recommendations of the Party, of Reich Governor (*Reichsstatthalter*) Arthur Seyss-Inquart and the relevant minister, Pfeiffer was named board of management member and director of the Creditanstalt. He was sworn in as Workplace Leader of the bank by *Gauleiter* Globocnik following the adoption of the law for 'organizing the national tasks of the *Ostmark*'.[29] In addition to all this, he also became – as of the end of December 1938 and with the consent of the Party – Deputy Spokesman of the Reich Group Banking for the economic district *Ostmark* and its representative assigned to the Economic Group for Private Banking, and chairman or administrative council member of a number of Creditanstalt's industrial holdings.

In appointing Pfeiffer as its Workplace Leader, Creditanstalt followed the recommendations of the Reich Labour Minister of 1934. Under National Socialism, the Workplace Leader was expected to fulfil a double duty, namely dealing with business and technical matters while also taking into account the concerns of the employees. This was a situation which offered advantages to the employer. In the conception of the State and of the DAF, these two roles were, in practice and to the extent possible, to be handled by one person. This stipulation, however, was directed mainly at legal persons, e.g. enterprises with multiple equally empowered board of management members, and to joint stock companies generally. Here the duties of the Workplace Leader could either be discharged by such equally authorized board members jointly or if the company's rules permitted it, severally. Either way, the Reich Labour Minister recommended that one board of management member, as per article 3.2 of the Labour Law (AOG, *Gesetz zur Ordnung der nationalen Arbeit*),[30] be both in charge of supervising the employees and also serve as a liaison to the DAF.

As Workplace Leader, Pfeiffer was responsible for looking after the interests of the employees and harmonizing the operation of the bank. While the principal goals of the Workplace Leader were to create and retain jobs, preserving internal procedures and practices was also important. The regime insisted that the managements in industry and business not only rely on their power to issue orders, but also work to strengthen a sense of unity between the employees and the enterprise. The unlimited right of the management to direct and order the organization was, however, not at issue; any right of co-determination for employees was rejected out of hand.[31] Decision-making authority for technical and organization matters rested and remained solely with the firms. Although all enterprises were taken under state supervision, the Labour Office, the Economics Ministry, and their subordinate officials steadfastly left the management of these enterprises to the enterprises themselves. 'Overall, therefore, the prevailing consensus was that by adopting the *Führer principle*, the power of the managers to rule over their employees should be reinforced and made more complete.'[32]

The DAF attached importance to the nature of its relationship with individual managements, and to what the possibilities were for it to structurally intervene in the internal affairs of the firms. The right of the manager to organize and run his company according to the *Führer principle* was not questioned. Within a company, the DAF claimed authority over employee training, the 'leadership of the people in the operation', and for reviewing the social services provided to the personnel including the so-called social responsibility (*Sozial-Bereitschaft*) of the management. Between 1934 and 1939, the ongoing attempts of DAF to get involved in corporate social policies led to numerous DAF initiatives designed to explain its sphere of influence over internal corporate affairs. Such efforts intensified during 1938–1939, but did not prevail. The authority to intermediate between company managements and employees was sought by the DAF, but this authority did not take hold institutionally, nor did the strengthened power of the DAF Workplace Spokesmen (*Betriebsobmänner*) that would have accompanied it.

A further example of the increasingly yet limited influence of DAF within firms is that of the obligatory membership. Mandatory membership of companies within it was a central priority of DAF but it could not fully overrule those firms who insisted that joining DAF remain voluntary.[33]

> By means of its regulations the DAF did manage, over the long term, to become an organization which companies were *de facto* compelled to belong to. Nevertheless, it was not able to fundamentally increase its power over labour relations within the enterprises, especially not when it came to choosing and determining the duties of the Workplace Leader.[34]

Concepts and contents

The company newspaper *Gemeinschaft* appeared quarterly during 1939, 1940 and 1941. In 1941 and 1942, it appeared only twice. The average length of a single issue was between 15 and 20 pages. The title page was labelled with the word *Gemeinschaft*, had wreathed swastikas encircling the logo of DAF and in many cases was decorated with photographs as well. The first two issues were bordered with red trimming, but thereafter this expensive coloration was abandoned. The first page consisted mainly of excerpts from Hitler's speeches (for example: 'It was never my intention to go to war, but rather to build up a new social state' or 'to overcome resistance is the most beautiful triumph of life'), along with 'guiding principles' from Hermann Göring, Robert Ley, Baldur von Schirach and the Austrian poet Peter Rosegger ('We best honour those who die for the Fatherland when we live for the Fatherland').

The newspaper was clearly structured in three sections. The first section had essays, articles, and speeches of a general type, designed to get alert readers interested in questions of finance, banking, funding for the war, the role of banks in the war, as well as themes related to a National Socialist worldview. The writers or the speakers quoted in these articles were mostly people from the top management of the bank, such as Rudolf Pfeiffer himself, or Supervisory Board President Franz Hasslacher and Director Ludwig Fritscher. Texts from Robert Ley were frequently cited, and on one occasion a full article by Carl Arnhold was published. Speeches from political personalities and special guests were also presented from time to time, for instance, that of Vienna Gauleiter Odilo Globocnik, who addressed Creditanstalt–Bankverein staff at the swearing-in ceremonies at a Workplace Assembly (*Betriebsappell*) for the trusteeship council (*Vertrauensrat*).[35] It is noteworthy that this event followed almost immediately the great pogrom of 9 November 1938.[36]

The second section, *Our Institute*, concerned internal organization matters such as information on the annual general meetings, financial results of the bank, reports on new branch openings and the presentation of achievement awards, general assemblies of the employees, employee training, career consulting programmes, and promotions, and reports about the 'political shock-troops' of the Creditanstalt–Bankverein.

The third section of the employee newspaper was devoted solely to information about the activities of bank employees, summarized under the heading 'from the community'. There were reports on the *Reich Vocational Competition* (*Reichsberufswettkampf*), company sports, concerts, assemblies, evening events, field trips, group hikes and ski tours, rest and recreation homes (*Erholungsheime*) of the bank, improvements to the organization's social infrastructure, along with information on air raid drills and on group snow-shovelling which was needed because of the shortage of janitorial personnel. The last page of every issue of Creditanstalt's employee newspaper was reserved for personal news. Service anniversaries were announced there as were marriages, births, and deaths.[37]

From the outset, the employee newspaper of Creditanstalt–Bankverein was influenced by various motivations of the bank's management, which can be summarized under the motto 'Comradery, the Joys of Work, and the Struggle to Improve Performance'. In full accord with the 'National Socialist concept of work', an organization set up along Taylorist lines, but wherein the 'joys of work' and the 'power of ambition' were promoted in juxtaposition to the Taylorite salary incentive (*Lohnanreiz*), and sought to bind all employees within a performance hierarchy (*Leistungshierarchie*).[38] Consistent with this philosophy, the bank adopted the performance-oriented hierarchical National Socialist concept of personnel leadership (*Menschenführung*) but coupled it with internal promotion incentives. The organization's social infrastructure was, however, used not only to compensate employees for the growing pressures of job performance and to forestall demands for higher wages, but also to strengthen the ties of the employees to the organization, a principle that managements had been promulgating already since the mid-19th century.

As a hierarchical principle within the bank, the *Führerprinzip* was also officially justified by the members of the board of management with reference to the *Leistungsprinzip* (performance principle). In his 11 November 1938 speech to Creditanstalt's general assembly, on the occasion of the swearing-in of the trusteeship council Odilo Globocnik, Gauleiter of Vienna, spoke generally about installing 'tried and tested men from the time of struggle [*Kampfzeit*]' at the top of all enterprises, but laid particular emphasis upon what he considered the decisive criteria for measuring performance.

> Not only that a company be led by National Socialists, but that all the work within the organization adhere to National Socialism and work towards promoting it… Clearly, disciplined conditions must prevail. There has to be everywhere a number one, a number two, and a number three. That is just the way it is in the world, and we certainly won't change things, especially since we, as advocates of the *Führerprinzip* do not recognize *Mr. Director* as such, but rather say that if you are the best, or the most capable, then you should be the leader of the organization and the retinue will then stand behind you. That should be our principle. (Heavy applause).[39]

Competition as a permanent motivation for improving performance represents an essential structural principle of National Socialist corporate policy. In addition to internal competition events, such as sports matches, there were two annual competitions for corporate employees that took place across the Reich: the Reich Professional Skills Competition (RBWK, *Reichsberufswettkampf*) which was first held in 1934[40] and initially intended only for young workers, and the German Enterprises Performance Competition (*Leistungskampf der deutschen Betriebe*) started in 1936.[41]

> Competitions weaken the individual employee's sense of solidarity and connection with his job, and bring on a greater sense of isolation. But at the same time, they should encourage a reinforced integration of the employee into the corporate culture and societal community which should encourage his efforts and improve his performance.[42]

DAF wanted to bring companies into this system of competitions in order to encourage ongoing efforts by employees and employers to improve performance, in a National Socialist sense, and thereby transform the workplace community into a 'performance community'. Success in the RBWK also improved chances for the personal advancement of employees; success in the German Enterprises Performance Competition enhanced the advertising and public relations of employers.

Non-Aryan organizations were excluded from participation in these competitions. 'Whether an organization is *Aryan* or *non-Aryan* depends, among other things, on the racial category of its top executive according to the Nuremberg laws and their implementing regulations'.[43] The number of competing firms rose steadily from 80,559 in 1937/38 to 164,239 in 1938/39 to 272,763 in 1939/40 (this includes the *Ostmark*). By 1940, 297 of these enterprises had earned the designation National Socialist model firm (*NS-Musterbetrieb*).[44]

The Creditanstalt–Bankverein had tremendous interest in capturing the 'golden flag of the DAF' and attaining the distinction of a 'National Socialist model firm'. In his function as Workplace Leader, Rudolf Pfeiffer called upon all bank employees, assembled at the commemorative gathering on 11 November 1938 to devote themselves fully to pursuing this targeted objective. In Pfeiffer's view, this required that the employees possess the 'correct' mentality.

> In this assessment, the decisive factor is the spirit prevailing amongst the workplace community. Contrary perceptions concerning relations between working people and regarding the essential functions of a bank, which had been abundant due to alien mentalities of a Jewish-international and Bolshevist sort, have now disappeared due to the expelling of foreign elements from the organization. The days of Bosel, Castiglioni, Popper, Ehrenfest, Rothschild and of liberal economic notions within banks are now finally and irrevocably behind us (energetic applause).[45]

In the 1939–1940 competitions of the German Enterprises Performance Competition Creditanstalt's Graz branch won an award for the 'professional strengthening of all members of the retinue, the pursuit of performance improvement, and the development of a workplace community.'[46]

The following year, the bank again participated in the annual competition; the appeal in the employee newspaper, *Gemeinschaft*, was bolstered by the war situation. Going ahead with the corporate competition, despite the war, was considered 'evidence' of 'how serious National Socialism is about implementing its societal goals'.

> For those of us who work, our shining example is the German soldier. He beats the enemies of Germany wherever he encounters them. What is the secret of his irresistible strength? Germans make the best soldiers… [and] … above all of them stands the military genius of the German field commander, Adolf Hitler. The German leader and the German soldier both represent the expression and the product of our race's discipline. Discipline is the prerequisite and the precondition for every achievement and every success. What applies to the fighting soldier, applies with equal measure to people who produce.[47]

In contrast to the large armaments manufacturers favoured by the National Socialist regime, which did not feel particularly compelled to participate in the German Enterprises Performance Competition,[48] Creditanstalt–Bankverein was not able or did not want, to miss this annual event. Nevertheless, the Bank considered itself 'essential to the war effort', and referred in various contexts to the importance of banking to the war economy.[49] When reporting on the annual competitions, and especially in its appeals for energetic participation in them by its employees, the Bank's management underscored the importance of the performance principle.

> National Socialism is rightly considered to be Performance Socialism, because at the core of its socialistic program is the performance which has been the principal reason for the advancement and freedom of the German people.[50]

In addition to awarding the designation National Socialist model firm, the DAF, from 1 May 1937 also gave out special commendations and *Gau* certificates (*Gaudiplome*). These had the purpose, firstly, of giving smaller, financially weaker enterprises incentives to integrate into DAF and secondly, of responding to general desires for commendations while still preserving the cachet of the National Socialist model firm category by strictly limiting the number of companies so designated.[51] Gau certificates were given out by local and regional offices of the DAF and were highly esteemed within the Creditanstalt–Bankverein. The Bank received many such awards for winning in sports competitions, and also for its efforts at job training. The competitions and awards were overall one of the most notable creations of the DAF for motivating and mobilizing firms and their employees towards increased on-the-job performance.

In addition to the annual German Enterprises Performance Competition, DAF also organized the previously mentioned *Reichsberufswettkampf.* The motivation behind this event was the development of the workers and employees in the sense of National Socialism, a goal which the DAF considered one of its most important. The DAF had enunciated this priority at its founding, at the beginning of 1933, and vocational training was, along with 'proclamation of the nature and purpose of the DAF', one its most central activities. The desire to monopolize the field of vocational training, however, was not limited to practical training of new employees. DAF also claimed principal responsibility for career counselling, labour inter-mediation, vocational schools, the whole area of employee training as well as guidance of trainees and young employees during their time outside of work.

Through a sort of comprehensive education, DAF sought to integrate employee training objectives such as improving physical fitness, building a political and spiritual outlook, and developing manual skills, in order to strengthen its influence over young employees, and thereby over their employers. The Hitler Youth (*Hitlerjugend*) was heavily involved in similar activities, but as of 1938 was required to acknowledge the primary position of DAF in employee training. Thereafter, the Hitler Youth was expressly prohibited from any involvement with companies that were not approved by DAF. The main sources of opposition to DAF's efforts at gaining a wide influence over employees were the business enterprises and state agencies, above all the Economics Ministry under Hjalmar Schacht. Fighting over lines of responsibility between DAF, the Reich ministries and Hermann Göring (in charge of implementing the four year plan prior to the outbreak of the war), continued unabated even after Schacht was replaced by Walther Funk in 1937.[52]

RBWK was heavily publicized and propagandized by DAF and managements were accordingly urged to motivate their employees taking part in the annual competitions. As with the Performance Competition, Creditanstalt–Bankverein explained its participation in RBWK as a form a performance improvement. After the *Anschluss* and the integration of Austria's economy into the *Großreich* (the Great Empire), the many-sided tasks facing the Bank were thought to require a 'particularly long yardstick'. To prepare for the 1939 RBWK, Creditanstalt organized events which young employees were expected to attend, alongside their normal training in the vocational school. The skills gained thereby were expected to help those competing in RBWK. Young employees were encouraged to sign up for the events at the assembly on 19 December 1938 where they were addressed by Pfeiffer. RBWK was held up as a 'competition that builds a path to the future'.[53]

On 5 February 1939, the first RBWK competition for employees in the credit and insurance sector was held in facilities of *Neue Wiener Handelsakademie* at Hamerlingplatz. Of 146 registered participants, 133 showed up to compete (22 were females). The event was organized by Mr Schwimann, and chaired by Workplace Spokesman (*Betriebsobmann*) Josef Dienst. A general written test of banking and accounting skills was followed by the career test (*berufskundliche Prüfung*). This part of the competition tested both specific vocational aptitude and general *Weltanschauung* (ideology). The young participants had to demonstrate their grasp of the 'nature' and 'elements' of the 'National Socialist community' as well as their knowledge of the 'development' of the *Großdeutsche Reich* and its four-year plan. Female test-takers were also examined n household economics, which required them to show their manual skills and answer questions on household management.[54]

Although the training and education of adult employees was, to companies, the State and the DAF, not as important as the schooling of teenagers, there were nevertheless training courses designed for more senior workers. From 1937 on, DAF's central programme for this sort of schooling were its so-called vocational development centres (*Berufserziehungswerke*). These training projects, described with great effort in the DAF press, received only a rather lukewarm response from companies in heavy industry. At the beginning of 1939, industry-wide and DAF sponsored vocational development centres numbered 231 compared to only 30 internal programmes of companies themselves. Only in 1940, with the drafting for the army and an increasing shortage of workers on the home front, did systematic in-house training operations develop widely, and by the end of 1940 they had grown to a total of 137.[55]

Based on numerous and lengthy articles and reports in its employee newspaper, *Gemeinschaft,* one may assume that Creditanstalt–Bankverein, in contrast to other firms, became involved in training adult employees relatively quickly and intensively. The Bank's management encouraged employees to participate in the annual Reich training courses held from mid-September to mid-October at University of Frankfurt am Main. These courses were established at the instigation of Wilhelm Kalveram of the Reich Group Banking, which then organized them with assistance from DAF's banking and insurance training division. These seminars were intended to instruct course participants from *Ostmark* into the highly developed art of German banking, in the role assigned to financial institutions within the German economy under National Socialism and in the laws for securing purity and independence.[56]

In 1938 only two bank officials from *Ostmark* took part in these courses (one of the two from Creditanstalt) whereupon the Bank's employee newspaper found it desirable that in 1939 a greater number of people take advantage of this 'opportunity for professional training'. In the summer of the same year the first series of courses was successfully concluded and a festive assembly to mark the occasion was held on 26 June 1939 in the large banking hall of the Bank's headquarters. Creditanstalt–Bankverein was the first bank in *Ostmark* to organize special in-house training for its employees.

At the beginning of 1939, the management and political leadership of the Bank decided to launch their own series of training courses, modelled after those of the training courses in Frankfurt. The provisions of the Old Reich (*Altreich*) were not to be followed in every particular, however, 'because the average preparatory schooling of Austrian banking and insurance officials was more highly rated'. The purpose of the in-house training course series was to identify and further develop talents, thereby raising the overall performance capability of the institution. The most important goal was the benefit conferred upon the 'whole social community as the result of a more joyful and skilfully run operation'.[57]

The organizational implementation of these courses was entrusted to G. Walde, and all lecturers were from Creditanstalt itself. Along with imparting, or further developing, purely technical knowledge, the courses were expected to deepen the 'inner relationship' of course-takers to their work and to the banking profession. Except for bank apprentices and errand boys (who were enrolled in the commercial vocational school and whose participation in the internal bank training courses was limited to typing, short-hand, and German language) all courses were open to any employee. In addition to those subjects just mentioned, the course offering consisted of banking math, introductory accounting, custodial accounting, account administration, postal (giro) banking, interbank payment transfers, as well as beginning language instruction in Italian, Romanian, Hungarian, and Croatian. Teaching south-eastern European languages to employees was in the Bank's interest, as its activities in Southeast Europe were being massively increased, especially in the early 1940s.[58] Regular attendance was required of all those who had decided to take a course. The instruction took place on the fourth floor of Creditanstalt's main office, in district 1 of Vienna on the Schottengasse, and also at DAF Vienna's facilities on Schottenbastei 7–9.[59] In the summer of the same year the first series of courses was successfully concluded and a festive assembly to mark the occasion was held on 26 June 1939 in the large banking hall of the Bank's headquarters. Creditanstalt–Bankverein was the first bank in the

Ostmark to organize special in-house training for its employees. At this gathering, special thanks were extended to DAF, whose contributions were emphasized.[60] To the extent permitted by local circumstances, Creditanstalt also wanted its regional branches to develop employee training, following the lead of the Vienna headquarter.[61]

At the start of 1940 Creditanstalt–Bankverein set up a further set of training courses, organized in conjunction with the training centre of DAF, the purpose of which was to convey to 'supervisors in the organization, National Socialist goals and philosophy'. On 12 January the first training sessions for Creditanstalt employees of managerial rank took place in the Bank's large conference room. All department and branch heads were there, as were all bank officers with signatory power and all officials from the local DAF. The opening remarks were given by Pfeiffer following a festive procession with flags. The principal purpose of this training was to orient the participants towards the National Socialist world view. This objective was literally underscored by a contemporaneous article in the employee newspaper *Gemeinschaft*, which reprinted a speech by DAF's regional training director and head of the *Neuwaldegg school* entitled: 'The all-encompassing National Socialist worldview'.[62]

These courses for management-level employees were further developed in 1941. The subjects covered included race doctrine (*Mendel's laws*, etc.), historical overviews of how the German tribes tried to unify and of the 'Teutonic Empire of the German Nation', National Socialist settlement policies, and the theory and practice of the German Enterprises Performance Competition.[63]

In March 1942, Creditanstalt–Bankverein's internal training programme received a certificate of commendation from the National Socialist *Gauleitung* of Vienna for its 'achievements up to that point in state-of-the-art employee training'. Senior *Gau* official Karl Schneeberger also designated the Bank an 'official Vocational Training Centre of the DAF'. At the same time, however, the Bank's training programmes were not unaffected by the military services duties of its employees. In 1942, declining enrolments and military absences caused many class sessions, and even entire courses, to be dropped.[64]

Beyond general and political education courses, the Bank also had an internal institution or association for the strengthening of the National Socialist worldview. The so-called *political shock troops*, made up mostly of old fighters, who held DAF posts within the Bank, were in charge of 'political motivation and attitude formation' and maintaining 'social peace' within the organization. The political *shock troops* of the Creditanstalt–Bankverein came into existence in January, 1941 and held a weekly assembly, divided into three working sections: 'vocational training, Strength through Joy (KdF, *Kraft durch Freude*), and social health and job safety'.[65]

Encouraging solidarity within the organization through reinforced development of internal social services and measures was (for the Bank, as for other enterprises) a useful means of heightening job satisfaction and organizational harmony, and helped increase performance and productivity. Enhancing work procedures and job productivity by providing company recreational facilities and improved workplace design was, in National Socialist Germany, under the authority of the Beauty of Labour Office (ASdA, *Amt Schönheit der Arbeit*). ASdA was founded on 27 November 1933 as a division within the leisure time and recreation organization. After some at first rather uncoordinated activities, ASdA grew rapidly in importance with accelerating armament and growing demands for output from workers after 1936. The National Socialist regime quickly recognized the initiatives of ASdA – in designing workplaces, sanitation arrangements, meal facilities, recreational areas and so forth – as an efficient and, more especially, cost effective means of offsetting the potentially negative effects on employee morale stemming from working hours being increased while wages were frozen. ASdA was, in turn, strengthened by the expanded and intensified involvement of DAF officials within companies that accompanied the building up of the German Enterprises Performance Competition.[66]

In addition to many more specialized activities, ASdA had launched seven main projects by 1938.[67] The last of these – *hot meals at work* – was supported by the Reich Labour Ministry, and provided an inexpensive cooked meal to all employees. This programme was put into effect in 1938 with the aims, firstly, of increasing employee performance through pre-planned nourishment, and, secondly, of making 'maximal use of foodstuffs' in a time of shortages.[68]

At its headquarters, Creditanstalt already had kitchen-servicing employees before the outbreak of the First World War. In the years following the war, this was expanded through extensive investment, and Creditanstalt's kitchen became exemplary for many other firms. The kitchen provided a warm lunch at an inexpensive price to employees of the Bank's headquarters and other branch offices in Vienna. In 1942, *Gemeinschaft* ran a full-page article praising this 'oldest' and 'most important' social provision of the Bank. The effect of the war was reflected in the menu, and the article made reference, accordingly, to the restrictions and difficulties of preparing the meals. The efforts of the kitchen staff to nonetheless 'put together an adequate and appetizing luncheon' were especially highlighted.

> In conclusion, it can be said that the employees of our institute have always known what they can expect from our kitchen. Of course there were occasions, during the tranquility of peacetime, when one employee or another may have not been completely satisfied with one dish or another, but today they really treasure these facilities and many an employee returns from a vacation with a sigh of relief and a 'Thank God, I am back', at his old familiar table surrounded by his fellow workers.[69]

By the end of 1939, the Graz branch was able to report that it had also established a dining room for 50 people; meals were provided by a central kitchen run by DAF and NSV (*Nationalsozialistische Volkswohlfahrt* – National Socialist Charity).[70]

Another project at the Bank that was mentioned in the employee newspaper was the company library and reading room, newly opened in October

1940. This small library was located in the main Creditanstalt–Bankverein building, room 303, on the third floor and could be reached through the entrance on Hessgasse 3. It was open from Monday through Friday between 4:30 pm and 5:30 pm. Books were lent out without fee, usually for up to two weeks, with a limit of one borrowed book per patron. An overdue fee of ten *Reichspfennige* per week was charged on books not returned on time, and borrowers had to pay for any lost or damaged books. Company vocational supervisor Johann Frisch seems to have been in charge of the library. It was, at any rate, he who wrote in the employee newspaper to tell employees about the library and encourage them to use it.[71]

Shortly after its opening, Rudolf Pfeiffer visited the library and borrowed, as 'reader number one', a volume from a series of technical works. At the outset, the library carried about 800 general and technical books. It had multiple copies of 'prominent works'.[72] In the first six months after it opened, the library had lent out 1,260 books to about 250 readers, and numerous additional books were purchased and donated by the Bank's management. In one of his appeals for greater use of the library, Frisch made mention of some of these new acquisitions, such as the *Heroic Battle of the German Destroyers, The Battle for the North Sea, Our Path to the Sea, Saxons and Anglo-Saxons, The North Germans* as well as *The Destiny of the German Race.* As a 'well-known' nature Guide in the Kosmo series, the cited 'Which star is that?', 'What tree is that?' and 'What's blossoming there?' and for 'books that tell us of our colonies', he recommended *Africa as a European Task* and *Rubber from Cameroon.* Because this was the library of a bank, acquisitions in the scientific section were also important. Among the new acquisitions in the fields of Law, Business, and Finance, were *Civil Law, a Guide for Businessmen, The Balance Sheet based on Trade and Tax Law* as well as *The Credit Committee.*[73]

As a demonstration of the solidarity of all employees with the organization, Creditanstalt–Bankverein held workplace assemblies since the National Socialists had taken over. As conceived by DAF, these assemblies were to be for all employees and to take place daily, and at the beginning and end of the workday, if possible. Originally, the idea behind this was that the 'roll calls' in these gatherings could replace punch clocks as a means of recording attendance. Such a substitution did not prove practical at Creditanstalt – or at any other firm – and the assemblies were mainly used for festive company events such as anniversaries, and also took place in conjunction with visits by high-ranking National Socialist officials.[74] Under National Socialism, workplace assemblies represented an ongoing and visible expression of the militarization of the daily work routine.

> The whole structure and practical execution of these assemblies, from the entrance in military formation, marching with flags, to the speech of the Workplace Leader, or a National Socialist official, was linked to a military model, and designed, even if the DAF officially disapproved, to instil [in the employees] discipline and obedience towards their superiors.[75]

Events such as the annual closing, festive occasions, swearings-in, the dedication or opening of new social facilities for employees, the assembly in March for the anniversary of '*Ostmark* returning home to the *Reich*,' youth assemblies and sports events were an opportunity for those in charge of the employee newspaper to provide full coverage. Articles on particularly festive events and bank-wide holidays, often celebrated at great expense and with politically prominent guests, were especially extensive and detailed. Speeches by well-known speakers and guest speakers from outside the Bank were often reprinted in full and accompanied by photographs. An example of such an event was the assembly of 11 November 1938, which was attended by all the employees of Creditanstalt–Bankverein in Vienna, numbering some 1,700 persons. Here the trusteeship council appointed according to the *Law on Organizing National Tasks* was festively sworn-in. The main room with the teller windows was decorated with 'flags of the movement', swastika emblems, and a huge statue of the Führer. The programme began with the entrance of the honoured guests, followed by a selection from Richard Wagner's opera *Tannhäuser*, performed by the Bank's band, continued with the greeting from the Workplace Leader, then the swearing-in of the trusteeship council, a speech by Gauleiter Odilo Globocnik, a speech by the Workplace Spokesman, and concluded with final words from the Workplace Leader. With the national anthem and the, played as a 'gesture of solidarity with the liberated Sudeten German Brothers'[76] the festivities were *Egerländer March* concluded.

Changes in management, especially in important positions such as those of the Workplace Leader and the Workplace Spokesman, were also celebrated by assemblies of the employees. When the ex-director of Deutsche Bank's Leipzig branch, Walter Tron, and the Reichsbankdirector Richard Buzzi were chosen to join Creditanstalt–Bankverein's board of management in 1942, the latter was also named new speaker and Workplace Leader of the Bank and officially greeted at a festive assembly on 24 June 1942. Workplace Spokesman Dienst had recently resigned his position as well, thus his replacement, Albert Nerber, was also announced on the same occasion.[77] Here again, the programme followed the general practice for mass assemblies. The entrance of the honoured guests, with flags and musical accompaniment, was followed by introductory remarks by the Workplace Leader and speeches by board of management representatives and political personalities of the Gau administration, and the festivities generally closed with music or an honouring of the *Führer*. Incidentally, credit for removing the 'party-appointed board of management director' Pfeiffer, and the 'radical Nazi Workplace Leader' Dienst, was claimed after 1945 by Franz Hasslacher.[78] This was confirmed by Josef Joham when he testified at Hasslacher's trial.[79]

If one were to judge the significance of the various subjects in the employee newspaper by the amount of coverage devoted to them, then one would have to assume that company sports within the Bank were on the top rung of importance. Coverage of sports activities and events filled pages and this was the topic best documented with photographs. Undoubtedly, group sports activities and competitions represented one of the strongest sources of attachment within the workplace community of Creditanstalt–Bankverein and was accordingly handled and publicized by the editors of the employee newspaper.

Since 1936, DAF had been trying to establish company sports programes, for all employees in Germany. Responsibility within DAF for these efforts shifted, meanwhile, to its sports division, Strength through Joy – but close ties between the company vocational supervisor, the company youth supervisor and the company manager in charge of sports continued. DAF left the decision of how best to set up and schedule these sports activities to the individual employers, but it promoted and publicized the construction of company sports facilities and the introduction of at least two hours of sports per week, during working hours, for employees. The emphasis here was on endurance and fitness sports. Promoting general, popular and inexpensive sports, such as athletics, gymnastics, soccer, handball and swimming, along with various military-oriented sports was not only expected to raise the performance capacity of the employees, but was also regarded as a successful means of education and for reinforcing a sense of community within the organization.[80]

After the regime change in Austria, Hans Korber took over the job of company manager in charge of sports (*Betriebsportwart*). Following Hitler's motto, 'One people in physical fitness training', he set the goal of motivating the Bank's employees to regular fitness exercises 'in order to preserve the body's flexibility and thereby also prevent its premature deterioration'.[81] The main rationale was, once again, to raise the performance capacity of the employees, as well as serving the interest of the management in having a 'healthy retinue', and reducing absences due to illness. By constructing sports areas and gymnasiums, the bank's management indicated its support for company sports. However, plans to build an exercise room in the Vienna headquarters fizzled out, and the expansion of the Vienna exhibition grounds also threatened to wipe out the existing sports facility in Prater-Krieau as well. Eventually, after protracted negotiations, Creditanstalt was nevertheless able to renew its rental agreement for that facility.

The sports facilities in Prater were available every Monday, Wednesday and Saturday to all employees in possession of an annual sports pass. For gymnastics, the Office of Physical Fitness's hall *Am Hof* was made available. Swimmers, or employees who wanted to learn how to swim, could use the *KdF-Bad Dianabad* for free every Thursday from 9 pm to 10.30 pm in the evening, although these swimming nights were not attended as heavily as had been expected. In winter, there was the additional possibility of skiing. The Bank organized group outings in the Vienna Woods and weekend excursions in the Vienna region. Multi-day ski courses for beginners, advanced skiers and touring skiers were also arranged. Ski cabins were rented from the *KdF* or the Alpine Club. In 1940, responding to pressure from skiers, the Bank acquired its own ski hut in the Styrian Salzkammergut on the Tauplitzalm. This *Torbauerhütte* could accommodate up to 20 overnight visitors in two sleeping rooms and was available for use by Bank employees from 1 December to 1 May.[82]

In addition to well-established sports such as soccer, handball, netball, athletics, gymnastics and swimming, the Bank's small-calibre sports-shooting also merits mention. On 21 September 1939, a small-calibre shooting gallery that had been built in the basement of Creditanstalt's headquarters building was officially opened. It had a shooting distance of 25 metres, meeting the regulations for small calibre shooting, and was envisioned for use by those employees serving in the war, for their specified shooting practice, and also by young employees and other interested Bank employees. At the opening ceremony, Pfeiffer praised the facility and stressed the importance of military-related sports training. There was also a moment's thought given for all employees serving on the front at that time. Supervision of the shooting gallery and those practicing in it was assumed by an in-house shooting supervisor. Shooting practice took place almost every day between 4 pm and 6 pm. Tuesdays were reserved for young employees. From its opening day through to the following November 38 practice sessions took place at the shooting gallery, the total number of participants was 460 people. Some 5,050 cartridges were fired during this time period, and in 1940 the Bank invested in an electrical target counter.[83]

The ambitions of Creditanstalt–Bankverein in the area of employee sports was further expressed in the numerous competitions held and honours bestowed: after their success at the 1939 Sport Gathering of the Enterprises, the male employees of the Graz branch received a commendation for their 'inspirational dedication', which simultaneously praised the management for its 'exemplary furtherance of physical fitness'.[84] At the 1940 Summer Sports Day of the Enterprises, which was put on by the Sports Office of the *KdF*, Creditanstalt-Bankverein was awarded the title Gau Champions for the 'inspirational efforts of the retinue' of the Bank. The certificate of commendation was officially presented to Pfeiffer and Dienst at a celebration honouring the 1940 Summer Sports Day champions, which took place on 25 November, 1940 in the large hall of Vienna's Konzerthaus.[85]

At the 1941 Sport Assembly, Creditanstalt–Bankverein won two Gau Champion commendations, one for the overall achievement of the Bank at the event and the other for its female participants' 'outstanding performance' in the team sport competitions. The women athletes were also awarded a certificate as District Champions and their male counterparts received a performance citation. On 12 April 1942, at the celebration in Vienna's Volkstheatre, Creditanstalt–Bankverein was feted as Gau Champion. The Bank's Workplace Leader and Workplace Spokesman were handed the commendations by Gau administrative head Karl Schneeberger. Two weeks later, at the Apollo Cinema, the three other awards were officially presented by city district administrator Rosenauer. At the Bank, special thanks in this connection were given to the sport officer Friedrich Marek, his helper Stehno, and the sports officers Elfriede Hauer, Christl Däger and Elsa Schroth, and the goal was set of eventually gaining the even higher distinction of *Reich Champions*.[86]

In 1942, at the Sport Assembly of the Enterprises, Creditanstalt's female team won the Gau Champions award. The victory celebration followed on 11 April 1943 in the Raimund Theatre in the course of a publicity event of the Vienna Gau entitled *Games and Sports of the German Woman*. After introductory remarks by a Gau official, the deputy Gauleiter of Vienna, Karl Scharizer, gave a speech, and then he and Karl Schneeberger presented the championship certificate to Creditanstalt's Workplace Leader Richard Buzzi and Workplace Spokesman Albert Nerber. As part of the festivities, women and girls of the honoured organization also performed for the gathering. Two employees demonstrated exercises on a rope apparatus (*Rundtau*) and three others gave a performance entitled: The Shaping of Movement (*Bewegungsgestaltung*).[87]

In National Socialist Germany, the Organization for Leisure Time for the Directed Recreation and Integration of Employees had been transferred over to the new DAF offices, Beauty of Labour and After Hours (*Feierabend*), which had previously been established in 1935 expressly for the purpose of that transfer. Companies largely left the organization of events for employees outside of working hours to the DAF: these included theatre and musical performances, organization sports, field trips, and also the so-called fellowship evenings (*Kameradschaftsabende*). Fellowship evenings took place outside of working hours, mostly on weekends. The idea behind them was that employees and managers could both get together, enjoy beer, music and dancing, that a feeling of organization solidarity would be imparted, and the common interest of all in the organization expressed.

These evening gatherings followed a general pattern that varied little from one organization to another. The evening was opened with speeches and remarks by the Workplace Leader, along with comments honouring those with service anniversaries, then followed presentations by individual employees, the company chorus and band, and music and dancing until the end of the evening. Fellowship evenings also came in for some criticism, however, often being described as 'unrewarding evenings of beer' or even as 'drunken orgies', during which all that mattered was the free beer dispensed. Such reservations applied mostly to the socializing that followed the official portion of the evening events.[88]

In the coverage by the employee newspaper, excessive alcohol consumption was certainly not a main theme. The first Fellowship Evening organized by the Bank took place on 8 March 1939 and was attended by about 400 employees. Small gatherings were more common, however, typically consisting of employees from a single department or branch office getting together in a restaurant.[89] By 1942, due to the wartime conditions, fellowship evenings were either completely prohibited, or were organized only at departmental level and held in small local bars or restaurants.[90]

Excursions and so-called retinue holiday trips received responses from employees similar to those given the fellowship evenings. Their judgments were based on how convivial the mood was and on the nature and quantity of the food and drink provided. Feelings of a special solidarity or interest in the workplace community cannot be automatically inferred based on the level of participation in the events.[91]

Creditanstalt organized diverse excursions for its employees. In 1939 it hired its own hiking guide to plan walks in the *Wiener Wald* (Vienna Woods) or on the *Hohe Wand*.[92] There were also cultural programmes, such as guided tours of museums and exhibits, visits to the theatre, to concerts, or sightseeing trips, for which the Bank's educational officer (*Volksbildungswart*) was responsible.[93] More substantial excursions such as pleasure cruises on steamboat through *Wachau* were organized jointly by the Bank management and DAF.[94]

Another type of employee excursion took place when the Bank's headquarters invited the branches to visit Vienna. In May 1941, for example, employees of the Salzburg and Crakow branches had the opportunity to get to know the headquarters – 'the heart of the Bank'. Visitors were guided through the individual departments of the Bank's offices on the Schottengasse and shown the technical infrastructure of the building. This was followed by a tour around Vienna, including visits to the Ringstraße, Schönbrunn castle, and St. Stephans Cathedral, where the southern tower was ascended so that 'everyone could enjoy a panoramic view of greater Vienna (*Groß-Wien*)'.[95] In the evening the guests attended a performance at the Vienna Opera. These excursions were popular amongst employees of the Bank's outlying branches. For many, this was the only possibility they had, for once, to visit Vienna.

In addition to the ski cabins already mentioned, the Bank also owned two recreational retreats, one in Zelking, near Vienna, and the other on the Klopeinersee in Carinthia. Here, in these retinue hostels, Creditanstalt employees and their family members could vacation. The ideological goal of these vacation retreats was 'National Socialist people-management', the 'mitigation of social differences' (there were subsidies for employees of lesser means), as well as 'deepening the sense of community'.

In 1941, for the first time, the hostel on the Klopeinersee had to be made available for the quartering of soldiers. As extensive precautionary arrangements developed for moving children out of urban regions subject to aerial bombing (especially northern and western Germany) and into the countryside, the management of Creditanstalt responded by making the retreats in Zelking und Klopein available to house them. On 23 March 1941, 50 girls from Northwest Germany, with accompanying adults, arrived and were housed at Zelking. The lodging of such children in the Bank's vacation hostels continued thereafter, but with some interruptions. For example, plans to take in 60 mothers with 140 small children at *Klopeinersee* had to be abandoned, because with German troops having marched into Yugoslavia on 6 April 1941, the hostel was suddenly only a few kilometres away from the war zone. In June 1942 the *Carinthian* rest and recreation home for employees again became a temporary recuperation spot for over 450 soldiers, most of them from the eastern front.[96]

Although the war received considerable coverage in the newspaper, *Gemeinschaft*, and across numerous categories and subject areas, the most current news items in this regard were the announcements of Creditanstalt employees dying in action. By the end of 1939, whole pages were being devoted to obituaries for fallen colleagues. In most cases, the deceased were introduced to the reader by identifying their areas of responsibility at the Bank, the department or branch where they worked. Personal and professional characteristics were also described. Details as to military rank, unit served in, where on the front they had been, and circumstances of their 'heroic death' were also disclosed and accompanied by photographs of them in uniform. These military obituaries were not relegated to the back pages of the newspaper, as was the case for obituaries generally (although a brief summarized reprise did appear there as well), but were instead placed either on the front page, or under a section headline *Reports from Our Comrades in the Field.*

This column, with published excerpts of letters from soldiers in the field, emerged out of the first Wartime Christmas at the end of 1939. The Bank's management and employees took up a collection in order to prepare and send two Christmas gift packages to every colleague who had been called into military service.

> Many diligent hands, loving female hands, were busy into the night, at the packing and preparation for mailing. The tender dedication of all those employed in the organization, who have found a sense of identity with the expression workplace community was put into this devoted work, and we can only hope that not only the practical value of the collection, but also the spiritual content of this work of love finds its way to the front.[97]

Creditanstalt–Bankverein received numerous thank-you letters in reply to the packages sent, and excerpts from those letters were published in the same issue of the newspaper. This practice continued with later issues, typically about 15 letters were featured. It is clear, both from the letters and the articles in the employee newspaper that copies of it were sent regularly to employees in the field.[98]

As far as can be determined – it is to be assumed that the published letters were very precisely selected – the employees at the frontline were happy to receive the newspaper. After all, it was a source of information about developments at the Bank and a connection to the previous job, and thereby to the homeland. The psychological effect of mailings to the employees serving actively in the war should also not be underestimated. The guarantee of a continuing contact to the enterprise, connection to goings-on at the Bank through ongoing information in the form of this newspaper, the feeling of still belonging to this *Gemeinschaft*, the appreciation, and the sense of not-being-forgotten are expressed in the many letters sent to the Bank from those employees in active military service. For Creditanstalt–Bankverein's part the letters were valued firstly as a way of remembering the 'comrades at the frontline' and secondly as means of motivating the employees still at the Bank. Those employees not called into military service were reminded of the efforts, the 'duty-fulfilment' and the sacrifices of their colleagues; efforts that had to be reciprocated on the 'home front.'[99]

Closing observations

In its conception and its content, the employee newspaper *Gemeinschaft* represented all the propositions and precepts of the National Socialist ethos and was an ideological instrument for the political and worldly indoctrination of Creditanstalt–Bankverein's employees. The persistent repetition of concepts like performance, competition, competitive struggle, organizational community, and working community throughout all the subject sections of the newspaper represents a continuous principle of its coverage. Its reporting and commentary emphasized internal organization-related matters. Day-to-day politics were avoided as a matter of principle. This was the case even during Creditanstalt's assembly of 11 November 1938 when the new trusteeship council was sworn in. The events of the pogrom two nights earlier were not mentioned by any of the speakers at the assembly, nor in any other article in this issue of the newspaper.

In comparison to the generally accepted press and other public media of the time, openly anti-Semitic agitation was rare in *Gemeinschaft.* Exceptions to this were reports concerning political training and gatherings of the *political shock troops* with the corresponding speeches about *racial doctrine* and *racial hygiene*, and the directly quoted positions taken in speeches, addresses, and commentaries, the selection of which depended on the editor. For example, the chairman of the Supervisory Board of Creditanstalt–Bankverein, Franz Hasslacher, in his speech on 'Current Problems in Finance and Politics', delivered at the University of Vienna on 14 May 1943, attributed the inflation and great crises of the 1920s and 1930s, among other factors, to the 'destructive influences of the Jews'.[100] A further example, reported in *Gemeinschaft*, was the speech of Rudolf Pfeiffer of 11 November 1938, on the occasion of the trusteeship council being sworn in. In his remarks, Pfeiffer spoke of the 'expulsion of foreign elements' and the removal of former Jewish directors and businessmen such as Bosel, Castiglioni, Popper, Ehrenfest and Rothschild. In the same address, he informed the employees of Creditanstalt:

> We have, without delay, filled the high-ranking positions in our organization that were held by the Jews with reliable National Socialists, or put monitoring procedures in place, so the expatriation of flight capital has been impossible. We have also sent our trustees to those companies connected to us, either by our provision of equity capital or extension of credit, and under Jewish direction, thus preventing the transferring out or liquidation of the people's wealth there as well. 180 Jews in the Vienna

organizations have been dismissed and replaced by deserving Party members, most of them former officials of our institute.[101]

Creditanstalt–Bankverein had, within a very short time, replaced people on its top-management boards, and fired its Jewish employees, so it is quite possible that verbal attacks in the employee newspaper were no longer 'a top priority'. The overall coverage of the organization – sports events, successful competitions, employee achievements, new social infrastructure and employee training – was (except for the obituaries of fallen colleagues) exclusively positive in nature. Creditanstalt–Bankverein portrayed itself in the newspaper as an exemplary, successful and 'Jew-free' enterprise.

How employees felt about the in-house newspaper cannot be clearly ascertained. Other than the consistently positive communications from soldiers at the frontline, happy to get news from home, there is no way to judge clearly whether employees accepted or rejected the newspaper. With 2,200 employees in 50 locations, the number of copies circulated was quite high. This, however, says little about how much the readers valued it, since it was distributed free of charge. It can nonetheless be assumed that *Gemeinschaft*, like in-house company newspapers in general, tended to be positively received. It was, after all, a free informational newsletter covering internal events at the organization.[102]

The final issue of *Gemeinschaft* appeared in July 1943, and the newspaper was then shut down. The reasons for this discontinuation cannot be traced in the sources, but war-related factors come readily to mind. The defeat at Stalingrad in January 1943, and Joseph Goebbels' proclamation of *total war*[103] in his speech of 18 February 1943 at the *Sportpalast*, was followed by the termination or absorption of numerous newspapers, as an emergency measure within the war economy. Although Deutsche Bank acquired majority control of Creditanstalt in 1942,[104] – its own employee newspaper *Schwibbogen* did not continue the features previously handled in *Gemeinschaft*.[105] There was also no new additional news coverage in *Schwibbogen*, in 1943 or thereafter, in the form of reports from Creditanstalt or even obituaries of the Viennese bank's employees, (which might indicate that Deutsche Bank's publication served as a replacement for Creditanstalt employees, following the demise of *Gemeinschaft*). In contrast to *Gemeinschaft*, Deutsche Bank's employee newspaper *Schwibbogen* continued until early 1945, although the size and frequency of its issues were reduced considerably from 1943 onwards as a result of the war situation and the associated restrictive measures taken by the German Reich.

Notes

1 Haller, K. 1982. *Werkzeitschriften in der BRD*. Berlin: Spiess, pp. 4ff.; Hilb, M. 1975. *Personalzeitschrift als Instrument innerbetrieblicher Informationspolitik*. Stuttgart/Bern: Paul Haupt, pp. 34–38; Hofer, C. 1969. *Wesen und Bedeutung der Werkzeitung als Zweig der betrieblichen Publizität*, PhD Thesis. Vienna University, pp. 9ff.

2 See Proksch, E. 1988. *Corporate Identity und Werkzeitschriften. Eine inhaltsanalytische Untersuchung*. Dipl. Thesis, Vienna University, pp. 6–11; see also Berzsenyi, C. 1988. *Die Mitarbeiterzeitschrift im Kontext interner Öffentlichkeit dargestellt am Beispiel der "Austria Tabak Information"; eine empirische Untersuchung zur Rolle einer Mitarbeiterzeitschrift aus dem Blickwinkel ihrer Rezipienten*. Dipl. Thesis, Vienna University; Polster, S., Tempelmayr, K. 2002. *Wirkung und Sinnhaftigkeit von Mitarbeiterzeitungen bzw. deren Einfluss auf Motivation und Zufriedenheit der Beschäftigten am Beispiel der Firma SKF in Steyr*. Dipl. Thesis, Vienna University; Schillerwein, H. 1997. *Innerbetriebliche Kommunikation unter besonderer Berücksichtigung der Mitarbeiterzeitschrift*. Dipl. Thesis, Vienna University; Slanic, R. 2000. *Mitarbeiterzeitschrift. Einfluss auf Einstellungsänderung durch Überzeugung*. Dipl. Thesis, University of Klagenfurt.

3 Among the first internal corporate or employee magazines in Austria were *Der rote Faden* of the Altmann-Arbeiterschaft starting in 1924 and *Werkzeitung der österreichischen Alpinen-Montangesellschaft* founded in 1926. These were followed by the *Werkzeitungen der Österreichischen Salinen* in 1928 and the *Brevillier-Urban* in 1929.

4 Later renamed to *Deutsches Institut für nationalsozialistische technische Arbeitsschulung*, hence the acronynm *DINTA* (German Institute for National Socialist Technical Work-Training).

5 Bunse, W. 1937. Die Werkzeitung im Dienste der Betriebsgemeinschaft, in Anon. ed. *Die erste Reichsarbeitstagung der Reichsbetriebsgemeinschaft Banken und Versicherungen in der DAF. Reichsbetriebsgemeinschaft Banken und Versicherungen in der DAF.* Berlin, p. 226.

6 Compare Frese, M. 1991. *Betriebspolitik im "Dritten Reich". Deutsche Arbeitsfront, Unternehmen und Staatsbürokratie in der westdeutschen Großindustrie 1933–1939.* Paderborn: Westfälisches Institut für Regionalgeschichte, Landschaftsverband Westfalen-Lippe Münster, Forschungen zur Regionalgeschichte 2, pp. 401–404; Nolan, M. 1994. *Visions of Modernity. American Business and Modernization of Germany.* Oxford: Oxford University Press, pp. 196–200; Reulecke, J. 1981. Die Fahne mit dem goldenen Zahnrad: Der 'Leistungskampf der deutschen Betriebe 1937–1939', in D. Peukert, J. Reulecke, eds. *Die Reihen fast geschlossen. Beiträge zur Geschichte des Alltags unterm Nationalsozialismus.* Wuppertal: Peter Hammer Verlag, p. 247; Hachtmann, R. 1996. Nazi-Deutschland und die *Amerikanisierung* der Produktionsstrukturen, in A. Lüdtke, I. Marßolek, A. von Saldern, eds. *Amerikanisierung. Traum und Alptraum im Deutschland des 20. Jahrhunderts.* Stuttgart: Franz Steiner Verlag, pp. 37–66.

7 Frese (1991), pp. 404–411.

8 The bank's name changed on 16 June 1939 from Austrian Creditanstalt–Wiener Bankverein (*Österreichische Creditanstalt–Wiener Bankverein*) to, simply, Creditanstalt–Bankverein. Creditanstalt–Bankverein is used here, from this point on.

9 The term 'community' (*Gemeinschaft*) is used here in the sense employed under National Socialism. *Gemeinschaft* according to National Socialists meant committing people to National Socialism and thereby extending the total control of the State, the Party, and their accomplices deep in people's most private concerns. Kranig, A. 1979. Arbeitnehmer, Arbeitsbeziehungen und Sozialpolitik unter dem Nationalsozialismus, in K.D. Bracher, M. Funke, H.-A. Jacobson, eds. *Deutschland 1933–1945. Neue Studien zur nationalsozialistischen Herrschaft*. Frankfurt am Main: Bonner Schriften zur Politik und Zeitgeschichte 23, p. 139.

10 Historisches Archiv der Bank Austria (BA), Creditanstalt–Bankverein (CA-BV) Sekretariat rot, Box 11/CA-BV XV, XVI/1–3, Folder Gefolgschaft, Werkzeitschriften, Gemeinschaft. Werkzeitschrift der Betriebsgemeinschaft der Österreichischen Creditanstalt-Wiener Bankverein. 1, H. 1 (Vienna, January 1939),

Rudolf Pfeiffer, *Zum Geleit*, S. 1. All employee newspapers of the Creditanstalt from 1939 to 1943 are located under the same catalogue number; referred to, in the notes following this one, simply as *Gemeinschaft*.

11 Bunse (1937), p. 227.

12 Pfeiffer, R. 1939. Zum Geleit. *Gemeinschaft*, vol. 1, nr. 1. Vienna, January, 1939, p. 1.

13 Ibid. Curriculum vitae, 27 March 1939.

14 Pfeiffer was a member of the Fatherland Front (*Vaterländische Front*, VF) from 1 December 1933 on and had the member number 192.308; Österreichisches Staatsarchiv/Archiv der Republik (ÖStA/AdR), Bundesministerium für Inneres (BMI), Gauakt Rudolf Pfeiffer Nr. 50.957, *Letter from the VF, Bezirk Innere Stadt, to the VF*, Landesführung für Vienna, of 16 October 1936.

15 Ibid. *Beurteilung durch Ortsgruppenleiter H. Mittendorfer und Organisationsleiter Trömel*, 14 October 1938.

16 Ibid. *Political Assessment of the NSDAP*, Gauleitung Vienna, 17 February 1943.

17 Ibid. *Ortsgruppenerhebungsbogen der NSDAP*, Gauleitung Vienna, 9 May 1942.

18 Ibid. Curriculum vitae of 27 March 1939.

19 See the political assessments in Pfeiffer's Gauakt (1936).

20 Ibid. *Ergänzender Bericht über meine nationale Betätigung nach dem Umbruch*, 29 June 1939.

21 On 1 September 1939, Dienst was appointed director of the Banking Trade Group (*Fachgruppenverwalter Banken*) for the Vienna Gau (district) of the DAF. BA, CA-BV Sekretariat rot, Kt. 11/CA-BV XV, XVI/1–3, folder Gefolgschaft, Allgemeines, *letter of Schwimanns* DAF, *Gauleitung Vienna, to Fischböck as Operating Manager of the Creditanstalt–Bankverein*, 5 October 1939.

22 ÖStA/AdR, BMI, Gauakt Rudolf Pfeiffer Nr. 50.957, *letter of 13 March 1938 from Pfeiffer to all employees of the Österreichischen Creditanstalt–Wiener Bankverein*.

23 See BA, Creditanstalt-Vorstandsarchiv (CA-V), *Verhandlungsschrift des Verwaltungsrates der Österreichischen Creditanstalt–Wiener Bankverein*, 7. April 1938.

24 Odilo Globocnik, born on 21 April 1904, was Gauleiter of Vienna from May 1938 to January 1939. On 1 November 1939 he was appointed by Heinrich Himmler to become SS and police chief for the Lublin district and thereby assigned to carry out *Aktion Reinhardt,* which resulted in the murder of at least 1.5 million Jews and the confiscation of Jewish property in the *Generalgouvernement.* After the conclusion of *Aktion Reinhardt* on 4 November 1943 he was transferred to a position as police chief in the Adriatic coastal operating zone. He committed suicide on 31 May 1945.

25 Hubert Klausner was born on 1 November 1938 in Raibl. He joined the Austrian National Socialist Party, left it in 1927 and rejoined on 14 February 1931. From January 1933 he was deputy Gauleiter for Carinthia. On 12 March 1938, one day after the *Anschluss*, he joined the SS, and on 13 March he was appointed minister for political decision-making (political *Willensbildung*) in the cabinet of Seyss-Inquart. He was the deputy of Reichs Commissar Josef Bürckel and from 22 May 1938, and until his death Gauleiter for Carinthia. Klausner died on 12 February 1939 from a stroke.

26 Robert Hammer rose to become an influential personality after the *Anschluss* due to his political connections in Vienna. He was a member of the German Club (*Deutscher Klub*) and he joined the NSDAP in 1932 which assessed him as 'without political or moral blemishes'. He was on the supervisory boards of numerous firms, including the Länderbank AG, and the Vienna Giro- und Cassen-Verein where he was board president. In his position as General Director of the Central Bank of the German Saving banks, and as chair of the review

board of the Vienna stock exchange, he was among the most prominent individuals in the banking sector. In this regard see the Gauakt: ÖStA/AdR, BMI, Gauakt Robert Hammer Nr. 279.749 (gem. mit Nr. 124.585), Kreisleitung Baden bei Vienna to the NSDAP, Gauleitung Niederdonau, Gaupersonalamt vom 1. Nov. 1941. Cited in Melichar, P. 2002. *Neuordnung im Bankwesen. Die NS-Maßnahmen und die Problematik der Restitution. Bericht an die Historikerkommission der Republik Österreich*. Vienna: Boehlau Verlag, p. 46. See also Schmidt, P.C.W., ed. 1940. *Wer leitet? Die Männer der Wirtschaft und der einschlägigen Verwaltung*. Berlin: Hoppenstedt & Co, S. 334ff.

27 ÖStA/AdR, BMI, Gauakt Rudolf Pfeiffer Nr. 50.957, *letter of Robert Hammer to Rudolf Pfeiffer* of 17 March 1938.

28 Franz Langoth was born in 1877 in Linz and trained as primary school teacher. He was a member of the Provincial Government of Upper Austria from 1918 to 1934, from 1918 to 1932 *Landeshauptmannstellvertreter* and 1932–1934 *Landrat*. In 1938 he became a member of the *Reichstag*, from 1939 to 1943 a member of the Creditanstalt–Bankverein supervisory board, and from 1943 Gau Head Office Director (*Gauhauptamtsleiter*) and Senior Administrative Director (*Oberbereichsleiter*) of the NSDAP and *SS Oberführer*.

29 The national labour law was adopted on 20 January 1934 by the National Socialist regime in Germany (Adolf Hitler, labour minister Franz Seldte, economic minister Kurt Schmitt, Justice minister Franz Gürtner, Finance minister Ludwig Graf von Schwerin von Krosigk und interior minister Willhelm Frick) and applied to the *Ostmark* after the *Anschluss*.

30 §§ 3 und 38 AOG, Erlass: Führer des Betriebes bei juristischen Personen, 1 March 1934, in *Reichsarbeitsblatt* (RABl.), T. I, 1934, p. 62.

31 Concerning the duties of the Workplace Leader, see Meyer, E.H. 1937. Die Aufgaben des Betriebsführers im Bankgewerbe, in Reichsbetriebsgemeinschaft Banken und Versicherungen in der DAF, ed. *Die erste Reichsarbeitstagung der Reichsbetriebsgemeinschaft Banken und Versicherungen in der DAF*. Berlin, pp.107–123. See also Adrian, H. 1937. Die Arbeitsbedingungen im Kreditwesen, in Reichsbetriebsgemeinschaft Banken und Versicherungen in der DAF, ed. *Die erste Reichsarbeitstagung der Reichsbetriebsgemeinschaft Banken und Versicherungen in der DAF*. Berlin, pp. 102ff., and Frese (1991), pp. 114–116, 128.

32 Frese (1991), p. 120.

33 Frese (1991), pp. 116–133, 162–168.

34 Frese (1991), p. 168.

35 *Gemeinschaft*, vol. 1 nr. 1 (Vienna, January 1939). We serve the people, pp. 3–8.

36 During the night of 9 to 10 November 1938 – referred to by the National Socialists as the *Reichskristallnacht* – there were targeted attacks against Jews across the German Reich. National Socialist propaganda described these as the 'spontaneous retaliation of the people' in response to the assassination in Paris of the German diplomat Ernst von Rath by the Jewish Pole Herschel Grünspan. In Vienna, Jewish synagogues were destroyed by the SA, SS, and security police, with the collaboration of the fire department. Jewish businesses and dwellings were plundered and destroyed; and six to eight thousand Jews were arrested and deported to concentration camps. The 'Rules for expelling Jews from German Economic Life' were put in place shortly thereafter.

37 See issues of *Gemeinschaft* from 1939 to 1943.

38 Frese (1991), p. 134; Siegel, T. 1990. *Industrielle Rationalisierung unter dem Nationalsozialismus*. Frankfurt am Main, Campus Verlag, p. 103.

39 *Gemeinschaft*, vol. 1, nr. 1 (Vienna, January, 1939), Gauleiter Globocnik spricht, pp. 6–8.

40 In March, 1938 participation in the RBWK was extended to include all employees. Despite intensive propaganda and psychological pressure by the

DAF, however, the competitions were never as popular among adult employees as among teenagers.

41 Decree of the *Führer* of 29 August 1936, reprinted in Landes, H. 1938. Der Leistungskampf der deutschen Betriebe, in *Sozialismus im Dritten Reich*, Vol 8, Berlin, p. 3; Concerning the rules and regulations see Landes (1938), pp. 7–18; Anon. 1941. *Durchführungsbestimmungen für den Leistungskampf der deutschen Betriebe: Nur für den Dienstgebrauch! Amt Soziale Selbstverantwortung, Der Beauftragte für die Durchführung des Leistungskampfes der deutschen Betriebe*. Berlin. In the appendix of the latter there is a complete list of rules and procedures for the *Leistungskampf der deutschen Betriebe*.

42 Frese (1991), p. 411.

43 Landes (1938), p. 9.

44 Frese (1991), p. 431; Reulecke (1981), p. 254.

45 *Gemeinschaft,* vol. 1, nr. 1 (Vienna, January 1939), Die Rede des Betriebsführers, pp. 4ff.

46 *Gemeinschaft*, vol. 2, nr. 3 (Vienna, June/September 1940), Auszeichnung unserer Filiale Graz, p. 43.

47 *Gemeinschaft*, vol. 2, nr. 3 (Vienna, June/September 1940), Leistungskampf der deutschen Betriebe 1940/41, pp. 41ff.

48 See Frese (1991), p. 423.

49 See, for example, *Gemeinschaft*, vol. 2, nr. 3 (Vienna, June/September 1940), Die Banken im Kriege, pp. 39–41.

50 *Gemeinschaft*, vol. 2, nr. 3 (Vienna, June/September 1940), Leistungskampf der deutschen Betriebe 1940/41, p. 42.

51 For the 'National Socialist model firm', see Lencer, R. 1937. Die Betriebs- und Leistungsgemeinschaft in der Bank- und Versicherungswirtschaft, in *Die erste Reichsarbeitstagung der Reichsbetriebsgemeinschaft Banken und Versicherungen in der DAF.* Part of the series *Reichsbetriebsgemeinschaft Banken und Versicherungen in der DAF.* Berlin, pp. 32ff On 'Reichsberufswettkampf und Leistungskampf der deutschen Betriebe', see Frese (1991), pp. 411–443; Kranig (1979), p. 142; Reulecke (1981), pp. 249–269.

52 On the vocational training of DAF, see Frese (1991), pp. 251–333; Siegel, T. 1989. Leistung und Lohn in der nationalsozialistischen 'Ordnung der Arbeit'. *Schriften des Zentralinstituts für sozialwissenschaftliche Forschung der Freien Universiät Berlin 57*, Opladen, pp. 62–124; Spohn, W. *Betriebsgemeinschaft und Volksgemeinschaft*. Berlin: Quorum Verlag, pp. 169, 1988.

53 *Gemeinschaft*, vol. 1, nr. 1 (Vienna, January 1939), Zum Reichsberufswettkampf 1939, pp.12ff; *Gemeinschaft*, vol. 1, nr. 2 (Vienna, April 1939), Zum Reichsberufswettkampf 1939, pp. 26ff.

54 *Gemeinschaft*, vol. 1, nr. 2 (Vienna, April 1939), Zum Reichsberufswettkampf 1939, pp. 26ff.

55 For further details, see Frese (1991), pp. 323–333.

56 *Gemeinschaft*, vol. 1, nr. 1 (Vienna, January 1939), Leopold Nahringbauer, Creditanstalt-Beamter beim Reichslehrgang, p. 13.

57 *Gemeinschaft*, vol. 1, nr. 2 (Vienna, April 1939), Förderung der Begabten, pp. 27ff; see also Ibid. Vera Oelmann, Von unserem Lehrgang. Eine Teilnehmerin aus dem Lehrkurs der Oesterr. Creditanstalt–Wiener Bankverein über den Lehrkurs, pp. 28ff.

58 See Feldman, G.D. 2004. *The Creditanstalt-Wiener Bankverein in the National Socialist Period, 1938–1945*. Vienna.

59 BA, CA-BV Sekretariat rot, Kt. 11/CA-BV XV, XVI/1–3, Mappe Gefolgschaft, Berufserziehungswerk, Berufserziehung und Berufsförderung in der Betriebsgemeinschaft Creditanstalt–Bankverein. Publ. by Berufserziehungswerk der Deutschen Arbeitsfront, Gau Vienna, Kreisverwaltung 1 (Vienna 1939); see

also *Gemeinschaft*, Vol. 3, H. 1 (Vienna, January/March 1941), Berufserziehung und Berufsförderung, S. 1–3.

60 See BA, CA-BV Sekretariat rot, Kt. 11/CA-BV XV, XVI/1–3, Mappe Gefolgschaft, Betriebsappelle, *Vortrag des Vorstandsmitgliedes und Direktors Dr. Rudolf Pfeiffer: 'Die Ordnung des Kreditwesens'* anlässlich des Abschlusses des ersten Lehrganges der Creditanstalt im Großen Kassensaale der Hauptanstalt am Montag, den 26. June 1939; Ibid. *Rede von Betriebsobmann Dienst.*

61 BA, CA-BV Sekretariat rot, Kt. 11/CA-BV XV, XVI/1–3, Mappe Gefolgschaft Berufserziehungswerk, Berufserziehung und Berufsförderung in der Betriebsgemeinschaft Creditanstalt–Bankverein. Herausgegeben vom Berufserziehungswerk der Deutschen Arbeitsfront, Gau Vienna, Kreisverwaltung 1 (Vienna, 1939).

62 *Gemeinschaft*, Vol. 2, H. 1 (Vienna, January/February 1940), Die Totalität der nationalsozialistischen Weltanschung, S. 1–4; Ibid. Betriebsschulung, p. 5. See also *Gemeinschaft*, vol. 2, H. 3 (June/September 1940), Politische Schulungsarbeit, p. 44.

63 In this regard, see the articles on political training (*politische Schulungsarbeit*) in subsequent issues of *Gemeinschaft*.

64 BA, CA-BV Sekretariat rot, Kt. 11/CA-BV XV, XVI/1–3, Mappe Gefolgschaft, Berufserziehungswerk, *correspondence between Gau Administrative Head (Gauobmann) Schneeberger, Gauberufsverwalter Hegert and Pfeiffer in March and April 1942*; See also *Gemeinschaft*, vol. 4, nr. 1/2 (Vienna, June 1942), Deutsches Berufserziehungswerk, p. 6.

65 *Gemeinschaft*, vol. 3, nr. 1 (Vienna, January/March 1941), Abnahme unseres Politischen Stoßtrupps, pp. 6ff.

66 For more on ASdA see Frese (1991), Betriebspolitik, pp. 334–351; von Hübbenet, A. 1938, ed. *Das Taschenbuch Schönheit der Arbeit. ASdA*. Berlin: Verlag der deutschen Arbeitsfront; Anon. ed. 1937. *Erlasse, Anordnungen, Aufrufe von Partei, Staat und Wehrmacht über Schönheit der Arbeit.* DAF. Berlin; Reichel, P. 1999. *Der schöne Schein des Dritten Reiches. Faszination und Gewalt des Faschismus.* Vienna, pp. 235–243.

67 These seven were 'Tidying up the office', 'Noise reduction week', 'Good lighting, good work', 'Clean people in a clean office', 'Healthy air in the workplace', 'Greenery in the workplace' and 'Hot meals at work'.

68 See also Amt Schönheit der Arbeit, ed. 1939. *Unser Ziel: Warmes Essen im Betrieb. KdF in der DAF.* Berlin: von Hübbenet, Taschenbuch, pp. 145–155.

69 *Gemeinschaft*, vol. 4, nr. 3 (Vienna, July/September 1942), Von unserer Gemeinschafts-Küche, p. 31.

70 *Gemeinschaft*, vol. 1, nr. 4 (Vienna, November/December 1939), Graz hat nun mehr auch seine Betriebsküche, p. 9.

71 *Gemeinschaft*, vol. 2, nr. 3 (Vienna, June/September 1940), Werkbücherei, p.54.

72 *Gemeinschaft,* vol. 2, nr. 4 (Vienna, October/December 1940), Werkbücherei, pp. 70ff.

73 *Gemeinschaft,* vol. 3, nr. 2 (Vienna, April/June 1941), Werkbücherei, p. 42.

74 See Frese (1991), pp. 367–371.

75 Frese (1991), p. 367.

76 *Gemeinschaft,* vol. 1, nr. 1 (Vienna, January 1939), Wir dienen dem Volke. Angelobung des Vertrauensrates, Gauleiter und Betriebsführer an die Gefolgschaft, pp. 3–8; ÖStA/AdR, BMI, Gauakt Rudolf Pfeiffer Nr. 50.957, Pfeiffer's invitation on 8 November 1938 to Peter Graf Czernin, SS-Hauptsturmführer, for the *Betriebsappell* of Österreichischen Creditanstalt–Wiener Bankverein held on 11 November 1938.

77 *Gemeinschaft*, vol. 4, nrs. 1/2 (Vienna, June 1942), Betriebsappell, pp. 2ff.

78 Steiermärkisches Landesarchiv (StmkLA), Landesgericht (LG) für Strafsachen Graz, Vr 734/1946 (Franz und Jakob Hasslacher), *Interrogation of Franz Hasslacher by the Landesgericht für Strafsachen in Graz* on May 34, 1946.

79 Ibid. *Testimony of Josef Johams to the Landesgericht für Strafsachen* in Vienna on 23 September 1946.

80 Compare Frese (1991), pp. 311–315, 395–404.

81 *Gemeinschaft*, vol. 1, nr. 1 (Vienna, January, 1939), Aufgabe und Ziel des Betriebssports, pp. 13ff.

82 See *Gemeinschaft*, vol. 1, nr. 1 (Vienna, January 1939), Aufgabe und Ziel des Betriebssports, pp. 13ff; *Gemeinschaft*, vol. 1, nr. 2 (Vienna, April 1939), Mitteilungen der Betriebssportgemeinschaft, pp. 30ff; *Gemeinschaft*, vol. 2 nr. 3 (June/September 1940), Unsere Skihütte, p. 51; *Gemeinschaft*, vol. 3, nr. 1 (January/March 1941), Jahresbericht der Betriebssportgemeinschaft, pp. 18ff.

83 *Gemeinschaft*, vol. 1, nr. 3 (Vienna, September/October 1939), Eröffnung einer Schießstätte, p. 10; *Gemeinschaft*, vol.1, nr. 4 (Vienna, November/December 1939), Kleinkaliberschießen, p. 11; *Gemeinschaft*, vol. 2, nr. 1 (Vienna, January/February 1940), Unsere Schießstätte, p. 14.

84 *Gemeinschaft*, vol. 2, H. 3 (Vienna, June/September 1940), Auszeichnung der Filiale Graz, pp. 43.

85 *Gemeinschaft*, vol. 2, nr. 4 (Vienna, October/December 1940), Der Sommersporttag unseres Betriebes, p. 71.

86 *Gemeinschaft*, vol. 4, nr. 1/2 (Vienna, June 1942), Auszeichnungen unseres Betriebes für den Sportappell 1941, p. 19.

87 *Gemeinschaft*, vol. 5, nr. 1/2 (Vienna, April 1943), Siegerehrung aus dem Sportappelle der Betriebe 1942, p. 15.

88 Frese (1991), pp. 255, 371–374, 383–389.

89 See for example, *Gemeinschaft*, vol. 1, nr. 4 (Vienna, November/December 1939), Vom Fröhlichsein im Kameradschaftskreise, pp. 13ff; *Gemeinschaft*, vol. 2, nr. 1 (January/February 1940), Kameradschaftsabend einzelner Abteilungen und Gruppen der CA, p. 15.

90 *Gemeinschaft*, vol. 4, nrs. 1/2 (Vienna, June 1942), Kameradschaftsabende, p. 20.

91 Compare Frese (1991), Betriebspolitik, pp. 389–395.

92 See *Gemeinschaft*, vol. 1, nr. 3 (Vienna, September/October 1939), Wanderungen, p. 11; *Gemeinschaft*, vol. 1, nr. 4 (Vienna, November/December 1939), Betriebswandern, p. 15; *Gemeinschaft*, vol. 4, nr. 1/2 (Vienna, June 1942), Kameradschaftsausflüge, pp. 21ff.

93 See, for example, *Gemeinschaft*, vol. 2, nr. 1 (Vienna, January/February 1940), Bericht des Volksbildungswartes, p. 10; Gemeinschaft, vol. 2, nr. 4 (October/December 1940), Bericht des Volksbildungswartes, p. 70; Ibid. Ausflug nach Carnuntum, p. 79.

94 *Gemeinschaft*, vol. 4, nr. 3 (Vienna, July/September 1942), Mit KdF in die schöne Wachau, p. 42.

95 *Gemeinschaft*, vol. 3, nr. 2 (Vienna, April/June 1941), Kameraden der Filialen in Vienna, p. 35.

96 See *Gemeinschaft*, vol. 1, nr. 3 (Vienna, September/October 1939), Von unseren Erholungsheimen, p. 10; *Gemeinschaft*, vol. 3, nr. 1 (Vienna, January/March 1941), Von unseren Gefolgschaftsheimen, p. 42; *Gemeinschaft*, vol. 4, nr. 1/2 (Vienna, June 1942), Von unseren Gefolgschaftsheimen, p. 17.

97 *Gemeinschaft*, vol. 1, nr. 4 (Vienna, November/December 1939), Für die an der Front, p.5.

98 See for instance *Gemeinschaft*, vol. 2, nr. 3 (Vienna, June/September 1940), p. 45.

99 Starting with *Gemeinschaft*, vol. 1, nr. 4 (Vienna, November/December 1939), letters were published in every issue. For general background on the propagandistic mobilization during the war, see: Wette, W. 1992. Ideologien, Propaganda und Innenpolitik als Voraussetzungen der Kriegspolitik des Dritten Reiches, in W. Deist, M. Messerschmidt, H. – E. Volkmann, W. Wette, 1992. *Ursachen und Voraussetzungen des Zweiten Weltkrieges.* Düsseldorf: Fischer, pp. 162–169.

100 *Gemeinschaft*, vol. 5, nr. 3 (Vienna, July 1943), Finanzwirtschaftliche Zeitprobleme, p. 29.

101 A verbatim citation of the speech is in *Gemeinschaft*, vol. 1, nr. 1 (Vienna, January 1939), Die Rede des Betriebsführers, pp. 4ff.

102 In this regard, see also Frese (1991), pp. 404–411.

103 The expression *total war* was used to refer to Germany's prosecution of the Second World War after Stalingrad, in which not only military means, but all social and political efforts were to be directed at achieving victory. A strict differentiation between *homeland* and *frontline* no longer applied; the entire civilian population was drawn into the war apparatus. In essence, this meant that instead of seeking to achieve concrete military objectives, the goal became the 'destruction of the enemy'. On the terminology, see Kleinhans, B. 2004. *Totaler Krieg*, [online]. Available at: <http://www.zukunft-braucht-erinnerung.de/totaler-krieg/> [Accessed 25 March 2016]. See further Herbst, L. 1982. *Der Totale Krieg und die Ordnung der Wirtschaft. Die Kriegswirtschaft im Spannungsfeld von Politik, Ideologie und Propaganda 1939–1945*, Stuttgart: Deutsche Verlagsanstalt.

104 See Feldman (2004).

105 *Schwibbogen* was published for employees of Deutsche Bank between 1934 and 1945. It was formed out of the merger of *Mitteilungen für die NSBO der Deutschen Bank und Disconto-Gesellschaft* (1931–1934) and the *Monatshefte für die Beamten der Deutschen Bank und Disconto-Gesellschaft* (1931–1934). See Historisches Archiv der Deutschen Bank (HADB*), Schwibbogen, Werkzeitschrift für die Betriebsgemeinschaft der Deutschen Bank*, vols 1–12 (1934–1945).

9 A non-neutral, non-belligerent country

Portugal during the Second World War from a financial viewpoint

Nuno Valério

During the Second World War, the Portuguese armed forces did not participate in military operations. Thus, Portugal was certainly a non-belligerent country. However, this does not mean it remained truly neutral. This is clear from a political viewpoint, as shown in section two, from an economic viewpoint, as shown in section three and especially from a financial viewpoint, as shown in sections four and five. Payment regimes provided credit to Great Britain and denied credit to other belligerent countries, as shown in section four. As a consequence, Portugal received huge gold and exchange inflows from the most important belligerent countries, with the exception of Great Britain, which accumulated a significant war debt towards Portugal, as shown in section five. Section six concludes that such a bias certainly favoured the acceptance of the Portuguese right-wing authoritarian regime in the post-war international order led by the United States of America.

The political viewpoint

From a political viewpoint, the evolution of the Portuguese position during the Second World War must be divided into three periods: an opening phase of biased neutrality until the summer of 1940; an intermediate phase of what was then called geometrical neutrality between the autumn of 1940 and the summer of 1943; and a closing phase of biased neutrality again after the autumn of 1943.[1]

Until the summer of 1940 there was no significant German military threat to Portugal. Consequently, the Portuguese government clung to its traditional alliance with Britain.

In the autumn of 1940, when it became clear that it would be impossible to undertake Operation Sea Lion against Britain, Operation Felix, which involved occupying the Iberian Peninsula and denying Britain access to the Mediterranean from the west, gained significance for Germany. However, Portuguese diplomacy played its part in convincing Spain that it was not wise to imitate Italy and side with Germany, and Operation Felix was abandoned in favour of Operation Barbarossa against the Soviet Union. However, the German military threat remained from both land and submarine war.

Moreover, the deleterious consequences for Portugal of Britain's enforcement of trade restrictions, in order to deprive Germany of valuable supplies, and the occupation of Portuguese Timor by Australia and the Netherlands (December 1941) as a precautionary (and ineffective) measure against Japanese invasion (March 1942) brought some friction to relations between Portugal and Britain.

Nevertheless, in the autumn of 1943, Portugal ceded military bases in the Azores to Britain (and in practice to the United States of America as well). Portuguese diplomacy managed to convince Germany that a regular supply of tungsten (sometimes known as wolfram) was preferable to retaliation (by way of comparison, it may be recalled that in 1916, during the First World War, Germany had declared war on Portugal when Portugal refused to guarantee that the German ships impounded in Portuguese harbours would not be lent to Britain). From then on, although non-belligerent, Portugal clearly sided again with the Anglo-Saxon allies. In the most important episode during the rest of the war, the supply of Portuguese tungsten to Germany was suspended in the spring of 1944 (in spite of the Portuguese undertaking not to cut it off), when the pressure exerted by the British on the Portuguese government in order to stop this flow became unbearable and the possibility of significant German retaliation had become remote.

The economic viewpoint

Legal foreign trade

Tables 9.1 and 9.2 present a summary of the available data on Portuguese legal foreign trade by country during the Second World War.

Great Britain remained the main foreign outlet for Portuguese goods until the end of the war (just as it had traditionally been for more than two centuries), except in 1941. However, the Portuguese colonial empire and the United States of America showed stable increases, and the former overtook Britain as the main outlet for Portuguese goods in the immediate post-war years (the United States of America also overtook Britain in 1946). Germany experienced very sharp fluctuations, depending on the state of communications between the two countries: the initial and closing periods of biased neutrality were periods of low Portuguese exports to Germany; during the middle period of geometrical neutrality, Portuguese exports to Germany increased, and Germany even became the main outlet for Portuguese goods in 1941.

Great Britain had also been the main supplier of Portuguese imports in the immediate pre-war years (as it had traditionally been for more than two centuries), but was overtaken from 1940 onwards by the United States of America, and from 1941 onwards by the Portuguese colonial empire, which became the main provider of Portuguese imports between 1942 and 1946 (in 1947, the United States of America took the lead once again and Great Britain regained second place). The fluctuations in imports from Germany

Table 9.1 Portuguese legal foreign trade, 1938–1947 (exports by country)

Year	*Portuguese colonial empire*	*Germany*	*United States of America*	*Great Britain*	*Other countries*	*Exports total*
1938	137	149	61	236	563	1,146
1939	173	121	121	359	565	1,339
1940	200	29	235	471	703	1,638
1941	323	565	547	526	1,012	2,973
1942	450	960	226	1,147	1,156	3,939
1943	546	855	388	1,230	1,016	4,035
1944	515	361	714	788	788	3,166
1945	768	+0	551	573	1,345	3,237
1946	1,032	3	685	659	2,208	4,587
1947	1,134	13	495	635	1,030	3,307

Source: Comércio Externo, various issues (1938–1947). Million escudos.

Table 9.2 Portuguese legal foreign trade, 1938–1947 (imports by country)

Year	*Portuguese colonial empire*	*Germany*	*United States of America*	*Great Britain*	*Other countries*	*Imports total*
1938	234	387	266	393	1,026	2,306
1939	253	276	219	394	940	2,082
1940	301	39	587	422	1,234	2,583
1941	426	200	629	375	839	2,469
1942	566	313	302	309	990	2,480
1943	562	481	464	516	1,318	3,341
1944	742	314	476	433	1,955	3,920
1945	759	14	778	444	2,061	4,056
1946	1,036	34	1,715	943	3,132	6,860
1947	744	51	2,993	1,122	4,552	9,462

Source: Comércio Externo, various issues (1938–1947). Million escudos.

mirror those in exports, although Germany never became the main source of Portuguese imports.

The fluctuations of Portuguese trade with Germany mirror the evolution of political relations: trade flows were minimal during the opening and closing phases of biased neutrality and became very important during the intermediate phase of geometrical neutrality. This was as much a consequence of the political influence on trade as a consequence of logistical possibilities. During the opening and closing phases of biased neutrality, there were no good overland communications between Portugal and Germany. During the intermediate phase of geometrical neutrality, non-belligerent, but pro-German, Spain and occupied France provided good overland communications between Portugal and Germany.

Illegal foreign trade

Of course, legal foreign trade was not the whole story. For several reasons, part of the trade flows with all belligerent countries escaped registration. In the case of Germany, good overland communications between Portugal and Germany during the intermediate phase of geometrical neutrality also meant that illegal trade between the two countries was possible. British efforts to deprive Germany of valuable supplies – in the form of navicerts, affidavits and the blacklisting of firms suspected of supplying Germany with forbidden commodities – led many Portuguese firms to avoid registering their profitable trade with Germany. A significant amount of German arms exports to Portugal also went unregistered. And, both in the case of Germany and Great Britain, an important question was, of course, tungsten.

During the war, the Portuguese government tried to implement a quota system for tungsten ore exports, which allowed each side in conflict to extract the ore from the mines owned by its nationals, and to obtain a percentage of the product of the mines owned by other proprietors. Germany received a favourable percentage of the product of other mines because it agreed, in exchange, to sell to Portugal those commodities that it badly needed. The Anglo-Saxon allies refrained from matching the German offers because they feared that part of the valuable supplies going to Portugal might end up in Germany through illegal channels. However, most of the legal production of tungsten ore was exported to the Anglo-Saxon allies. The total legal production of tungsten ore reached 22.8 thousand tons, of which 14 thousand tons were exported to Great Britain, 1.6 thousand tons were exported to the United States of America and 6.2 thousand tons were exported to Germany (to which may be added a further three hundred tons exported to Italy and five hundred tons exported to France; the remaining two hundred tons were exported to other countries). As was to be expected, a lot of illegally mined ore escaped this quota system. The greater financial capacity of the Anglo-Saxon allies favoured them in transactions on the black market. Thus, it may be said that the quota system worked to the advantage of Germany, in spite of its lower share in the market. As a consequence, Portugal was Germany's main supplier of tungsten ore until the spring of 1944. Thereafter, legal prohibition (even if not fully enforced) and subsequently the lack of serviceable overland communications between the two countries soon stifled the flow of Portuguese tungsten to Germany.

Payment regimes

Free convertibility had been the normal regime for external payments from the Portuguese perspective ever since Decree-Law 28088, of 18 October 1937, had abolished all exchange controls dating back to the time of the First World War, allowing for the unrestricted buying and selling of foreign exchange on the market. However, as most other countries had either already established exchange controls before the war or did so soon after the conflict started, the Bank of Portugal had to organize its own counterpart to these controls by signing payment agreements with the central banks of these countries.

The payment agreement with Germany was approved by Decree-Law 25418, of 29 May 1935, and remained in force until the collapse of Germany on 9 May 1945. It did not include any provision for stabilizing the exchange rate, included provisions to balance payment flows between the two countries, and called for any outstanding balances to be settled in gold or convertible foreign exchange within three months. In peacetime, the outstanding balances usually favoured Germany, but the situation changed during wartime whenever overland communications between the two countries were relatively easy (roughly from the summer of 1940 until the summer of 1944, as mentioned above).

The payment agreement with Great Britain was signed on 29 July 1940 and remained in force until the devaluation of the pound sterling on 18 September 1949. It established a fixed exchange rate (1 pound sterling = 100 Portuguese escudos), did not include any provisions designed to balance the payment flows between the two countries, and allowed Britain to borrow any amount at all from the Bank of Portugal without having to service this debt until the end of the European war. Notice that, until the beginning of the war, the Portuguese monetary authorities had kept the Portuguese escudo pegged to the pound sterling at a rate of 1 pound sterling = 110 Portuguese escudos, but the Portuguese escudo rapidly appreciated against the pound sterling between September 1939 and July 1940. Only the stabilization of the pound sterling against the American dollar (1 pound sterling = 4 American dollars), which was agreed on 18 July 1940, allowed for the stabilization of the pound sterling against the Portuguese escudo.

In spite of German pressure to obtain more favourable conditions for the settlement of its outstanding balances with Portugal, and Portuguese dissatisfaction with British interference in Portuguese imports from overseas (of course, these interferences were part of the British economic warfare apparatus, designed to deprive Germany of valuable supplies), both agreements were maintained. This means that Portuguese neutrality was never geometrical and always favoured Britain in the financial field.

Financial flows: the balance of payments

Table 9.3 presents a summary of the available data on Portuguese (legal) trade balances by country and the Portuguese balance of payments during the Second World War.

An analysis of trade balances by country shows that all balances were negative on the eve of the Second World War. During the war, surpluses were obtained between 1940 and 1945 with Great Britain, between 1941 and 1944 with Germany, in 1941 and 1942 with other countries, in 1944 with the United States of America and in 1945 with the Portuguese Colonial Empire. After the end of the war, the typical peacetime situation of negative trade balances with all partners returned, except for a positive balance with the Portuguese Colonial Empire in 1947.

Aggregation of trade balances over the war years (1940–1945) shows that only Great Britain and Germany provided overall positive figures (2,236 million escudos and 1,409 million escudos, respectively), while the United States of America, the Portuguese Colonial Empire and the rest of the world had overall negative figures (575 million escudos, 556 million escudos and 2,377 million escudos, respectively). Thus, the overall positive trade balance during the war years was almost negligible (139 million escudos). It should also be noted that overall surpluses in the trade balance only existed in the years of geometrical neutrality, which in turn roughly coincided with the period during which there was serviceable overland communication with Germany, the country that was most in need of Portuguese supplies, especially tungsten ore.

Invisible flows were traditionally favourable to Portugal, mainly because of the remittances sent by the Portuguese emigrant communities that had settled in Brazil and the United States of America. The war did cause a significant increase and some changes to the composition of the invisible flows within the Portuguese balance of payments. For a while, the capital inflows resulting from money seeking refuge in a neutral economy or brought to the country by refugees, plus aid to refugees (which is supposed to have been given mainly by the American Jewish community to Jewish refugees trying either to go to America or stay in the country) overtook emigrants' remittances as the main items. Unfortunately, although such a development seems quite plausible, and was taken for granted at the time (the annual reports of the Bank of Portugal and the Ministry of Finance's reports on public accounts often present this phenomenon as the explanation for the inflationary process occurring during the war), there are no statistical data available to prove or illustrate this theory. And it must not be forgotten that the payment of illegal trade flows was certainly another important item contributing to the increase and change of the composition of the invisible flows within the Portuguese balance of payments.

Table 9.3 Trade balance by country and balance of payments

Year	*Portuguese Colonial Empire*	*Germany*	*United States of America*	*Great Britain*	*Other countries*	*Legal trade balance total*	*Invisible flows total*	*Balance of payments total*
1938	–97	–238	–205	–157	–463	–1,160	+995	–165
1939	–80	–155	–98	–35	–375	–743	+1,134	+391
1940	–101	–10	–352	+49	–531	–945	+1,604	+659
1941	–103	+365	–82	+151	+173	+504	+3,214	+3,718
1942	–116	+647	–76	+838	+166	+1,459	+3,069	+4,528
1943	–16	+374	–76	+714	–302	+694	+1,011	+1,705
1944	–227	+47	+238	+355	–1,167	–754	+3,429	+2,675
1945	+7	–14	–227	+129	–716	–819	+2,675	+1,856
1946	–4	–30	–1,030	–284	–924	–2,273	+2,775	+502
1947	+390	–38	–2,498	+487	–3,522	–5,155	+2,356	–2,799

Source: Relatório do Conselho de Administração do Banco de Portugal, various issues (1938–1947). Million escudos.

Aggregation of invisible flows during the war years (1940–1945) shows that the overall positive balances reached a figure slightly above 15 billion escudos. This figure is roughly similar to the overall surplus of the Portuguese balance of payments during the same years. Unfortunately, there are no data available on invisible flows (or total flows) by country. Thus, to have some idea about its distribution, we must rely on the figures relating to the war debt (the money borrowed by the Bank of England, according to the payment agreement of 29 July 1940, as explained above) and the gold inflows from other central banks to the Bank of Portugal. As Table 9.4 shows, these foreign payments amounted to a total of around 17.9 billion escudos, almost three billion escudos above the overall surplus of the Portuguese balance of payments.

As could be expected from the payment regimes, while Great Britain paid trade deficits and invisible flows to Portugal by accumulating war debt, other countries sent gold and convertible exchange, which the Portuguese monetary authorities tried to convert into gold or gold certificates as soon as possible. Of course, gold payments from Europe meant the physical shipment of gold, while gold payments from America meant the acquisition of certificates over gold that never physically left America. As a matter of fact, the Portuguese authorities even sent part of their gold reserves across the Atlantic in 1940, fearful that the Portuguese gold reserves would share the same fate as the gold reserves of countries occupied by Germany in the event of Operation Felix being implemented.

British payments amounted to almost half of total inflows, and American payments exceeded one fourth of total inflows, leaving less than one third of the total for Germany and the rest of the world. Both British and American

Table 9.4 Foreign payments by country during the war years, 1940–1945

Country	*War debt (million pounds)*	*Gold flows (metric tons)*	*Total payments (billion escudos)*	*Trade balance (billion escudos)*	*Invisible flows (billion escudos)*
Great Britain	81	—	8.1	+2.2	+5.9
USA	—	167	4.7	–0.6	+5.3
Switzerland	—	104	2.9	+0.5	+2.4
Germany	—	49	1.4	+1.4	≈0
Others	—	28	0.8	–2.9	+3.7
Total	81	348	17.9	+0.6	+17.3

Sources: Table 9.3 and Report of the Commission of Research on Gold Transactions between Portuguese and German Authorities during the Period between 1936 and 1945. Lisbon: Banco de Portugal, 1999.

Notes: 1 gold metric ton = 28.132 million escudos (1 metric ton = 32,151 ounces troy; 1 gold ounce troy = 35 American dollars; 4 American dollars = 1 pound sterling; 1 pound sterling = 100 escudos).

invisible flows were very important, suggesting that either unregistered exports or aid to refugees was quite significant (very likely mostly the former in the British case, and the latter in the American case). The most interesting point is the absence of significant invisible flows from Germany, and the huge gold inflows from Switzerland. In the case of the Swiss National Bank (and other sources), it is likely that Portuguese gold acquisitions were financed partly by Swiss francs obtained from the German State Bank, partly by foreign exchange brought into the country by refugees. As a matter of fact, Portuguese refusal to award any long-term credit to Germany or to accept unconvertible marks forced this country to pay Portugal in both Swiss francs and gold. Notice that all gold and foreign exchange payments by the German State Bank to the Bank of Portugal were made through the Swiss National Bank.

Using these figures, and the amount of unregistered German arms exports to Portugal (666 million escudos),[2] it is possible to estimate that the accumulated net amount of Portuguese illegal exports to Germany during the war might have reached a maximum figure slightly above three billion escudos. Very likely, the real figure for illegal exports to Germany remained somewhat below the figure for legal exports, and also below the figures for legal and illegal exports to Great Britain.

The main consequence of the evolution of the balance of payments for the Portuguese economy was that the Portuguese capital market was characterized by a glut of savings opportunities and a shortage of investment opportunities. The glut of savings opportunities was caused by surpluses in the balance of payments, which resulted from Portugal's capacity to supply valuable commodities and to remain a relatively safe refuge in troubled times. The shortage of investment opportunities derived from the economy's overall stagnant performance and the lack of adequate supplies from abroad. As a consequence, there was a downward trend in interest rates, despite the increase in price levels, and investors concentrated on public bonds and construction. It may, however, be argued that this process acted as a kind of prior accumulation of international means of payment that facilitated the take-off of modern economic growth that was to occur in the Portuguese economy during the post-war years.[3]

Portugal and looted Nazi gold

German payments to Portugal during the Second World War gave rise to the Portuguese involvement in the notorious question of looted Nazi gold (which included the gold reserves of occupied countries extracted in payment for the costs of occupation, and even gold from private persons, either extracted against payment in local currencies or confiscated from prisoners). When these transactions came under the scrutiny of the Allied Tripartite Commission after the end of the war, the Portuguese government refused to accept the principle of giving back looted gold, arguing that it had acted in good faith in its legal international transactions. For a while, the American government froze Portuguese holdings in the United States as a means of pressure, but at the same time allowed Portugal to be a beneficiary of Marshall aid. As a matter of fact, the crucial point of the whole negotiations from the American point of view was not Nazi gold, but the wish to encourage Portugal to accept the American military bases in the Azores as permanent in practice. The whole question was not settled until the early 1950s. In the end, four metric tons of gold were acknowledged as having been looted from the Netherlands Central Bank and were given back, together with the payment of compensation by the Federal Republic of Germany. Payments were made only in the late 1950s.[4]

Conclusion

During the Second World War, Portugal remained formally neutral, but clearly favoured Great Britain from a financial viewpoint. Of course, as the figures presented in this paper show, this bias represented a minor contribution to both the British war finance and German financial worries during the conflict. However, it certainly favoured the acceptance of the Portuguese right-wing authoritarian regime in the post-war international order led by the United States of America.

Notes

1 For a general analysis of Portugal's situation during the Second World War, especially from a political and an economic viewpoint, see Telo, A. 1991. *Portugal na Segunda Guerra*. 2 volumes. Lisbon: Vega; and Telo, A. and de la Torre Gómez, H. 2000. *Portugal e Espanha nos sistemas internacionais contemporâneos*. Lisbon: Cosmos.

2 The amount of unregistered German arms exports to Portugal was obtained from Louçã, A. 2000. *Hitler e Salazar – comércio em tempo de Guerra*. Lisbon: Terramar.

3 On the Portuguese capital market during the Second World War and the long-term consequences of these processes for the Portuguese economy, see Valério, N. 2005. *The Portuguese Capital Market during the Second World War*. Gabinete de História Económica e Social, Instituto Superior de Economia e Gestão, working paper no. 24.

4 On Portugal and looted Nazi gold, see Telo, A. 2000. *A neutralidade portuguesa e o ouro nazi*. Lisbon: Quetzal.

Index

For Product Safety Concerns and Information please contact our
EU representative GPSR@taylorandfrancis.com Taylor & Francis
Verlag GmbH, Kaufingerstraße 24, 80331 München, Germany